VIKING REVALUATIONS

Bessastaðir, 15th May 1992.

To my fellow Vikings!

My warmest congratulations, personally and on behalf of the people of Iceland, on the centenary of the Viking Society - or should I say, on the first centenary, the opening chapter of your Saga. To say that the Icelanders have regarded you as kindred spirits during the past one hundred years would not do justice to the grandeur of your work. Your devotion to illuminating the Icelandic experience has been an important stimulus for the Icelanders themselves to remember, respect and advance the unique heritage with which they have been entrusted. The Icelandic cultural heritage today is built on the notion of keeping an ancient language and literature alive, vital, fresh and relevant, built on transforming the past into both present and future. Your enthusiasm, encouragement and scholarship have been invaluable to us the people of Iceland.

Til hamingju með næstu hundrað árin!

Vigdís Finnbogadóttir

VIKING REVALUATIONS

VIKING SOCIETY CENTENARY SYMPOSIUM
14–15 May 1992

Edited by
Anthony Faulkes and Richard Perkins

VIKING SOCIETY FOR NORTHERN RESEARCH
UNIVERSITY COLLEGE LONDON
1993

© Viking Society for Northern Research 1993

Printed in the University of Birmingham

ISBN 0 903521 28 8

The Society acknowledges with gratitude the grants of the British Academy towards the expenses of the symposium and of Seðlabanki Íslands towards the cost of publication of this volume

The cover design is by Calum Campbell

CONTENTS

A letter from the President of Iceland ....*frontispiece*

FOREWORD vii

CENTENARY REVALUATIONS

KNUT HELLE. Norway, 800–1200 1
GUNNAR KARLSSON. A century of research on early Icelandic society 15
VÉSTEINN ÓLASON. The Sagas of Icelanders 26
DIANA WHALEY. The Kings' Sagas 43
MICHAEL BARNES. Norse in the British Isles 65
CHRISTINE FELL. Norse studies: then, now and hereafter 85

CURRENT PROBLEMS (1): PAGAN BELIEFS AND CHRISTIAN IMPACT

BJARNE FIDJESTØL. The contribution of scaldic studies 100
URSULA DRONKE. The contribution of Eddic studies 121
ELSE ROESDAHL. Pagan beliefs, Christian impact and archaeology—a Danish view 128
PETER FOOTE. Historical studies: conversion moment and conversion period 137

CURRENT PROBLEMS (2): SCANDINAVIAN SOCIETY 800–1100

R. I. PAGE. Scandinavian society, 800–1100: the contribution of runic studies 145
JUDITH JESCH. Skaldic verse and Viking semantics 160
PREBEN MEULENGRACHT SØRENSEN. Historical reality and literary form 172
BJØRN MYHRE. The beginning of the Viking Age—some current archaeological problems 182
    Figures .... *after page* 204

FOREWORD

THE Viking Society for Northern Research celebrated its centenary by publishing a Centenary Saga-Book (XXIII 4, 1992) and by holding an international symposium on 13–15 May 1992. This was arranged in collaboration with the Department of Scandinavian Studies, University College London, and the meetings were held in Birkbeck College. Speakers were invited from Denmark, Iceland and Norway, and from among members of the Society. The papers given, variously revised, make the contents of the present volume.

The Society gave a reception for foreign guests on the evening of Wednesday, 13 May. Members of the symposium were the guests of H.E. Helgi Ágústsson, Icelandic Ambassador, and Mme Hervör Jónsdóttir, at their residence on the evening of Thursday, 14 May.

The principal *blót*, however, was the Centenary Dinner, held in University College on the evening of Friday, 15 May, and well attended by symposium participants and members of the Society at large. The principal guests were Dr Sveinbjörn Björnsson, Rector of the University of Iceland, and his wife, Guðlaug Einarsdóttir; H.E. Kjell Eliassen, Norwegian Ambassador, and Mme Eliassen; H.E. Helgi Ágústsson, Icelandic Ambassador, and his wife, Hervör Jónsdóttir; H.E. Ólafur Egilsson, and his wife, Ragna Ragnars; and Dr Jóhannes Nordal, Chairman of the Central Bank of Iceland and of Hið Íslenzka Fornritafélag, and his wife, Dóra Guðjónsdóttir.

In addition to the symposium speakers, Professor Bjarne Fidjestøl and Professor Knut Helle, both of Bergen University, Professor Gunnar Karlsson and Professor Vésteinn Ólason, both of the University of Iceland, Else Roesdahl and Preben Meulengracht Sørensen, both of Århus University, and Professor Bjørn Myhre of Oslo University, a number of other scholars were especially invited to join the Society in its celebrations. At the dinner they were welcomed because of their distinction in fields of endeavour matching the aims and interests of the Society, and some of them in particular because they recalled its foundation as a 'social and literary' branch of the Orkney and Shetland Society of London: Professor Bo Almqvist (University College, Dublin), Professor Hans Bekker-Nielsen (Odense University, and representing the Danish Ministry of Education), Dr Barbara E. Crawford (St Andrews University, and sometime President of the Scottish Society for Northern Studies), Professor Lennart Elmevik (Uppsala University, and representing Kungl. Gustav Adolfs Akademien för Folklivsforskning), Dr Thomas Fanning (University College, Galway), Professor Jan Ragnar Hagland (Trondheim University), Professor Eyvind Fjeld Halvorsen (Oslo University), Helgi Þorláksson (Stofnun Árna Magnússonar, Reykjavík), Professor Finn Hødnebø (Oslo University), Professor Jónas Kristjánsson (University of Iceland), Professor Bengt R. Jonsson (Svenskt Visarkiv, Stockholm), Professor Else Mundal (Oslo

University), Dr Lena Peterson (Uppsala University), Professor Bo Ralph (Gothenburg University), Professor Hubert Seelow (Erlangen University), Brian Smith (Shetland Archivist, Lerwick), Stefán Karlsson (Stofnun Árna Magnússonar, Reykjavík), William P. L. Thomson (Orkney), and Arne Thorsteinsson (State Antiquary, Faroe Islands).

The President presided. He extended a warm welcome to all and warm thanks to many: to the speakers, to H.E. Helgi Ágústsson for his reception and for his never-failing help in the course of the symposium preparations, to the officers of the Society who had worked hard and willingly to make the occasion a success, and to the British Academy and the Central Bank of Iceland for their generous subventions. Speeches of congratulation were made by Dr Sveinbjörn Björnsson and H.E. Kjell Eliassen. Toasts were frequently and enthusiastically drunk, to the health of heads of state, to the Society's guests and to the Society's future. H.E. Helgi Ágústsson read a message from H.E. Vigdís Finnbogadóttir, President of Iceland, and another from Davíð Oddsson, Iceland's Prime Minister. On behalf of the President of Iceland, Helgi took the opportunity to decorate three senior members of the Society, Professor Michael Barnes, Dr (now Professor) Anthony Faulkes and Professor emeritus Desmond Slay, with the knight's cross of the Order of the Falcon 'for services to Icelandic scholarship'.

Other presentations were made: Professor Elmevik brought medals issued by Kungl. Gustav Adolfs Akademien and by Uppsala University as congratulatory tokens of esteem; Professor Hans Bekker-Nielsen a gift of books for the Society's Library from the Danish Ministry of Education; Professor Finn Hødnebø facsimile editions of early Norwegian texts and the volumes of *Regesta Norvegica*; and subsequently, through the good offices of Dr Sveinbjörn Björnsson, the Society received from the University of Iceland a facsimile edition of the Konungsbók of the Eddaic poems 'in gratitude for the excellent achievements of the Viking Society in fostering *íslensk fræði*'. Inadequate thanks were expressed on the Society's behalf at the time, later confirmed by letters of more eloquent gratitude.

The officers of the Society were content to think that their efforts, in straitened circumstances, to make the centenary celebration a worthy commemoration had not been unsuccessful, and they were deeply gratified by the ready goodwill they met on every hand, both before and during the symposium, most especially from the friendly scholars who agreed to contribute the papers now found in this volume. I should like to thank them yet again and also acknowledge the debt I personally owe, along with every member of the Society, to the editors, Anthony Faulkes and Richard Perkins.

Peter Foote
President 1990–92

KNUT HELLE

NORWAY, 800-1200

IN 1891, the year before the Viking Club was founded, Ernst Sars published the fourth and last volume of his monumental *Udsigt* or 'survey' of Norwegian history (Sars, 1873-91). In Sars's presentation, the nationally oriented Norwegian history writing of the nineteenth century reached its peak. This was a historiography which consciously served the purpose of creating a national identity within the young Norwegian state that had emerged after the Napoleonic Wars.

In 1814 the long-lasting union with Denmark had been dissolved and Norway had declared its independence, only to be forced into a new union with Sweden which lasted until 1905. The first generation of Norwegian historians after 1814 set out to show that their people constituted an old and venerable nation, historically entitled to statehood. In pursuit of this goal they turned to the Middle Ages, the only period when Norway had formed an independent state. Led by the founding fathers of Norwegian historical research, Rudolf Keyser (1865-70; 1867; 1868) and Peter Andreas Munch (1852-63), they not only made extensive and learned contributions to medieval studies by publishing collections of original sources and producing detailed accounts of historical events and conditions, they also attached great importance to developing general interpretations of Norwegian medieval society (Dahl 1959, 36-69).

The next generation of historians, to which Sars belonged, started to explore also the following period of the Danish-Norwegian union. This they did without any loss of interest in the Middle Ages. In keeping with contemporary evolutionist ideas, they stressed the coherence and continuity of Norwegian history from the Middle Ages through the union period down to the nineteenth century (Dahl 1959, 81-83).

Sars was the greatest evolutionist of them all (Dahl 1959, 157-61, 165-69). In his four-volume survey he brought Norwegian history up to 1814 and suggested some major themes of its further course. One of his main propositions was that Norwegian society had already in the Middle Ages assumed the basic 'democratic' character which was to be its strength in the nineteenth century. A strong aristocracy was lacking and the peasants enjoyed greater freedom and independence than in most other European societies (Sars 1911-12, I 594-95, II 284, 306, III 153; cf. Seip 1940, 50-51). This was a view in accordance with a general assumption shared by most nineteenth-century Norwegian historians, namely that medieval Norway was unique among the neighbouring Danish and Swedish societies and the rest of Europe.

What Sars regarded as democratic conditions were in his view an outcome of historical development within precisely the span of time which I have been asked to deal with in this paper, namely the period from the beginning of the Viking Age and down to about 1200. For Sars, Norway was at the beginning of the historical period the most aristocratic part of Scandinavia. Local affairs were determined by an old and hereditary tribal aristocracy of Germanic type that recruited the military, judicial and religious leaders of independent *fylki* or counties. They controlled a peasantry of which the majority were already by now tenant farmers. As a consequence not least of the fragmented topography of Norway, the native tribal aristocracy had kept its local power and independence better than in the neighbouring countries and it became the chief adversary of a monarchy which from the Viking Age onwards strove to unite the whole of the country under its rule (Sars 1911–12, I 97–202, 595–96; cf. Dahl 1959, 169–75).

From these considerations Sars concluded that the main theme of Norwegian history between 800 and 1200 was the struggle between royal and aristocratic power. This was a view which went back to Munch, whereas Keyser had thought more in terms of a confrontation between royal and popular power, since he regarded the magnates of the period as patriarchal leaders of the people more than as an aristocracy (Dahl 1959, 60–63). All three, however, agreed that the struggle ended in victory for the monarchy. It made its first forward thrust to rule the whole of the country in the days of Harald Finehair in the late ninth and early tenth centuries, progressed further a hundred years later in the reign of Olaf Haraldsson, and gained its conclusive victory over the aristocracy or the local leaders of the people with King Sverre around 1200 (Sars 1911–12, I 132–59, 211–460). This was the main course of events agreed upon by other nineteenth-century historians as well. What there was of a service aristocracy in the thirteenth century was generally considered to have been too weak to play an independent political role and form the basis for a nobility which could in the late Middle Ages hold its own in relation to the Danish and Swedish aristocracy (Sars 1911–12, 559–99; cf. Dahl 1959, 50–51, 63–64, 119–20, 175–77).

Nineteenth-century Norwegian historians were not, of course, uninterested in natural and socio-economic conditions, but their main interest was clearly political. In most cases it was also idealistic in the sense that historical explanations were sought in ideas, human motives and mental attitudes more than in material conditions. This applies particularly to Sars, whose writings avowedly abound in such explanations. Natural environment and socio-economic realities could impede or facilitate historical development, but the real motive powers were to be found in the dominant intellectual and moral ideas and the mental attitudes of the period in question (Dahl 1959, 110–11, 115, 117, 157).

There was, however, one important exception to this way of thinking. Sars encountered opposition from a group of contemporary and politically conservative historians who considered themselves to be greater realists than him and also more empirical. Led by T. H. Aschehoug, they explained the weakness of the medieval

Norwegian aristocracy by pointing to its relative poverty. This was, in turn, a consequence of natural conditions, notably the scarcity of cultivable soil in Norway as compared with Denmark and Sweden. Nor did they accept the idea of a general tension between monarchy and aristocracy; rather they thought that a national medieval kingdom had been built up in cooperation with the secular and clerical aristocracy of the land (Aschehoug 1966, 78–79, 119–24; cf. Dahl 1959, 115, 117, 119–20). In both these respects they were ahead of their times.

The dominant political outlook of nineteenth century medieval historians made them to a large extent dependent on narrative sources, notably the sagas. In their use of sources such as these they were on a par with contemporary European historical criticism. Starting with Keyser and more particularly with Munch, they worked constantly to purge the saga tradition of unhistorical accretions and misunderstandings (Dahl 1959, 65–69). But their criticism of the sagas was never radical. Even Gustav Storm, who in 1869 decisively rejected the customary conception of the sagas as direct representations of fixed and worked-up entities of oral tradition, tended to rely on saga narratives, even those relating to a distant past, unless there was specific reason to disbelieve them (Storm 1869, 5, 36; cf. Dahl 1959, 90–91, 198–205).

Up to the very end of the nineteenth century, then, historians found it possible to render, on the basis of what they considered to be 'historical' sagas, coherent and detailed accounts of political events and conditions from the beginning of the Viking Age onwards.

The dissolution of the union with Sweden in 1905 led to a change in the political and ideological climate of Norway. The main democratic issues had mostly been resolved in the preceding period and the national problems could largely be removed from the political agenda. At the same time a rapid wave of industrialization made economic and social problems loom larger in political life than before.

The change of climate made itself felt within Norwegian historiography as well. From the second decade of the new century historical research was comparatively strongly influenced by the Marxist approach to history and by materialist historical thinking in general. The foremost proponents of change were Halvdan Koht and Edvard Bull, professors at the University of Oslo, who were both also prominent figures in the Norwegian labour movement of the interwar period (Dahl 1959, 231–32).

As historians, Koht and Bull were far from dogmatic Marxists. But the influence of historical materialism on their thought is clear enough and can be seen in their belief that economic conditions were decisive for the course of historical development, in their use of the concepts of class and class-struggle and not least in their adoption of the Marxist model of base and superstructure and the Marxist view of the State as an instrument of class interests (Dahl 1952).

Koht and Bull's historical thinking is relevant to my theme because they made medieval history the chief proving ground for their more general concepts. In their view, Norwegian medieval society was basically shaped by the pattern of the ownership of land, the most important means of production. Whereas most nineteenth-century historians had seen a general tension between the monarchy and what there was of an aristocracy, Koht and Bull undertook what may be described as a materialist rewriting of one of the basic conceptions of Aschehoug and his conservative colleagues: they assumed an essential solidarity between the crown, the clergy and the magnates conditioned by the fact that they were all landowners. The monarchy of the High Middle Ages was created by the landowning upper class and served to enhance its domination over the peasants. One consequence of this interpretation was that Norwegian medieval society was no longer considered unique; its development was conceived as more in line with that of the neighbouring Scandinavian societies and the rest of Europe (Seip 1940, 52–56; Dahl 1959, 247–52).

The classical statement of the materialist interpretation was given by one of Bull's pupils, Andreas Holmsen, in his survey of Norwegian history before 1660 which appeared first in 1939 and subsequently in three new and only slightly revised editions up to 1977 (Holmsen 1977). Other Norwegian medievalists have offered variations of the same interpretation (among them Lunden 1976; cf. Helle 1961, 349–52). But important aspects of it have also been challenged, first by the leading figure of Norwegian historical research in the second half of this century, Jens Arup Seip (1940), and later by others, including myself (Helle 1960; 1972; 1981). Nevertheless, we have all been influenced by this interpretation and have adopted parts of it. In wider perspective historical materialism should be seen as one of several influences which have, in the twentieth century, contributed to what may be termed a general sociological approach to Norwegian medieval history. Medieval society has increasingly been studied as a totality in which there is a functional connection between all occurrences—including economic and social as well as political and cultural phenomena. At the same time there has been a movement away from the study of political events to research into structural and institutional aspects of society.

In connection with these developments there have also been changes in the selection and treatment of historical evidence. The principles of nineteenth-century historical criticism were radically sharpened by Koht and Bull, under considerable debate and in interaction with similar tendencies in Swedish and Danish historical research, above all represented by the Swedish historian Lauritz Weibull (Dahl 1959, 236–42).

Koht's main contribution was to apply more consistently the principle of regarding the contents of historical narratives as coloured by the circumstances under which they originated. Thus he thought it possible to group the sagas and chronicles of Norwegian kings according to the influence of contemporary politics on their presentations of past and contemporary history (Koht 1921, 76–91, 156–81). His practical applications of this principle have met with opposition. But the principle has in itself become an integral part of historical research, namely that the contents of sagas and other narratives should be critically interpreted in the light of their genesis and that one should always be aware of contemporary influences on presentations of the past. This is an approach which has also contributed to a more conscious use of medieval literary works as sources for the study of various aspects of the milieux which produced them.

Bull carried historical saga criticism to a more radical conclusion than Koht. In 1931 he commented upon the fact that Norwegian political history from the ninth to the twelfth century had previously been presented coherently on the basis of sagas written in the thirteenth century, above all Snorri Sturluson's *Heimskringla*. 'We now know,' he continued, 'that this is due to a failure to appreciate the true character both of this literature in itself and of the tradition on which it builds ... We should therefore abandon any illusion that Snorri's masterly historical narrative bears any deep resemblance to what actually happened in the period between the Battle of Hafrsfjord and the Battle of Re' (i. e. from about 900 to 1177) (Bull 1931, 9; my translation).

Bull's statement has been rejected as too sweeping. For my own part, I would hesitate to include most of the twelfth century in the period about which thirteenth-century Kings' Sagas can provide no deeper knowledge. But it would be hardly wise to deny the soundness of his implication that sagas of a more distant past should not be taken at face value unless there are specific reasons for doing so. In the twentieth century such reasons have increasingly, and more consistently than before, been sought by confronting later saga narratives with information that can be derived from contemporary written evidence, fragmentary as it is, and from archaeological material.

The more radical historical criticism of the twentieth century and the parallel movement away from the study of political events have made medieval historians attach increasing importance to other types of historical evidence than the sagas. For the period before 1200 place-names, law texts and archaeological material have been used as well as skaldic and Eddic verse, annalistic notices, runic and other inscriptions. In their studies of presumably slowly changing or fairly constant features of social structure Norwegian historians have also made frequent use of the so-called 'regressive' or 'retrospective' method, in the sense that they have drawn inferences about both early and high medieval conditions from later records, land-registers, tax-lists, public accounts etc.

One might think that the development of twentieth-century medieval research has made the historiography of the preceding century obsolete; this, however, is not the case. There is still much to be learned from the detailed and penetrating research of Munch and others into political events and biographical matters. And today's general sociological approach to medieval society is quite clearly indebted to the general interpretations put forward by Sars and his predecessors; we still identify many of the same problems and have also adopted, or at least adapted, some of their solutions to them. Still, there is no doubt that any survey of Norwegian medieval history would today be written in quite another fashion than was the case a hundred years ago.

At this juncture I would like to illustrate the point by giving some samples of my own presentation of the main historical developments and conditions in the period 800–1200, as it was published last year in a volume of Norwegian history from the Vikings to the present day (Helle 1991). I do not, of course, expect other Norwegian medievalists to agree with me on everything; they will definitely not. But I nevertheless think it is right to say that I have written a survey within the mainstream of current research.

I begin my book with a brief presentation of the Norwegian natural environment at the beginning of the Viking Age (Helle 1991, 13–19). What concern me are the natural conditions for mixed farming and other means of subsistence, communications and social life in general. Like the conservative historians of the late nineteenth century I seek to stress the scarcity of cultivable soil in Norway, but also to identify where such soil was to be found. Historical geography was a field of interest for nineteenth-century historians too. There can, however, be little doubt that my environmental sketch, in which I try to conjure up a picture of Norway's geography at the beginning of the historical period by thinking away the changes man has been responsible for since then, is typical of an ecological approach belonging to the late twentieth century.

Demographic studies form an important part of current historical research in Norway and have also given a new dimension to medieval history. Throughout the whole of the Middle Ages, Norway was a predominantly agrarian society in which towns were few and small and in which the agricultural population was settled on separate farms and not in villages as was the case in most of Denmark, the central parts of Sweden and most of the rest of Europe. This pattern of settlement, determined by the fragmented topography of the country, was an impediment to the formation of large, compact estates in the hands of aristocratic landowners. It also makes it possible to work out the volume of settlement in terms of the number of farms with their own names at given times, as they are indicated by place-names and other information in both contemporary and later sources. We cannot determine with any accuracy the extent to which the farms named in extant sources were divided into holdings, i. e. actual working units occupied by separate households, without names of their own having been recorded. Nor do we know the average number of people living on each holding. Still, the demographic research of the last three decades has laid the foundations for a rough estimate of the population of medieval Norway at somewhere between 300,000 and 550,000 when it peaked around 1300 (Helle 1991, 35–37). This may have been about double the early Viking-Age population. In the interval there had, therefore, been a very considerable growth of population and a corresponding expansion of agrarian settlement.

We are ignorant of the causes of this growth. From what we know of the contemporary European situation and conditions in Norway in the early modern period, there can be little doubt that the average expectation of life at birth was very low. The examination of skeletal material from a number of medieval Scandinavian graveyards suggests it lay well under 30 years. It was kept low above all by high infant mortality and deaths amongst young people. When, in spite of this, the population rose, it must have been because a high death rate was more than matched by an even higher birth rate. Women must, for the most part, have begun to produce children on reaching child-bearing age. Early and frequent child-bearing seems to have been the main cause of a lower expectation of life amongst women than amongst men, at least in the High Middle Ages and possibly earlier as well (Helle 1991, 41–42).

This, by the way, is one instance of the growing interest in the medieval history of gender in recent years. In my survey I also touch upon the role of women in agricultural and urban work, their social position and their economic rights according to medieval law texts (Helle 1991, 56–58).

In recent research the Norwegian expansion overseas in the Viking Age has been explained as being a consequence of demographic conditions: the increase of population and the resulting pressure on resources, particularly in western Norway. Here, the reserves of cultivable land appear to have been modest already in the Viking Age, and it was from here that the bulk of Viking expeditions set out. This is an explanation that does not preclude other causes and motives having contributed to Viking expansionism. We should not dismiss the possibility that it was to some extent the result of political unrest at home, as was believed by Icelandic historians of the twelfth and thirteenth centuries. The Vikings were also undoubtedly driven by a spirit of adventure. They partly followed old trade routes, lured by the riches they knew were to be found along them. Plunder was often the motive, but also more peaceful trade. On the other hand, the Norse colonization of the Atlantic islands can hardly be explained except within a context of less favourable economic conditions at home than in the areas which attracted the broad mass of colonists (Helle 1991, 26–27, 39).

In modern Norwegian archaeological and historical research into the Viking Age attention has generally been given more to conditions and developments at home than to Viking activity abroad. In my own survey, I stress the fact that it was during the Viking Age that Norway was first opened to Europe on a significant scale. Christian influences began to trickle in and led eventually to what amounted to a cultural revolution. It is also relevant that Norwegians abroad became aware of more sophisticated forms of political organization under princely power and in co-operation with a Christian Church. Among other things they discovered too the role that urban centres could play in this context (Helle 1991, 27).

The study of the Conversion and of urbanization are both good examples of the shift of weight of historical research away from later saga evidence to other types of source material, in these cases particularly archaeological material. In accordance with the saga tradition, nineteenth-century historians considered the conversion of Norway to be the work of the two missionary kings Olaf Tryggvason and Olaf Haraldsson in the last years of the tenth and the early decades of the eleventh centuries. In modern research the change of burial customs and the existence of early stone crosses in western Norway have been used to support the view that Christianity started to extend itself to the coastal districts of southern and western Norway earlier in the Viking Age (Helle 1987, 89). In the same way the extensive urban archaeological excavations of recent decades have in some cases made it possible to uncover earlier stages of urbanization than the royal foundations mentioned in later sagas and chronicles of towns from about AD 1000 onwards (Øye 1992).

As to the social structure of Viking-Age Norway, a crucial question is this: to what extent were the broad mass of people, the peasants, already at that time tenant farmers and so to what extent was there a basis for a Viking-Age aristocracy in the payments and services of such farmers? The tenancy system existed as far back as it is possible to go with the help of written records, but it is not possible to measure just how widespread it was, relative to the freeholder system, before 1300 or thereabouts, by which time the great majority of Norwegian farmers were obviously renting their land, in whole or in part, from clerical or secular landowners.

There have been two main schools of thought on this issue. The older one, represented by among others Munch and Sars, suggests that the tenancy system was well developed and probably embraced the majority of the country's farmers well before the twelfth century. A more recent view, held by Bull and the younger Holmsen, suggests that a shift from freeholder to tenant status only took place, for the majority of farmers, in the last two or three centuries before 1300. According to this view, which has one of its roots in the writings of Keyser, the starting-point of Norwegian social history was a society of freeholding peasants all with holdings of more or less equal size. In the course of the High Middle Ages the majority of these peasants were then reduced from freeholders to tenants. This development created a clerical and lay aristocracy which separated itself from the broad mass of the population and ruled the people through the Church and State (Helle 1961, 350–53).

Neither of these hypotheses has much in the way of evidence to support it, and my own suggestion is that the truth lies somewhere in between. The growth of population from the seventh century onwards, and for that matter even in earlier periods, may have led to the creation of a number of subordinate and dependent holdings; in other words to an early form of the tenancy system. There are indications, emphasized not least by the elder Holmsen, that from the Viking Age, at the latest, collections of dependant holdings were to be found at least in the coastal districts of western Norway around seats of landed proprietors.

Later the system of tenant farmers spread more widely. The colonization of new land led to more and more tenants under public or private landowners. The larger landowners could find it more profitable to rent out their lands than to farm them on their own account in a time of rising population and high land rents. This, together with the clearing of land, could be the main reason why the unfree largely disappeared in the course of the twelfth century; in economic terms it paid to put freed slaves on rented land rather than to work that land with the help of slaves. In accordance with recent research, I consider slavery to have been of some economic significance in the Viking Age, although its importance cannot of course be assessed exactly (Helle 1991, 51–54).

What, then, of the development of a Norwegian aristocracy? Today most Norwegian historians would probably agree that Viking-Age society must to some extent have been an aristocratic society. The Viking expeditions abroad could hardly have been feasible without the organising capacity of chiefs and leaders over groups of men who stood in a dependent, patron–client relationship to them at home as well. Gradually as the Viking expeditions increased they produced their own warrior chiefs. The foremost among them were able to found kingdoms both at home and abroad. Viking wealth acquired by warfare and trade was an effective means of winning support and building up power and prestige within the social system at home (Helle 1991, 26).

All in all, it is difficult today to maintain the view that the starting point of Norwegian social history was a society of more or less equal freeholders. There is relatively sound evidence from the Viking Age and even earlier for a more differentiated social structure with a family aristocracy at the top led by regional chieftains and slaves at the bottom. In between there was a peasantry of both freeholders and tenant farmers.

It should, however, be stressed that the tenants, as we meet them in the provincial law codes representative of the twelfth century, were legally free individuals and in no way personally beholden to the landowners. They cultivated the soil they leased independently on a contract basis. In other words, there was no serfdom or villainage in medieval Norway. Moreover, what there were of economic and social differences among the peasantry of the time probably owed as much to the size and qualities of the holdings as to whether one enjoyed the status of freeholder or tenant. This would seem to support the time-honoured view that medieval Norwegian peasant society was, after all, relatively egalitarian and not dominated by the native aristocracy to the degree that was usual in contemporary Europe. And Sars was probably right in suggesting that this has affected the further development of Norwegian society down towards our own times (Helle 1991, 50–51, 61).

In all probability there existed, at the beginning of the historical period, a number of local and regional chieftainships in Norway. The inbuilt tendency for some chieftaincies to expand at the cost of their rivals increased in the Viking Age and was the starting point for the development of more extensive political and social units (Helle 1991, 24–26).

According to texts of the twelfth and thirteenth centuries, Harald Finehair was the first king to rule over the whole of Norway. And Snorri Sturluson in *Heimskringla* is the first saga-writer to describe in detail, more than three centuries after the events, Harald's conquest of one *fylki* after another until his final victory in Hafrsfjord in south-western Norway towards the end of the ninth century. Today, Snorri's presentation of Harald's systematic unification of the realm must be rejected as an unhistorical reconstruction. But it is still reasonable to regard Harald as a ruler who took an important early step in the building up of a national kingdom (Helle 1991, 28–29).

As I see it, the actual royal unification of Norwegian territory was a politico-military process that took more than three hundred years to complete. Roughly speaking it fell into two main phases. The first phase began in earnest with Harald Finehair and stretched down to the middle of the eleventh century. For this phase I agree with Bull that we must abandon any illusion that the detailed accounts of later sagas bear any *close* resemblance to the actual course of events. But there are indications that through most of the period a kingdom with roots in the west Norwegian coastal districts sought to win control over other parts of the country with varying but never permanent success. It may well be that Olaf Haraldsson was the first Norwegian king to assert himself over most of the country at one and the same time, in the second and third decades of the eleventh century. But we have to admit, as Norwegian historians have been rather reluctant to do, that his rule was merely an interval in a period extending from the beginning of the Viking Age onwards when Danish kings were the strongest political factor in Scandinavia, frequently with authority over greater or lesser parts of Norway, especially Viken (the Oslofjord area), which was closest to them.

It was not until the dissolution of the Danes' North-Sea empire on the death of King Cnut in 1035 that it was possible for the Norwegian royal power to obtain permanent control over the bulk of Norwegian territory. For a time in the eleventh century, in the reigns of Magnus Olafsson and Harald Sigurdsson ('Hardrada'), Norway was even on the offensive against its neighbours and Norwegian territory was secured to the south along the present Swedish coast to the Göta älv. At the same time the monarchy managed to take control of the whole kingdom including the rich agricultural inland districts in eastern Norway and in Trøndelag to the north.

Earlier historiography tended to regard the political unification of Norway as complete by about the middle of the eleventh century. There then followed a period of relative political stability and peace. But there were times when two or more kings, each with their power base in different parts of the country, ruled at one and the same time, which, in my view, is clear evidence that political unity was far from complete. This becomes even clearer from the 1130s onwards. A series of disputes over the throne then began which were to occupy the next hundred years and have subsequently been termed the 'Civil Wars'.

The Civil Wars may be regarded as the second and final phase of the unification struggle. They ended, in the first half of the thirteenth century, with victory and exclusive control over the whole country for the kingdom of the Sverre family (the 'Birchlegs'). I find it natural to enlarge on a point first made by Bull, namely that it was not until well into the thirteenth century that there had finally been built up a social and political organization, and, I would add, an associated ideology, which could bind the kingdom permanently together (Helle 1991, 29–30).

An important aspect of the development of a national kingdom was the relationship between royal power and the secular aristocracy. Most nineteenth-century historians stressed, as we have seen, what they considered to have been a continuing conflict between the two parties, which led eventually to a clear weakening (in Sars's view almost an elimination) of the aristocratic element of society. The twentieth-century materialists were of the opposite opinion: the aristocracy, and indeed the clergy, were strengthened through the growth of the tenancy system and contributed fundamentally to the development of a national kingdom which came to act as an instrument of their own interests.

Personally, I would tend to follow the materialists so far as to regard a Norwegian aristocracy with local and regional influence as a necessary precondition for the unification of the kingdom. There were, no doubt, frequent conflicts between kings and more independent chieftains and magnates, as is testified by skaldic verse and sagas. Even so, royal power could hardly be built up over a major part of the country without some kind of organizational arrangement between the early kings and a local aristocracy which had a power base the kings themselves still lacked outside their core territory. In the long run this was achieved by incorporating the magnates of the country into the royal *hirð* or body of retainers.

The *hirð* originally served as the bodyguard and household of an itinerant king and constituted the core of his military power. In the course of time, however, it came to function as a corps of administrative personnel as well, comprising royal officials and helpers in the local districts. The termination of the first phase of the unification struggle in the eleventh century was connected with the downfall of the last of the more independent local chieftains of the land and the subordination of other magnates under the king as *lendir menn* or 'landed men', i.e. men who in return for fealty and service were provided with an income from royal land in addition to their own. In the following period royal service in the *hirð* increasingly attracted magnates and leading peasants from all over the country, so that already before Sverre's reign *hirð* membership had come a long way towards becoming the criterion of lay aristocratic status, thus transforming the earlier local family aristocracy into a service aristocracy. During the civil wars this aristocracy was as yet divided between rival kings and pretenders. The wars ended when it had been united under one king, Haakon Haakonsson, in the 1220s (Helle 1991, 28–31).

It is my conclusion, then, that Aschehoug was right when, in the 1860s, he stressed that the increasing medieval royal power was built on cooperation with a lay aristocracy. Whether the transformation of a local family aristocracy into a service aristocracy led to a strengthening or weakening of the aristocratic element of Norwegian society is difficult to say. In my judgement, this was an element of great internal political importance throughout the whole of the Middle Ages, but perhaps never a particularly strong element socially compared with the contemporary aristocracy of other European countries. At least from the twelfth century, when contemporary written evidence begins to shed more light upon them, Norwegian magnates appear to have been relatively few in number and largely without the private economic resources that would have enabled them to play an independent political role. The Viking-Age sources of wealth had largely dried up and the country lacked the natural conditions for a strong and numerous landed aristocracy. This may again explain the willingness of the existing aristocracy to serve the monarchy and thereby obtain a share of royal income and power (Helle 1991, 30–31, 58–61, 79).

Another condition necessary for the development of a national system of government was the collaboration of the Church and the clergy with the monarchy. Since the impact of Christianity is given separate treatment elsewhere in this volume I shall not go into details on this matter here. I would only stress, as Sars has already pointed out, that the introduction of Christianity and a national Church organization must have served the interests of the monarchy. It helped to break down the old pagan organization of society, led by local chiefs and magnates, wherever it opposed the king. Everywhere the conversion to Christianity could be made a factor in the reorganization of local communities and their incorporation into the kingdom. As the protector and head of the Church, the king acquired both power and an exalted position in society. In a wider sense the clergy were advocates to the nation for the king's cause and were instrumental in creating a monarchical political ideology. Christian teaching allowed itself without difficulty to be enlisted in support of the more permanent secular arrangement of society that the monarchy stood for (Helle 1991, 31–33).

Even if the *hirð* aristocracy and the clergy played key roles in the political unification of Norway, they were in themselves too slender a basis on which to build national royal power. Norway was and continued to be throughout the Middle Ages predominantly a peasant society. No significant official authority could be established and maintained without positive support from the agrarian population. The peasantry's need for a minimum level of peace and tranquillity, for legal and political stability, was an essential feature of politico-administrative development. As the process of unification progressed, this need came to be regarded as best met by the king in his capacity of upholder of the law and military leader. In this way he took on social functions which produced the conditions required for a more lasting support of the monarchy as an institution (Helle 1991, 71–72, 76–79). This functional relationship was first stressed by Jens Arup Seip in the first serious challenge made to the Marxist interpretation of Norwegian medieval history (1940, 55–56, 97–110).

In my view, Seip's idea of a functional relationship between the monarchy and the peasantry is a necessary part of a fuller explanation of why the kingdom succeeded in its endeavours for unification. It was this relationship that made possible the establishment of the *leiðangr* or naval levy under royal command and of the regional representative assemblies called *lǫgþing*, for a time the highest judicial assemblies in the land and the only ones that could ratify laws. Through them the peasantry of larger parts of the country could be legally associated with important royal initiatives, such as the establishment of the *leiðangr* and the adoption of Christianity and its Church organization. At the same time they promoted the maintenance of law and order according to regulations which brought the king income from legal fines and confiscations, created the conditions for the development of a royal judicial power apparatus and gave the king an enhanced ideological position as the enforcer and also, as time went on, the source of justice (Helle 1991, 33–34).

The development of a national monarchy, then, rested on a broader power base than the interests of the aristocracy and the clergy. The monarchy met serious needs of a peasantry which had greater political influence and military importance than that in almost any other contemporary European kingdom. This does not mean that the relationship between monarchy and peasantry was ever free from tension. But it had a positively functional aspect which procured for the monarchy a basic and necessary support. In this sense there may be a considerable element of truth in Sars's contention, which I mentioned at the start, namely that Norwegian society in the period 800–1200 assumed, or perhaps rather had, a basic 'democratic' character. In my own words I would characterize it as a not particularly aristocratic society (Helle 1991, 61, 75–78).

BIBLIOGRAPHY

Aschehoug, Torkel Halvorsen. 1866. *Statsforfatningen i Norge og Danmark indtil 1814.*
Bull, Edvard. 1931. *Fra omkring 1000 til 1280. Det norske folks liv og historie gjennem tidene* II.
Dahl, Ottar. 1952. *Historisk materialisme: historieoppfatningen hos Edvard Bull og Halvdan Koht.*
Dahl, Ottar. 1959. *Norsk historieforskning i 19. og 20. århundre.*
Helle, Knut. 1961. 'Tendenser i nyere norsk høymiddelalderforskning', [Norwegian] *Historisk Tidsskrift* XL, 337–70.
Helle, Knut. 1972. *Konge og gode menn i norsk riksstyring ca. 1150–1319.*
Helle, Knut. 1981. 'Norway in the High Middle Ages: recent views on the structure of society', *Scandinavian Journal of History* VI, 161–89.
Helle, Knut. 1987. 'Da Rogaland var Rygjafylke', *Fra Vistehola til Ekofisk: Rogaland gjennom tidene* I, 72–138.
Helle, Knut. 1991. 'Tiden fram til 1536', in Rolf Danielsen et al., *Grunntrekk i norsk historie fra vikingtid til våre dager*, 13–106.
Holmsen, Andreas. 1977. *Norges historie. Fra de eldste tider til 1660.*
Keyser, Rudolf. 1865–70. *Norges Historie* I–II.
Keyser, Rudolf. 1867. 'Norges Stats- og Retsforfatning i Middelalderen', *Efterladte Skrifter* I, 3–403.
Keyser, Rudolf. 1868. 'Udsigt over den norske Samfundsordens Udvikling i Middelalderen', *Samlede Afhandlinger*, 403–51.
Lunden, Kåre. 1976. *Norge under Sverreætten. Norges historie* III.
Munch, Peter Andreas. 1852–63. *Det norske Folks Historie* I–VI.
Sars, Johan Ernst. 1873–91. *Udsigt over den norske Historie* I–IV.
Sars, Johan Ernst. 1911–12. *Samlede Værker* I–IV.
Seip, Jens Arup. 1940. 'Problemer og metode i norsk middelalderforskning', [Norwegian] *Historisk tidsskrift* XXXII, 49–133.
Storm, Gustav. 1869. *Om den gamle norrøne Literatur.*
Øye, Ingvild (ed.). 1992. *Våre eldste byer. Onsdagskvelder i Bryggens Museum* VII.

GUNNAR KARLSSON

A CENTURY OF RESEARCH ON EARLY ICELANDIC SOCIETY

IT IS difficult to imagine a scholarly book which is, in a way, more thoroughly outdated than *Gullöld Íslendinga*, 'The Golden Age of Iceland', a collection of public lectures by Jón Jónsson Aðils, published for the first time in 1906. It is totally uncritical in its use of the sagas as historical sources, and nationalistic in a way that now sounds naive and, after the age of Fascism, almost blasphemous. Jón Aðils never doubted that a nationalistic sentiment was inherent in people. He was absolutely convinced that Icelandic society had lived a real golden age in the tenth and eleventh centuries; and he probably never suspected, what has been made clear by sociologists since his time (cf. Smith 1986, 191–200), that every population which adopts the idea of nationhood and fights for political independence always discovers a golden age in its past, whether supported by genuine historical evidence or not.

So, there can be no doubt that *Gullöld Íslendinga* is an outdated work. Nevertheless, if I were to write an essay on the social history of early Iceland, on daily life and social relations, one of the very first books I would consult would be Jón Aðils's *Gullöld Íslendinga*. I might not use many of Jón's interpretations, but his narrative would give me a good survey of the written sources, reliable or not, and his conclusions might make the best starting-point so far available for such a study. The comprehensiveness of his work, his consistent point of view and his optimism about what it is possible for us to know, make Jón Aðils still a good companion for a scholar who sets out to study any field he has dealt with.

Jón Aðils was one of the two Icelanders who first specialized in history at the University of Copenhagen. The other was Bogi Th. Melsteð, and they were both about to start their careers as historians when the Viking Society was established here in London (Ingi Sigurðsson 1986, 22). That of course was not the beginning of the study of early Icelandic society. It stretches back at least as far as to Arngrímur Jónsson lærði towards the end of the 16th century. In the 19th century, before the beginning of the period which I hope to evaluate here, a relatively solid basis had been laid for early Icelandic history with editions of texts and studies of source-material by Jón Sigurðsson, Konrad Maurer, Vilhjálmur Finsen and others. It was a basis which owed much to the German critical school of history. Against that background the works of the first professional Icelandic historians, Jón Aðils and Bogi Melsteð, may look somewhat primitive. In a preface to the second volume of his *Íslendinga saga*, published in 1910, Bogi Melsteð made a laudatory remark about the status of historical studies in Denmark where, he added, Professor Kristian Erslev had now founded a critical school of history. But the rest of Bogi's volume, some 570 pages, consists of little more than extracts from the Icelandic sagas, and it is not at all critical either with regard to the trustworthiness of the material or to its historical importance. It seems as if this first generation of professionally educated Icelandic historians was too anxious to give the Icelandic people a national history to be able to observe the time-honoured principles of source-criticism. In a way, this makes their works look more archaic now than they would do otherwise. But sometimes their determination to squeeze as much as possible out of any kind of early writing has enabled them to make contributions that are still of considerable value.

Fortunately, the first generation of Icelandic historians was not left isolated in their study of early Icelandic society. The very strong interest in saga-literature in western and northern Europe in the first decades of the 20th century gave rise to a number of studies of relevance to Icelandic history. One need only recall the works on legal history by Andreas Heusler or Hjalmar Falk's research into material culture.[1] Admittedly most of these non-Icelandic works were relatively limited in scope, and more often than not their ultimate aim was to improve the understanding of the sagas. Whereas Jón Aðils wanted to use the sagas to throw light on early Icelandic society, these foreign authors wanted to establish a knowledge of the society to throw light on the sagas. Nevertheless, these men wrote much valuable history. It is incredible how often, if one sets out to study an aspect of early Icelandic society, even a seemingly novel one, sooner or later one finds out that some German professor has written an article or a book about it more than half a century ago. To mention only one example: in 1926, about four decades before women's history became a fashionable subject in European universities, Professor Wolfgang Krause published a book in Göttingen which he called *Die Frau in der Sprache der altisländischen Familiengeschichten*. Professor Krause was a grammarian, and in the preface to his book he states that it 'is written from the viewpoint of the linguist; it is not intended to be in itself a work of cultural history, but to contribute with linguistic material to such a history' (my translation). And of course by modern standards there is not much proper history in Krause's book. But it is an organized collection of saga-episodes where women play a considerable role, and as such it could have become a valid contribution to cultural history if some institution somewhere had existed to collect such individual pieces of research and make a whole out of them. The lack of such an institution was extremely detrimental to the development of the study of Iceland's early history.

For all this work never developed into a coherent cultural history of Iceland. After Bogi Melsteð's rather unsuccessful attempt to write a comprehensive work on early Icelandic history, which ended with the third volume of his *Íslendinga saga* in 1930, no one else tried their hand at it until the 1950s. Then Björn

Þorsteinsson and Jón Jóhannesson wrote their books on the Icelandic commonwealth, Björn *Íslenzka þjóðveldið* in 1953 and Jón the first volume of his *Íslendinga saga* in 1956. When these books were written, the products of the three decades from the 1890s to the 1920s were considered largely outdated, and it was very evident that the three succeeding decades, from the 1920s to the 1950s, had produced no satisfactory substitute for them. Constitutional and political history was still largely based on the works of Konrad Maurer and Vilhjálmur Finsen, agricultural history on *Lýsing Íslands* III–IV by Þorvaldur Thoroddsen (1919–22) and the history of trade on the works of Bogi Melsteð, all works written before or around 1920. History of daily life had relied almost exclusively on *Íslendingasögur* and was therefore considered out of date in the 1950s. The new books contained no such history because the authors had no available knowledge to replace what had become obsolete. And this was not the end of the period of stagnation. In 1972 I was persuaded to write a survey of the political and economic history of the 12th and 13th centuries for *Saga Íslands*. I was a young and inexperienced scholar, and completely unable to create a new account on the basis of original sources. Consequently I found it very difficult to make my survey anything more than a retelling of Jón Jóhannesson's *Íslendinga saga*, and probably did not succeed in that aim at all. So little had happened in the field since he wrote his book almost twenty years before.

I am of course exaggerating. In fact, the period from the 1920s to the 1970s produced a number of important works. One can mention, for instance, the excellent studies of Ólafur Lárusson, the reports of archaeological excavations in Iceland in 1939 which appeared in *Forntida gårdar i Island* (1943), and the numerous detailed studies contributed to *Kulturhistorisk leksikon for nordisk middelalder* by Magnús Már Lárusson, Jakob Benediktsson, Björn Þorsteinsson and many others. But the scope of this paper does not allow me to go into detail, and I think that it is fair to say that the half-century from the 1920s to the 1970s was a period of stagnation. From some points of view it might even be regarded as a period of regress. What we thought we knew about early Icelandic society in the 1970s was probably far less than Bogi Melsteð and his contemporaries thought they knew about the same subject in the 1920s.

What was the reason for this long period of stagnation? The most obvious culprit is the book-prose theory in saga-studies. It forbade historians the use of *Íslendingasögur* as sources in the way they had used them before, and thus deprived them of their richest and most inspiring kind of evidence. Jón Jóhannesson was probably the most consistent of the book-prose theorists in Icelandic historiography, and therefore its consequences for the pursuit of history are very evident in his works. They also offer a good example of the shortcomings of his school of history, for there is no doubt that Jón was a first-class scholar, and no one could have done better within the limits set by the circumstances. First, he relied heavily on the historical works of the 12th and 13th centuries, *Íslendingabók* and *Landnámabók*. It is no coincidence that Jón wrote his doctoral dissertation on the relationships of the redactions of *Landnámabók* to each other, and attempted to get closer to the original 12th-century text. Second, constitutional history, based on the law code *Grágás*, loomed rather large in his *Íslendinga saga*, where constitutional details are given considerable space. And third, political events of the Sturlung Age were given great prominence, obviously because the book-prose theorists did not classify *Sturlunga saga* as a piece of fiction. Those parts of the account which were derived from what were now regarded as reliable written sources tended to swell, those that were based on evidence from *Íslendingasögur*, especially any aspect of social history, were reduced to little or nothing.

Thus historians lost interest in the sagas, and what was even more detrimental to the study of history, saga-scholars lost interest in society. The sagas were mainly (although not exclusively) considered to be the achievements of individual minds. They were no longer something that had happened in a society, been transformed into a text by a society and been remembered and retold in a society. Even the very few attempts that were made to explore the social background of the sagas as book-prose seem to have appeared useless to historians. Einar Ólafur Sveinsson, for instance, published in 1940 a slim volume called *Sturlungaöld*, to explain the background of *Njáls saga*, but there is no reference to this book in Jón Jóhannesson's *Íslendinga saga*. There are a few more signs of influence from Sigurður Nordal's *Íslenzk menning* in Jón Jóhannesson's book, but they are entirely restricted to the field of constitutional history. The historians of the period defined their subject in a peculiarly narrow way and left all history of ideas to the students of literature.

The book-prose theory can hardly be held totally responsible for this narrow definition of history, and in other respects that theory is an unsatisfactory explanation of the stagnation in Icelandic historiography. If historians had really felt inhibited by a lack of sources after the sagas had been excluded, they could have learned to utilize the immense potential hidden in *Grágás* and *Sturlunga saga* as sources for social history. They could also have learned to use the *Íslendingasögur* in a new way, as what is called *Überreste* in German and *levninger* in Danish. I do not know whether there is a technical term for this in English—'relics' perhaps—but the meaning is simply that we can use the sagas as sources for the ideas of their authors, not least about their own society, irrespective of whether the events described in the sagas actually took place. This use of *Íslendingasögur* is, if not completely absent, at least very rare in Icelandic historiography before the 1970s. And finally, if historians had really felt inhibited by a lack of sources, they could have done more to dig them up by promoting or conducting archaeological research.

The reason why historians did not feel inhibited by a lack of sources was the lack of historians. There were simply too few people working in Icelandic history, and there was no academic institution where the results of individual studies could be discussed and gathered into coherent wholes. It would hardly be realistic to expect to find such an institution anywhere outside Iceland, so we can say that the principal reason for the lack of progress in this field was the miserable state of the University of Iceland. For the first three decades of its existence, from 1911 to 1944, the University had only one chair of Icelandic history and none of foreign history. At this time there had been little good investigation of the later periods of Icelandic history (which is to a certain extent still the case), and the most prolific occupants of the chair, such as Páll Eggert Ólason (1921 to 1929), found it more important to study them than the early period which had previously got far more attention. A mistake in appointment happens now and then at any university without doing serious harm, but in such a small institution it can paralyse a branch of study for years. It is for instance rather obvious now that Árni Pálsson was the least well qualified of the three applicants when he was appointed professor of Icelandic history in 1931, and the story goes that the Faculty of Arts recommended him in order to deprive the then Minister of Education, Jónas Jónsson, of an opportunity to appoint a political follower, Þorkell Jóhannesson. However that may be, the consequence was that practically no work was done in history in the Faculty for a decade. From 1944 to the late 1960s there were two chairs of Icelandic history at the University, and it was not until the appointment of Jón Jóhannesson in 1943 that anything of importance was written there about the early, pre-1264 history.

This wretched state of affairs in the Faculty of Arts did not mean a complete stop to work on early history in Iceland because there were people active in the field outside the small group of professional historians. The Faculty of Law, with men like Ólafur Lárusson and Einar Arnórsson, contributed much more in this field during this period than the Faculty of Arts. We also have in Iceland a tradition of natural scientists studying history, mainly specialists in different branches of the earth sciences. I have already mentioned Þorvaldur Thoroddsen, a geologist who wrote what is still the most extensive history of Icelandic agriculture. This tradition was kept up during the period in question by people like Sigurður Þórarinsson and Trausti Einarsson, to name but two, and I should add that it has been maintained by younger scholars since: Þorleifur Einarsson, a geologist, Páll Bergþórsson, a meteorologist, Stefán Aðalsteinsson, a biologist, and many others have made invaluable contributions to our history.

In the late 1960s the status of history was radically altered at the University. A chair was established in foreign history, and history, foreign and Icelandic, was made into a separate discipline. For the first time we had a real forum for history in Iceland. A little later, in the 1970s, a Faculty of Social Sciences was established at the University, and a few people interested in early Icelandic society have worked, and still work, there. At about the same time we got a Faculty of Science, and there links between natural and human history are still maintained. Our Department of History has also grown considerably; there are now around ten of us working in it, so maybe we are now capable, for the first time, of constituting the necessary central institution for the study of early Icelandic society, if we prove to be sufficiently interested in this earliest part of our history.

It might be tempting for me as an Icelander to attribute the revival of the study of early Icelandic history and society since the 1970s to the growth of the University of Iceland. But, alas, it would not be true. Although a considerable part of the production of knowledge is ours, the new impulses, the ways of writing a new kind of history, have for the most part originated in other countries. This novelty consists principally in a new attitude towards the sagas, particularly the Íslendingasögur, and a rehabilitation of the sagas as historical sources. My colleague, Helgi Þorláksson, described this new movement in the Icelandic periodical Ný saga four years ago (1987) and attributed the innovation to a linking of traditional history and anthropology. Anthropological findings, which can be based on evidence from any society anywhere in the world, are used to confirm the evidence of the sagas. Because Helgi wrote this in an Icelandic periodical and can hardly be suspected of wanting to flatter our present hosts, as I may be, I can quote him on the point that the first authors who suggested this method for the study of early Icelandic society were two prominent English members of the Viking Society, Peter Foote and David Wilson, in The Viking Achievement in 1970. But the first to use the Íslendingasögur and back up their evidence with anthropological material was, according to Helgi, the Norwegian archaeologist and anthropologist Knut Odner. A year after The Viking Achievement appeared, in 1971, Odner published a study of economic structures in Western Norway in the period from about AD 200 to 600, using evidence from Egils saga and Landnámabók about the households of Skalla-Grímr and Geirmundr heljarskinn in the light of theories elaborated by the American anthropologist Karl Polanyi.

I do not doubt Helgi's statements about these early instances of an anthropological approach. But in general I prefer to see the new developments in early Icelandic history as coming primarily from two disciplines, literary study of the sagas and anthropology, and principally from two countries, Denmark and the United States.

As Helgi Þorláksson mentions in his article, the rehabilitation of the sagas within the domain of literary studies partly originated in the so-called new free-prose theory, whose proponents were more willing to see traditional material in the sagas than the typical book-prose scholars had done. In 1976 Óskar Halldórsson argued for the view that Hrafnkels saga Freysgoða, the saga which had been considered the purest fiction of all the sagas, was in fact based on oral tradition, and Óskar urged scholars to use the methods of folklore in studies of the sagas. A part of Óskar's argument was closely related to the anthropological approach. The story of Hrafnkell's attitude to his horse Freyfaxi reminds us strongly of what we know about horse-worship among other Indo-European peoples. Therefore, Óskar maintained, the story must be based on tradition. Here, as in the anthropological approach, the historical reality is tested by sources which are useful because they are about something other than, and remote from, Icelandic history. Apart from such cases the new free-prose theory, as represented by Óskar Halldórsson, does not seem to have much to offer historians. In principle the method is the same as that recommended by the book-prose theorists, to study each saga and each episode separately, and that has proved to lead to more uncertainties than we historians like to live with. Nevertheless I think that one can discern a certain influence from this new free-prose approach in the writings of some Icelandic scholars. I refer for instance to the ethnologist Jón Hnefill Aðalsteinsson who is mainly active in the study of heathen and folk religion.

Another movement has originated among scholars of Old Icelandic literature who have shown more interest in the society behind the sagas than the first generation of book-prose theorists did. A good example of this recent interest is Preben Meulengracht Sørensen's book, *Saga og samfund* (1977), an introduction to Old Icelandic literature based on an inspiring and original interpretation of the society that produced it. But such an interest of course does not in itself solve problems of sources or form a school of study, although it may provide new insights into neglected aspects of social history. And maybe if we examine these studies closely, it will emerge that the novel things in them owe their novelty to what Helgi Þorláksson designated the anthropological approach, namely the method of comparing with and confirming by something distant and unrelated.

My ponderings have thus led me to the conclusion that this general approach to the subject is *the* novelty in the studies of early Icelandic society since the 1970s. We could call it a structuralist approach, because it lies in discovering structures rather than in explaining events, and the proof of the existence of these structures lies partly in seeing them as instances of still larger structures. Sometimes it is a question of structures which in certain circumstances can occur anywhere in the world and can thus be called anthropological. It is not for that reason, though, that I choose to describe this new movement as an anthropological one, but because the discipline of social anthropology has contributed more to it than any other branch of learning, and this new school is, I suppose, part of a world-wide growth of interest in anthropology.

I have already said that the new movement originated in Denmark and America. From Denmark we have the works of Kirsten Hastrup, her book, *Culture and History in Medieval Iceland* (1985), and a number of interesting articles. From America we have the works of Jesse Byock, Carol Clover, William Ian Miller and

Paul Durrenberger, of whom as far as I know only Durrenberger is educated as an anthropologist. Kirsten Hastrup has dealt with very general systems of thought in early Iceland, systems of time and space, ethnicity and so on. She has not made much use of the sagas, so we cannot say that she has contributed to their reinstatement as historical sources. But she has made a very serious attempt to use the structuralist approach of social anthropology to extract a new kind of knowledge from the legislation and the learned, scientific literature of medieval Iceland. The American scholars have thrown new light on subjects as varied as bloodfeud, revenge, honour, exposure of babies, gift-exchange and means of keeping warfare within tolerable limits. This is a major achievement which could form the basis of a brand-new social history of early Iceland. On some of these subjects considerable knowledge can be found in sources which Jón Jóhannesson could have used, especially *Grágás* and *Sturlunga saga*. But the success of the American scholars depends mainly on their use of the *Íslendingasögur* in a way that was unknown until the 1970s.

Now I am not saying that anything new or successful is necessarily good or right. I do not mean to say that the scholars who have adopted an anthropological approach have said the last word on the subjects they have dealt with. All theories of systems of thought beg serious questions about the very existence of such systems. For instance, when the early Icelanders built a wall, *garðr*, around their hay-making *tún* or *taða*, they certainly did it for practical purposes, to keep the sheep and cattle out while the grass was growing and the hay was being made. When they decided in their legislation that certain legal procedures should take place outside this wall, *útangarðs*, and at a minimum distance from it, they probably did so to minimize the risk of violence. I find it difficult to accept that this entirely practical distinction between what was *útangarðs* and *innangarðs* could symbolize a general distinction between the world of human and the world of non-human beings, as Kirsten Hastrup maintains in her book (1985, 140–43). I cannot imagine that any early Icelander ever thought of his or her *útangarðs* area as a 'dangerous, unknown, and non-human wild space' (after all it was a part of the farm, often within a hundred yards of the house-door). And if no one ever thought this thought, where did the system of thought exist until the anthropologist discovered it?

As a further criticism I would note that anthropologists are often remarkably vague in describing how they mean to use the sagas: whether they think of them as *Traditionen* or *Überreste*, in the German terminology, whether they think that sagas describe the operations of structures as they actually existed in the tenth and eleventh centuries, or as the saga authors of the thirteenth or fourteenth centuries believed or imagined them to have been. In many cases it perhaps makes no great difference which of the two possibilities one has in mind, for we are dealing with long-lived structures that were most likely active throughout both periods, if they were active at all. Nevertheless it must be considered a scholarly duty to make clear in which sense the sources are taken to be valid, especially if these same sources have been deemed unreliable by earlier scholars. Often the proponents of anthropological methods seem to care rather little for the tradition of previous research, especially the tradition of Icelandic historiography. Some of these authors make little use of or reference to earlier work in Icelandic at all. This may be partly due to the scarcity of good Icelandic collections in foreign libraries, but partly, one suspects, to an inadequate knowledge of the Icelandic language. I stress, of course, that this is by no means true of all scholars in the field.[2] All the same, it is an important consideration. I was brought up to believe that learning the language of the natives was a basic rule of social anthropology. I hope that rule is not outmoded, and that the discipline will be more sternly maintained in future.

I was explicitly asked to give here a 'sweepingly authoritative review' of my subject. Trying to meet that demand, I would like to say that foreign students of early Icelandic society tend to go about their work with a bold inventiveness which we in Iceland deem somewhat irresponsible. Naturally, we feel more keenly than foreigners do that we are not merely stating something about people who died a thousand years ago and who will never find out—or care—what we say about them. We have a strong feeling, when we make statements on our history, that we are coming to grips with the cultural heritage of a nation. To give just one example: history education in schools requires a certain degree of consensus about national history. I am not recommending that we should go on writing and teaching obsolete history to secure this consensus; I am only making an observation. Nor do I maintain that we have been completely without bold and inventive ideas about our early history in Iceland. Þórhallur Vilmundarson's theory about Icelandic place-names could in its most drastic form invalidate all written sources about the settlement and the early constitutional and political history of the country. But in a way Þórhallur's theory is the exception that proves my rule, because it was received with quite remarkable hostility by many Icelanders. 'Just think what it leads to if it is true,' is said to have been the first comment of one of Þórhallur's colleagues. This comment is, of course, undocumented, and the story may be apocryphal. But if it is, it is a fiction of the kind that contains more truth than many an authenticated statement.

For these reasons it is to be expected that new approaches, new ways of thinking about Icelandic history, will generally originate outside Iceland, as long as we are so lucky that people outside the country find it worth while to think about our history. On the other hand, the University of Iceland is the institution which is best suited to collecting the information into a coherent whole and securing a necessary continuity of research. Thus I anticipate a fruitful division of labour between foreigners and Icelanders, which of course is not to be applied rigorously or deliberately, but may be none the less successful for that.

Finally, as a further hope I would like to remark that our sagas and our lawbooks *Grágás* and *Jónsbók* are far from exhausted as sources for history. They have immense potential as material for the history of the daily life of ordinary people, a potential which as yet has not been exploited to the full. I would prefer such a history to a new, hard critical school which could also emerge as a reaction to the present trend and more or less forbid the use of the sagas as historical sources altogether. Nevertheless we must remain a little careful in our use of the sagas. Sooner or later the anthropological history of Iceland will enter the international body of anthropological knowledge. We shall not only have a sort of science where knowledge about Indonesians is used to explain and confirm historical data about Icelanders. Knowledge about Icelanders will also be used to explain and confirm data about Indonesians. Thus, knowledge culled from Iceland will be— or at least ought to be—subjected to international criticism. We must at least try to ensure that it is as reliable as it claims.

NOTES

[1] For examples of works on Icelandic history by authors mentioned in this paper, down to 1980, see Gunnar Karlsson (1981).

[2] For instance, Jesse Byock (1988) has over 90 secondary works in Modern Icelandic in his bibliography. On the other hand William Ian Miller (1990) has only 23 and Kirsten Hastrup (1985) only 14. All three bibliographies include some 250–70 works each in other languages. Carol Clover (1988) wrote an article on 'The Politics of Scarcity: Notes on the Sex Ratio in early Scandinavia'—admittedly not in Iceland alone—with three references to scholarly works in Icelandic but 75 to those in other languages. Durrenberger (1992) has one work in Modern Icelandic in his bibliography.

BIBLIOGRAPHY

Björn Þorsteinsson. 1953. *Íslenzka þjóðveldið.*
Byock, Jesse L. 1988. *Medieval Iceland. Society, Sagas, and Power.*
Clover, Carol J. 1988. 'The Politics of Scarcity: Notes on the Sex Ratio in Early Scandinavia', *Scandinavian Studies* LX, 147–88.
Durrenberger, E. Paul. 1992. *The Dynamics of Medieval Iceland. Political Economy & Literature.*
Einar Ól. Sveinsson. 1940. *Sturlungaöld. Drög um íslenzka menningu á þrettándu öld.*
Guðni Jónsson. 1961. *Saga Háskóla Íslands. Yfirlit um hálfrar aldar starf.*
Gunnar Karlsson. 1981. *Hvarstæða. Leiðbeiningar um bókanotkun í sagnfræði.*
Hastrup, Kirsten. 1984. 'Defining a Society: the Icelandic Free State Between two Worlds', *Scandinavian Studies* LVI, 235–55.
Hastrup, Kirsten. 1985. *Culture and History in Medieval Iceland. An Anthropological Analysis of Structure and Change.*
Helgi Þorláksson. 1987. 'Að vita sann á sögunum. Hvaða vitneskju geta Íslendingasögurnar veitt um íslenskt þjóðfélag fyrir 1200?' *Ný saga* I, 87–96.
Ingi Sigurðsson. 1986. *Íslenzk sagnfræði frá miðri 19. öld til miðrar 20. aldar.*

Jón Hnefill Aðalsteinsson. 1985. 'Blót og þing. Trúarlegt og félagslegt hlutverk goða á tíundu öld', *Skírnir* CLIX, 123–42.
Jón Jónsson [Aðils]. 1906. *Gullöld Íslendinga. Menning og lífshættir feðra vorra á söguöldinni.*
Jón Jóhannesson. 1941. *Gerðir Landnámabókar.*
Jón Jóhannesson. 1956. *Íslendinga saga* I. *Þjóðveldisöld.*
Krause, Wolfgang. 1926. *Die Frau in der Sprache der altisländischen Familiengeschichten.*
Kulturhistorisk leksikon for nordisk middelalder fra vikingetid til reformationstid I–XXII. 1956–78.
Melsteð, Bogi Th. 1903–30. *Íslendinga saga* I–III.
Meulengracht Sørensen, Preben. 1977. *Saga og samfund. En indføring i oldislandsk litteratur.*
Miller, William Ian. 1990. *Bloodtaking and Peacemaking. Feud, Law, and Society in Saga Iceland.*
Nordal, Sigurður. 1942. *Íslenzk menning.*
Óskar Halldórsson. 1976. *Uppruni og þema Hrafnkels sögu.*
Smith, Anthony D. 1986. *The Ethnic Origins of Nations.*
Stenberger, Mårten (ed.). 1943. *Forntida gårdar i Island. Meddelanden från den nordiska arkeologiska undersökningen i Island sommaren 1939.*
Thoroddsen, Þorvaldur. 1919–22. *Landbúnaður á Íslandi. Sögulegt yfirlit* I–II. [*Lýsing Íslands* III–IV.]

VÉSTEINN ÓLASON

THE SAGAS OF ICELANDERS

IN DISCUSSIONS about the fate of the Sagas of Icelanders—or *Íslendingasögur*, as I shall call them here—no one seems to have wondered or worried about the fact that no *Íslendingasögur* have been written for ages. Much has been written about things that have happened to Icelanders, and stories have been written about the Middle Ages, even with characters that also appear in *Íslendingasögur*, but no one seriously considers these stories as genuine sagas, not even Halldór Laxness's *Gerpla*. It would be an interesting exercise for a student to prove that *Gerpla* is not an *Íslendingasaga*, but I dare not try the patience of my readers with such pedantry. No one could be more aware than competent modern novelists, like, say, Laxness or Sigrid Undset, that the writing of 'sagas' in our age is out of the question, because their world is no more.

The narrative art of the sagas, however modern it may seem in some respects, is part of a world of the past, a world we neither can nor will bring back to life, except in our imagination, but the sagas are one of the roads that are open to us if we want to travel in our minds to this world, either to study it for its own sake or even to try to view the present in the light of the past. Such a venture is fraught with dangers and difficulties, but during the last century a large number of scholars have been occupied in the study of the *Íslendingasögur*. It is of course a hopeless task to try to summarize or describe their work in a few pages, even if we have read it in its entirety, which I certainly have not. On the other hand, I think that there are many interesting topics for consideration, and I shall proceed to discuss some of them.

No small part of the debate about *Íslendingasögur* has revolved around one issue: the question of *Freiprosa* or *Buchprosa*, to use Heusler's well known terms (Heusler 1913, 53-55). The debate up to the 1960s has been conveniently summarized (Andersson 1964, Mundal 1977), and I shall try to avoid this issue here. I tend to look at this question as finally unanswerable and hence not worth pursuing at present at the expense of other issues, although our general ideas about the origin of sagas inevitably influence our understanding of them.

However that may be, I intend to concentrate on two objectives of saga studies which I choose to call 'appreciation' and 'interpretation'. The first is basically aesthetic and involves an attempt to understand and define the narrative art of the *Íslendingasögur* as an aesthetic form. The second is basically philosophical or moral, and involves an attempt to understand the message of the sagas, to reveal the kind of truth they tell. The distinction is obviously theoretical, because in the text the aesthetic and the moral, the form and the content, are unified. In considering these objectives I shall pay attention to another distinction, the one between the individual voice and character of a saga and the more abstract 'collective' voice and character of the genre as a whole. This distinction bears some relation to the *Buchprosa/Freiprosa* debate, but individual and collective voices are not mutually exclusive, though it may be difficult to listen carefully to both at the same time.

I find it not only appropriate but inevitable to begin my survey with *Epic and Romance*, Ker's classic study, which he seems to have begun exactly one hundred years ago here in London. In the preface to the first edition of 1896 Ker writes: 'Some of these notes have been already used, in a course of three lectures at the Royal Institution, in March 1892 . . . and in lectures given at University College and elsewhere.'[1] The inevitability of beginning with *Epic and Romance* does not only stem from its proximity in time and place to the founding of the distinguished society we are celebrating, but also from the conviction I assume I share with many students of the sagas, that Ker is the finest literary critic who has written about the Icelandic sagas, and that his insights and comments have retained their value to this day. It is therefore natural to use his work as a yardstick against which to measure other contributions.

Ker saw clearly what many later critics have dealt with, that the effect of the sagas arises in part from the conflict or contrast between sophisticated narrative art and matter that seems intractable and often trivial:

> It is no small part of the force of the Sagas, and at the same time a difficulty and an embarrassment, that they have so much of reality behind them. The element of history in them, and their close relation to the lives of those for whom they were made, have given them a substance and solidity beyond anything else in the imaginative stories of the Middle Ages (1957, 184).

The implications of this statement are spelt out in comments on individual sagas which at the same time give a clear picture of Ker's preferences: *Njáls saga* is 'the greatest of all the Sagas', yet 'carries an even greater burden of particulars' (190) than other sagas. *Víga-Glúms saga* has 'biographical unity' and 'interest of character', but does 'not attain to tragedy', and he places it 'midway between the closer knit texture of *Gísla saga* and the laxity of construction in the stories without a hero, or with more than one' (193–94). *Gísla saga* and *Grettis saga* produce 'one single impressive and tragical effect, leaving the mind with a sense of definite and necessary movement towards a tragic conclusion' (195). But he has no taste for 'the imbecile continuation of the story after Grettir's death and his brother's vengeance' (195). *Hrafnkels saga* and *Bandamanna saga* 'appear to have discovered and fixed for themselves the canons of good imaginative narrative in short compass, and to have freed themselves, in a more summary way than *Njála*, from the encumbrances of traditional history, and the distracting interests of the antiquarian and the genealogist' (199).[2]

In his chapter about matter and form Ker discusses a conflict between 'the difficulties of reluctant subject-matter' and 'that sense of form which was revealed in the older poetic designs' (199). His aesthetics are those of the classicist and appear in his emphasis on 'sense of form', his preference for good taste and moderation, and for a balanced composition. Although some readers may share his aesthetic standards today, many of us no doubt disagree with him on the ending of *Grettis saga*, which is delightful reading and probably significant for the structure and meaning of the saga (Hume 1974; Guðmundur Andri Thorsson 1990). Ker's emphasis on balanced composition may also have made it impossible for him fully to appreciate what I experience as narrative excellence in *Egils saga*. He praises the composition of the first part of the saga, and adds: 'After this compact and splendid piece of work the adventures of Egil Skallagrimsson appear rather ineffectual and erratic, in spite of some brilliant episodes' (192–93). Later (220) he talks of 'want of comprehensive imagination in the author' (of *Egils saga*). In a way he is right here as usual, but nevertheless I feel that he fails to do justice to the sustained brilliance of the description of Egill in this saga, which has been recognized by many of its readers. The reason for this difference of opinion can hardly be that Egill is more appealing from a moral than from an aesthetic point of view. It must stem from different aesthetic standards.

In his discussion of the heroic ideal of the sagas Ker again remarks on what he sees more of in the sagas than in any other heroic literature and calls 'the meanness of reality', but he adds:

> . . . no appreciation of this 'common life' in the Sagas can be just, if it ignores the essentially 'heroic' nature of the moral laws under which the Icelandic narratives are conducted . . . there can be no doubt that the Sagas were composed under the direction of an heroic ideal, identical in most respects with that of the older heroic poetry (202).

At the same time he notes a phenomenon which is more easily explained by what is now known of the sagas' literary history than it was in his day: sometimes they seem to move on the 'brink of decay', to be on the verge of formal heroics where the emphasis is more on external signs of heroism as an abstract phenomenon than on its integration of ideal and conduct. His example, which will spring to the mind of other saga readers too, is Kjartan Óláfsson in *Laxdœla saga*. In the treatment of comedy it becomes clear, however, that Ker does not feel that the sagas have crossed this boundary (no one would deny that some fourteenth-century sagas have done so):

> The Sagas have comedy in them, comic incidents and characters, because they have no notion of the dignity of abstract and limited heroics; because they cannot understand the life of Iceland otherwise than in full, with all its elements together (229).

It would be easy to continue quoting Ker. There is practically no end to memorable formulations in the chapters with the headings 'Tragic Imagination', 'Comedy', and 'The Art of Narrative', but I assume that many of them are either vividly remembered by most of my readers or stored somewhere in the mind with the wisdom whose origin one has forgotten. I should like to add one more quotation though, which I think states very succinctly Ker's views on the development of the form:

> The relation of the Sagas to the older poetry may be expressed in this way, perhaps, that they are the last stage in a progress from the earliest mythical imagination, and the earliest dirges and encomiums of the great men of a tribe, to a consistent and orderly form of narrative literature, attained by the direction of a critical faculty which kept out absurdities, without impairing the dramatic energy of the story (210).

Although Ker was more aware of the differences between individual sagas than many of his contemporaries and had a keen perception of their varying purity of tone, he was not primarily interested in the individuality of the voices of the sagamen, but rather in what might be called their collective voice. He had an unusual knowledge of medieval literature—and not only medieval I am sure—and his aim was to place the sagas as a specific type of narrative art. His success was remarkable.

Ker's cultural orientation was European in the best sense, as far as can be judged from the periphery. He had great knowledge of the whole field of Germanic literature in the Middle Ages, but his approach was not particularly Germanic. He was not interested in the sagas as products of a Germanic spirit, but rather in their own right as a form of narrative art.

Around the turn of the century German and Scandinavian scholars, at least, were generally more interested in literary works as expressions of a spirit, either of an individual, of a nation or of a period, than in aesthetic form for its own sake. The *Íslendingasögur* were considered prime examples of pre-Christian Germanic spirit and eagerly studied as such. Rather than dwell on the excesses and distortions this approach could sometimes lead to, I should like to discuss two of its best representatives. The obvious choice is Andreas Heusler. A highly cultivated and sensitive man, he seems to have felt deeply that what he saw as Germanic values and Germanic style needed to be defined and defended in opposition to culture of Mediterranean origin, and in the *Íslendingasögur*, as well as in Germanic heroic poetry, he found the purest examples of what he called *Germanentum* (1934).[3] We may find this interest in *Germanentum* objectionable in the light of a history we see from a point of view that was not his, but we must not let that blind us to Heusler's great learning and his feeling for the qualities of Germanic literature including the sagas. His contribution to the description and analysis of Iceland's legal system and the system of feud according to the sagas has lasting value as interpretation and as social history, although he draws conclusions from it about Germanic society in general which are probably too far-reaching (Heusler 1911 and 1912). His description of the sagas in *Altgermanische Dichtung* (1941) is brilliant and more systematic than Ker's description in *Epic and Romance*. Along with the above mentioned studies it shows that Heusler's greatest strength may, after all, have been in his appreciation of aesthetic as well as social forms rather than in the interpretation of Germanic spirit. Although he had a firm belief in oral sagas, he had a nuanced attitude to the preserved texts, and he was open to consideration of some influence of the time of writing. We may feel that his interest in the sagas was somewhat biased and that he underestimated their debt to Mediterranean culture, but he had a sharp eye for many of their most interesting features, and it is always worth while to see what he has to say on a particular subject.

While Heusler is well known and frequently quoted in saga scholarship, the same can hardly be said of another scholar who studied the world view or culture of the Germanic peoples in pre-Christian times, although he probably did not value it any higher than other cultures. I am referring to the Danish linguist and historian of religion Vilhelm Grønbech.

Grønbech did not study the sagas for their own sake. In his great work, *Vor folkeæt i oldtiden*, which first appeared in four volumes in the years 1909–12, he sought to describe the native pre-Christian culture of the Germanic peoples.[4] The *Íslendingasögur* were among his most important sources, and therefore his interpretation of Germanic or Teutonic culture is to a considerable degree an interpretation of the sagas. This applies particularly to the first volume, *Lykkemand og niding*, from 1909. I dare not say how accurate Grønbech's description of the world and world view of the Teutons is, but he is always specific about his sources, and his interpretation of the sagas retains its value independently of the validity of his more general statements.

Grønbech's interest was historical and philosophical. He wanted to reveal the truth the sagas had to tell about our forefathers and consequently about humanity and culture in general. He may have had a stronger belief in the historicity of the sagas than is now current, but this is mostly irrelevant because he is not interested in isolated facts but in a world view, in the ideas and feelings governing the acts of men. He understood that one does not find new truths in the texts by using them as a mirror, looking for the familiar, but rather by concentrating on the strange and unfamiliar. He puts it this way:

> Sagen er den at Nordboernes særhed, snæverhed, ensidighed, det inhumane ved dem er begrundet i selve deres kulturs væsen. De er karakterer, men på et grundlag som slet ikke kunne bære et menneskeliv nu. Deres liv er i kultur, men denne kultur har et helt andet centrum end vor. Deres harmoni er grundforskellig fra alt hvad vi besidder eller stræber efter. Deres kultur har sin skønhed, og den havde i sin glanstid livets ubestridelige berettigelse; men den var bunden til en form for selvhævdelse og selvvurdering som, indsat i vor verden, vilde få plads blandt de nedbrydende magter.
> Man kan ikke gå fra dem til os, eller omvendt, uden at afklæde sig sin menneskelighed og iføre sig en anden (1909, 18–19).

THE SAGAS OF ICELANDERS

However people read the *Íslendingasögur*, it can hardly escape notice that at the core of their world view lie ideas and feelings about the individual's relationship to his family or kin, about the honour of individual and kin, about the necessity and moral value of revenge for harm done to the kin, and about good fortune and bad. These concepts form the moral norm against which men's lives are judged. The semantics and coherence of these concepts are analysed by Grønbech in *Lykkemand og niding* under the chapter headings 'Fred' (Peace), 'Ære' (Honour), and 'Lykke' (Good Fortune). These are positive values and followed or conditioned by their opposites. No one has to my knowledge analysed this world view as thoroughly as Grønbech, and demonstrated how the key concepts come together in a unified moral code where the taking of life for revenge can be a holy duty, a categorical imperative.

Grønbech speaks without reservation about the importance of honour for the individual in this culture, and we recognize his individual from our reading of the *Íslendingasögur*:

> Han har kun eet syn på mennesket: mennesket som hævdende sig selv, hævdende sin ære, som han kalder det. Alt hvad der rører sig i manden, det må snos om, til det bliver en egenskab ved æren, førend han kan få fat på det, og al hans lidenskab gennes inde, til den finder ud til den bestemte side. Det punkt der samler alle linjer i sig er hævnen. Fordi hans hævn ikke er en tom, retlinet gentagelse af gjort uret, men en personlig genoprejsning, en åndelig selvhævdelse, betoning af kraft, værdi, ide: ære, derfor bliver hans hævndigtning aldrig gold, altid menneskelig; men ensidigheden viser sig deri, at kun det der gør manden til hævner og hjælper med til hævnens fuldbringelse, kun det der driver, inspirerer manden til selvhævdelse, kun det får udtryk; alt andet falder helt i skygge (1909, 15).

Grønbech continues by emphasizing that the world he is describing is a man's world where women play a limited role; although—I should like to add—the sagas often make women the most eloquent spokesmen for exactly this ideology. At the basis of this ideology lies the importance of kin, the peaceful love which is supposed to dominate the relationship of kinsmen. From the mutual obligations of kinsmen follows the idea of honour and the need for revenge as a bond of insurance; finally, the success of the kin in guarding their honour and keeping their peace is linked to their fortune. He compares this situation to modern culture: we need to be human beings to function as *frændr*, 'relatives'; they had to be *frændr*, 'kinsmen', to be human beings (1909, 208).

Grønbech's reader must realize that he is not describing reality as lived, not even as it is described in the sagas, but an ideology or system of norms by which reality is interpreted in life and in books and which modern readers must understand to be able to interpret these books correctly. He never claims that his description fits all life in the sagas. He says about Bolli and Kjartan in *Laxdæla saga*: 'Når først frændeuenigheden bevidst udnyttes som digterisk sujet, som i Laxdølas skildring af de to fætre der hidses op imod hinanden for en kvindes skyld, da befinder vi os i en ny verden' (59). About *Njáls saga* he says: 'den sentimentalt overarbejdede Njals saga lader jeg ude af betragtning; som *helhed* tilhører den en anden verden' (120).

These comments show that Grønbech was aware that individual sagas did not necessarily reflect the ideology he describes in a mechanical way, but he probably saw the conflicting elements as superficial. When he makes this comment on *Njáls saga*, he has already demonstrated how deeply rooted the morality of revenge is in this saga.

We shall probably never know to what extent the free farmers of Scandinavia in the Viking Age and their colleagues among other Germanic peoples conducted their lives in accordance with the moral code Grønbech describes, but no reader of the *Íslendingasögur* can deny that it seems real enough in the society they depict. And indeed his conclusions seem to be confirmed by many other sources. This moral code could hardly have been constructed by Christian authors in thirteenth-century Iceland.

Having perused the central works of these three scholars from the first decades of the century (although Heusler's summing up in the second edition of *Altgermanische Dichtung* only appeared in 1941), one can begin to wonder how much we have achieved in the way of appreciation and interpretation since their time. There is no denying, however, that our understanding of the *Íslendingasögur* has been radically changed by the discussion about their origins and nature, a discussion which has affected every aspect of research in this field.

When Heusler published the second edition of *Altgermanische Dichtung*, some of the most influential studies of the so-called 'Icelandic School' had already appeared or were about to appear: Einar Ólafur Sveinsson's *Um Njálu* (1933), the first volumes in the *Íslenzk fornrit* series, as well as a few slim volumes of *Studia Islandica*, both series edited by Sigurður Nordal. Heusler did not like the tendency of this school, and the disagreement was mainly about the existence and nature of 'oral sagas' as opposed to the role of a creative author. The Icelandic school was very influential for a while and has now suffered the fate of most conquerors in scholarly debates: new generations revolt against them and accuse them of simplifying the issues; and now their ideas are being simplified and even distorted.[5]

The traditional attitude to the *Íslendingasögur* in Iceland is in many ways quite opposite to the one current among non-Icelanders. The reader who comes to the sagas from the outside, as it were, immediately feels how different they are from most other literature, and the need to explain to oneself how one can enjoy stories about such wild and strange people has no doubt been the beginning of many a love affair with the sagas. Initially, such a reader will experience one saga as very similar to all the others, and only gradually begin to discern their individual voices. For generations of Icelanders, on the other hand, who were brought up reading or hearing the sagas, they were the narrative norm; people felt that the world of the sagas was their own; the geography was the same, the heroes were ancestors and models. There was great knowledge of the detail in the sagas, the acts and words of people were admired or criticized in the same way as those of politicians, film stars or athletes in our time. This naïve attitude was common when the Icelandic school started its work, and there still survive some remnants of it, although everyone knows by now that men of learning do not agree.

The Icelandic School was fighting on two fronts: against Icelandic naïveté, and against the belief in the sagas as vessels for a common Germanic or Nordic spirit. In place of these ideas they wanted to posit a model in which the *Íslendingasögur* were seen as thirteenth-century creations from material drawn from books and oral tradition, and even in some cases as fictional. The model in itself was not new. It had been adumbrated by Konrad Maurer and extended by Björn M. Ólsen and others. What was new was rather that a group of scholars were working along the same lines in the same place and publishing their work with the Icelandic public as their primary target. Moreover, the consequences of the new model for the appreciation and interpretation of the sagas began to appear more clearly. The nationalistic and ideological background for this work has been pointed out, and sometimes simplified; it is certainly important, although time does not allow me to enter into that debate.[6] It would also be tempting to discuss the introductions and commentaries of *Íslenzk fornrit*. Their paradox is that from the point of view of the new model they are burdened with many remains from the past; in the words of Ker one could say that they are 'immersed in matter', matter which from the point of view of literary criticism is often irrelevant; but that is another story.

The work of Sigurður Nordal, after his edition of *Orkneyinga saga* (1913–16) and his dissertation on the Olaf sagas (1914), has a strong anti-positivistic trend: he was an adherent of an aesthetics of expression in a romanticist vein, that is, he saw great works of art primarily as the expression of individual poetic genius, and the role of the critic was, with the help of intuition and learning, to recreate the original poetic vision and the personality of the poet or author. He did not, however, see the individual poet as above time and surroundings; on the contrary, he emphasized the relationship between genius and its age. This approach is nowhere more clearly to be seen than in his work on *Völuspá* (1923), but it is also manifest in his book on Snorri Sturluson (1920) and in several essays on modern Icelandic literature.

In view of this attitude of his to literature it may seem strange that Nordal never attempted the spiritual reconstruction of a saga author. His attempt to prove that Snorri is the author of *Egils saga* may be seen as part of such a project, since he had already written a book about Snorri, and his conclusion was, among other things, based on the personality of Snorri he had already constructed. The eagerness of his pupils to find authors for other *Íslendingasögur* can be explained by the need of the biographical school of criticism for an author as creator (Vésteinn Ólason 1984).

Nordal admitted his debt to both Ker and Heusler, but he did not have their interest in or keen eye for form. He could write a competent literary analysis if he needed to, as is shown by 25 pages of his *Hrafnkatla* essay (1940), but his basic interest was cultural interpretation, *Geistesgeschichte* if you like, and in this he is closely related to Grønbech. His most important contribution to the interpretation of *Íslendingasögur* may be his *Íslenzk menning* (1942), although he never wrote the volume containing an interpretation of the *Íslendingasögur* themselves. I have often wondered if the giving up of that project as well as the rather disappointing essay on saga literature in *Nordisk kultur* (1953), may not be explained by the fact that the *Íslendingasögur* are basically resistant to his analytical method: the authors were able to hide between the lines. Through essays and personal influence Sigurður Nordal made a significant contribution to the new understanding of *Íslendingasögur*, but his contribution to the appreciation and interpretation of the genre is mainly indirect.

Although Einar Ólafur Sveinsson worked in close cooperation with Sigurður Nordal when he was launching *Íslenzk fornrit* and *Studia Islandica*, they were quite different as scholars. Einar Ólafur was more of a literary critic in the usual sense. The literary critic appears in the introductions to his volumes in *Íslenzk fornrit*, where he differs from all the other editors to this day in the depth and scope of his comments on style, characterization, and in general on the specific literary qualities of each saga. His greatest achievement is his *Njála* research, summed up in the introduction to his edition (1954). From our present point of view he may sometimes go too far—especially in *Á Njálsbúð* (1943)—in treating the *Njála* characters as living personalities and furnishing them with modern psychology.[7] This tendency is less discernible in the introduction to the *Íslenzk fornrit* edition of *Njála*, where he skilfully combines appreciation and interpretation; I feel that it is a major contribution to saga studies. Needless to say, faults can be found, and later critics have explained several aspects better than he did,[8] but together with Ker and Heusler he stands, I think, as one of the literary critics of *Íslendingasögur* that scholars neglect at their own cost. He does not see the sagas from the same high perspective as Ker and Heusler do, but his great knowledge, and his closeness, enable him to appreciate the individual voice of sagas like *Njáls saga* or *Laxdœla saga* with a deeper and more nuanced perception and understanding.

The scholars forming the Icelandic school were not interested in theory, and we can blame them for not stating explicitly some of the basic assumptions they were making, but that was indeed a characteristic of scholarship in their time. It seems obvious to me, however, that the anti-theoretical bias, as well as the fact that these scholars were born and bred with the traditional Icelandic closeness to the sagas, made it difficult for them to keep the sagas and the saga world at a necessary distance, and consequently they tend to project their modern attitudes on to that world.

The Icelandic school became known for its disbelief in oral sagas, and for its source analysis and acceptance of fiction as one possible element in the creation of *Íslendingasögur*. Such ideas had appeared earlier, as already noted, and were evident also in the work of many non-Icelanders. But the change in attitudes affected all aspects of saga studies. An interesting attempt to revive the idea of unconscious art in the sagas was made in 1971 by Steblin-Kamenskij in his *Saga Mind*, which is the title of his book in the English translation (1973). Although I suspect that he is wrong on many of his main points, I consider his book healthy and entertaining reading for all saga scholars. Above all it highlights the vital importance of what his countryman A. J. Gurevitch (1985) calls 'categories of medieval culture' for the analysis of the products of that culture.

Studies in *Íslendingasögur* up to the 1950s, including the work of the Icelandic school, were dominated by an interest in origins and background. I have mentioned two notable exceptions: Ker's and Heusler's descriptions of the sagas as a form of narrative art. In literary studies in general the focus of interest had by the 1950s for some time been moving from origins to texts, and the movement continued from texts to audience, or to the whole literary process from origin to reception. In the last forty years we have seen an increasing flow of books and articles about the *Íslendingasögur* with literary analysis and interpretation as their main topic. It is impossible to do justice to this activity here, although there are many studies worthy of note that fall within the boundaries I have drawn for my discussion.[9]

The growth and diversity of theoretical debate in humanistic studies has necessarily influenced saga studies. New Criticism, Formalism, Structuralism, Narratology, Hermeneutics, Reader–Response Criticism, Feminist Criticism, Poststructuralism— the influence of all these schools or approaches can be detected in articles on the sagas. I have not yet seen a deconstruction of a saga, however, and one can always hope to be spared that experience. Instead of classifying saga criticism under such headings, I would like to use the rest of my space to point out three tendencies in saga criticism that have been influential and have yielded interesting results. I call them the European approach, the formalist approach, and the sociological approach. Many of the finest pieces of criticism and scholarship are not easily classified and are not caught by this net of mine.

The first school are the Europeans or Latinists. In revolt against the old Germanic preoccupation and an Icelandic nationalist bias, these scholars try to clarify the debt of the *Íslendingasögur* to religious literature and the European tradition. This is partly done by pointing out specific instances of loans and influences, partly through new interpretations of saga texts, which are supposed to exemplify Christian teaching and other ideas current in medieval Europe or to carry a hidden message in the allegorical tradition of the Middle Ages. Earlier generations of scholars had, of course, seen many instances of direct and indirect influence from religious literature in the *Íslendingasögur*. The Germanic school, and early bookprosaists such as Finnur Jónsson, had considered such elements as superficial and secondary, having been smuggled into the sagas by clerical scribes. The Icelandic school was in principle more open-minded towards seeing Christian ideas and literary influence as part of a saga from its creation, but interpreted the sagas in general as secular and dominated by heroic and political themes. Many of the scholars who have contributed significantly to clarifying the relationship of Old Icelandic literature and European learning, such as G. Turville-Petre and Peter Foote and many of their students, have done so without rejecting the insights of the Icelandic school.[10] Others, like Hermann Pálsson and Lars Lönnroth, have taken a step further in the direction of criticizing the basic assumptions of the Icelandic school about the indigenous culture of Iceland and see the sagas as permeated with Christian ideas and attitudes.[11]

In my opinion the European approach has yielded many interesting results which must be taken into account in the interpretation of individual sagas and in any attempt to define the dialectical relationship between indigenous Icelandic culture with Nordic and Germanic roots and the southern culture of mixed Christian/Jewish and Classical origin brought to the North with Christianity. Increased knowledge of medieval culture in general has opened new possibilities of interpreting the background of the sagas as well as their meaning. These possibilities are being used by many scholars and will undoubtedly bring important new results. But it must certainly be a case of 'both . . . and' rather than 'either . . . or'. Allegorical interpretation of the *Íslendingasögur* has in my opinion not been successful. The heroic and social interest is undeniably of overriding importance in the sagas, even the ones most clearly influenced by Christian morality like *Njáls saga*.

The Romanticists of the early 19th century saw the Eddas and sagas as *Volksdichtung*, and what I have called the Germanic school is a continuation of that attitude in a modified form. There are many links: the anonymity or absence of authors to mention only one. Many of the scholars writing about *Íslendingasögur* have been folklorists as well as philologists. Knut Liestøl is an outstanding example, and in his study of the origins of the *Íslendingasögur* (1929) he compares several features of narrative technique in sagas and folktales. Throughout this century the simple forms of folk narrative have been eagerly studied, narrative structure as well as textual patterns. Scholars have developed methods and terminology for the systematic study of narrative which have had some influence on saga studies. Partly it has been a question of applying to the study of sagas methods which in principle should apply to all narrative, such as ways of appreciating the function of time (e.g. van den Toorn 1961, Röhn 1976). Such methods are useful for exact description although they do not necessarily reveal features specific to sagas.

THE SAGAS OF ICELANDERS 37

In the sagas action dominates other aspects. The action revolves around conflict acted out as feud which follows certain rules as in a game. This makes the action of the sagas a challenge for narratology, and during the last quarter of a century several attempts have been made to formalize description of saga action through structural analysis. When Theodore Andersson introduced his 'feud pattern' in 1967 many of us received it with optimism. For one thing, it seemed an efficient tool for formal analysis which revealed a fixed pattern of composition in the *Íslendingasögur*; secondly, it seemed to strengthen the case for fully formed sagas in oral tradition, because it could be found in the oldest sagas. But it very soon appeared that the optimism was unfounded. On the one hand, this pattern was a rather crude tool and lacked the flexibility of the structural models that have been used with most success in the analysis of simpler forms of narrative.[12] Anderson's model does not function properly unless one can determine one or possibly two central climaxes around which the saga can be arranged in a nice pyramid. In many instances this can only be done by force and then the result conflicts with the impression given by the text. On the other hand, it is highly doubtful whether such a pattern, even if it were real, has any value as an argument for oral origin. In a widely read book on *Orality and Literacy*, Walter J. Ong argues that a pyramid form, such as the one Anderson finds, is characteristic of literary as opposed to oral composition (1982, 141–47).

Andersson's method was improved by Lars Lönnroth in his study of *Njáls saga* (1976), and similar methods have been applied by Joseph Harris in a study of *Íslendingaþættir* (1972). It is my belief that formal analysis of this sort can bring interesting results and will be continued, although some people may find such work tedious reading; it does have obvious limitations. Having read a structural analysis one is often tempted to ask: So what? What is the use of models and diagrams if and when they function? The answer is, in my opinion, that they are not an end in themselves but tools that ought to enable us to answer more exactly several kinds of questions. On the one hand, it is important to be able to discuss the form of *Íslendingasögur* in terms which make them easily comparable to other narrative forms. On the other hand, structural analysis of the action can help us to reveal important structures in the content, and thus lead us forward in the project of interpreting the sagas and their world. Attempts have been made, by Jesse Byock (1982), for instance, to combine the formal analysis of the action of feud with the underlying social realities. Although his model is very simple, too simple perhaps, it does not do violence to the narrative, and it focuses the attention on essential aspects of the conflicts.

This brings me to the third and last of the tendencies I want to mention. Grønbech and Heusler, Sigurður Nordal and Einar Ólafur Sveinsson were all, for different reasons and in different ways, interested in the social and intellectual world of the sagas. Such interest has greatly increased in recent years, mainly as a result of changes of emphasis in the study of medieval history. Anthropologists and historians have realized that although the sagas may be untrustworthy on particular facts, they are a mine of information about social mechanisms and mentality. In contrast to earlier generations of scholars, people now realize that the use of sagas as a source of information demands awareness of their literary form and sophisticated methods of analysis.[13] This has called for cooperation between literary scholarship and neighbouring disciplines, a cooperation that has only just begun but which may hold great promise. In addition to Jesse Byock (1982 and 1988) I should like to mention here the work of William Ian Miller (Andersson and Miller 1989 and Miller 1990), an American legal historian. It is, for instance, quite interesting to compare his analysis of the function of honour in saga society with Grønbech's. Although Grønbech was well aware of the economical and social conditions of the acquisition and maintenance of honour, his analysis is conducted in idealistic terms, making honour an existential question for individual and kin. Miller deals with honour in materialistic and political terms from the point of view of the community, seeing honour as a limited resource fought over by members of the ruling class (1990, 29–34). Miller's approach does not bring us nearer to the truth than Grønbech's, it tells a different truth. It is an interesting confirmation of his quantitative theory of honour, although he does not mention in it, as far as I have noticed, that it explains the need of young heroes to go abroad to renew and increase the supply of honour which is a recurrent theme in *Íslendingasögur* and *Íslendingaþættir*.

An important aspect of the modern social approach to the sagas is that it does not limit its interest to the question of origins, but is equally or even more interested in the audience.[14] The ideas presented in the sagas must have had resonance in the minds of the audiences for which they were originally intended, and their study must take into consideration a long process, comprising (1) the forming of tradition in the centuries prior to saga writing and its nature in that early society, (2) the development of a literary tradition from the introduction of Christianity onwards, (3) the rise and development of the writing of *Íslendingasögur* in the 13th century, and (4) the conditions of reception at the time of writing.

I have now entered the field of current problems, and it is high time to end this very selective survey. I hope I have been able to remind you that already in the first decades of the century we are commemorating, brilliant scholars and men of great learning had acquired a deep understanding of the art of the sagas and the world they describe. Nevertheless, I feel that a century of research has brought a considerable harvest, and that we now understand and appreciate many things better than people did one hundred years ago, and I have no doubt that the *Íslendingasögur* are going to interest scholars as well as the general reading public for many years to come. An attempt at a survey of research, imperfect though it may be, will at least reinforce one's strong feeling of how dependent scholarship is on time and circumstance. Historical and literary research has become more international in the years since the war, and this trend will continue. It would certainly be an anachronism now to name schools of research in national terms: a German school, a British school, or an American school are terms that no longer make sense, any more than a Scandinavian or an Icelandic school does. There are good grounds for welcoming this diversity. Whatever theories are current, there is only good scholarship or bad. In our field it can never be too forcefully emphasized that research should be based on sound knowledge and good understanding of the primary sources. Let me therefore end with the words of Brother Eysteinn in *Lilja*:

> Varðar mest til allra orða
> undirstaðan sé réttlig fundin.

NOTES

[1] The page references are to the 1957 Dover edition which is a reprint of the second edition of 1908.

[2] It is interesting to note this characterization of two sagas which at the time were considered historically very reliable but have later been shown to be fictional with more solid arguments than most other sagas (Nordal 1940; Magerøy 1957 and 1981).

[3] He chose this word as the title of a series of lectures printed in 1934. Heusler gives an interesting description of himself and his attitude to his work in a brief autobiographical essay written in his old age (1943–69, II 3–13).

[4] English translation: *The Culture of the Teutons*, London 1931.

[5] In her very informative survey of research (Clover and Lindow 1985), Carol Clover says: 'Nordalian doctrine holds that the sagas are in effect historical novels . . .' (272). In the introduction to Lindow, Lönnroth and Weber 1986 the editors speak of 'the so-called *Icelandic School's* predilection for the realistic modern novel, to which it would compare and by whose standards it would generically categorize the Icelandic family sagas. This entailed the distressing consequence of belittling sagas such as *Heiðarvíga saga* because of their seemingly primitive style and clumsy mode of narrative and plot' (8). Both these statements are misleading. Nordal was anything but doctrinaire, and it would never have occurred to him, or to Einar Ólafur Sveinsson, to equate sagas with modern novels, although they like many other scholars were aware of certain parallells. Anyone who has read Nordal's introduction to *Heiðarvíga saga* in *Íslenzk fornrit* will know how far he was from 'belittling' this saga in any way; on the contrary, he has many words of praise for it. It seems to me obvious that such criticism of *Heiðarvíga saga* as there is to be found in Sigurður Nordal's introduction to the *Fornrit* edition, or in his 'Sagalitteraturen' in *Nordisk kultur* VIII:B, is based on the standard set by the sagas themselves rather than by modern novels. True, Nordal speaks of *Hrafnkels saga* as a 'short novel' (my translation) in his *Hrafnkatla* essay, but it seems to me that all he is saying there is that it is a piece of short fictional narrative. It is of course important to realize that Sigurður Nordal never claimed that *Hrafnkels saga* was a paradigmatic case. Many other sagas had much 'history' in them

in his view, and I see it as misleading when Andersson and Miller talk about a reaction against 'the Icelandic school's idea of free fiction' (1989, xii). I also find it strange when they say about the same school: 'Unfortunately, the scholars who established this view had rather narrow conceptions of what history was. To them it was mainly political, biographical, or constitutional history' (x). Modern historians may have their disagreements with Nordal's *Íslenzk menning* and Einar Ólafur Sveinsson's *Sturlungaöld* because of what many of them see as their romanticized picture of Icelandic culture, but these works remain among the most interesting attempts to deal with the history of Icelandic mentality in the Commonwealth. Sigurður Nordal, as a matter of fact, was frequently ironic about the narrow positivistic concept of history about which Andersson and Miller are complaining. His irony may sometimes have passed unnoticed by readers not too familiar with his work, as certainly is the case with Jesse Byock, who quotes a description of the attitude of modern historians from *The Historical Element in the Icelandic Family Saga* (Sigurður Nordal 1957) and takes it as Nordal's description of what ought to be the interest of historians (1988, 40). The fact is that Nordal is describing a historical method which he despised for its pedantry and lack of *esprit*, and several of his statements, as well as his own practice, show that he himself had very different aims and principles as a historian.

[6] The ideological importance attributed in Iceland to the *Íslendingasögur* as the cream of the national heritage from the early 19th century to the present day is indisputable and has been of benefit to the funding of scholarship in the field. Scholars like Lönnroth and some others sometimes seem to think that this ideological importance was greatly enhanced by the theories of the Icelandic school. It was not understood to that effect by the common Icelandic public at the time. I suspect any people would prefer to have as monuments of its history named and known real persons of excellence with regard to beauty, bravery and wisdom than a handful of outstanding but nameless writers. There is no doubt that scholars of the Icelandic school were nationalists, as most Icelanders are to this day, and they were proud of the sagas. But I cannot see that their basic conclusions about the origin of the sagas would have been different had they been less nationalistic. These conclusions are an inevitable outcome of general trends in scholarship and would have been reached sooner or later anyway. It should also be kept in mind that a scrutiny of the specific Icelandic background of the sagas was a healthy reaction to the equally ideologically biased and more simplistic views of the 'Germanic' or 'Nordic' school.

[7] It is probably this part of his criticism which has brought on him the blame for treating the sagas as modern novels. I see it rather as general influence from a certain type of psychological criticism much practised in the first half of the century. *Á Njálsbúð* frequently reminds the reader of the Shakespeare criticism of A. C. Bradley.

[8] An early and convincing example is Maxwell 1957–61.

[9] A selection of titles would be incomplete and arbitrary, and I must refer my readers to bibliographies and bibliographical studies, especially Jóhann S. Hannesson 1957 and Clover and Lindow 1985.

[10] See, e.g., Turville-Petre 1953, 213–53, and Foote 1984, passim.

[11] See, e.g., Hermann Pálsson 1971 and Lönnroth 1965 and 1976.

[12] Propp 1968, Greimas 1966 and 1970, have probably been most influential, although a great number of other contributions deserve to be mentioned.

[13] A few years ago I attempted a summary of recent saga scholarship of relevance to the use of the sagas as sources for writers of history (Vésteinn Ólason 1987).

[14] A good example of general attention to this aspect is Foote 1974 (reprinted 1984); an interesting application of reader-response criticism in the reading of a particular saga is Cook 1982–85.

THE SAGAS OF ICELANDERS 41

BIBLIOGRAPHY

Andersson, Theodore M. 1964. *The Problem of Icelandic Saga Origins. A Historical Survey.*
Andersson, Theodore M. 1967. *The Icelandic Family Saga. An Analytic Reading.*
Andersson, Theodore M. and Miller, William Ian. 1989. *Law and Literature in Medieval Iceland. Ljósvetninga saga and Valla-Ljóts saga.*
Byock, Jesse L. 1982. *Feud in the Icelandic Saga.*
Byock, Jesse L. 1988. *Medieval Iceland. Society, Sagas, and Power.*
Clover, Carol J. and Lindow, John (eds.). 1985. *Old Norse–Icelandic Literature. A Critical Guide.* Islandica XLV.
Cook, Robert. 1982–85. 'The Reader in *Grettis Saga*', *Saga-Book* XXI, 133–54.
Einar Ól. Sveinsson. 1933. *Um Njálu* I.
Einar Ól. Sveinsson. 1940. *Sturlungaöld. Drög um íslenzka menningu á þrettándu öld.*
Einar Ól. Sveinsson. 1943. *Á Njálsbúð. Bók um mikið listaverk.*
Einar Ól. Sveinsson (ed.). 1954. *Brennu-Njáls saga.* Íslenzk fornrit XII.
Foote, Peter. 1974. 'The audience and vogue of the Sagas of Icelanders—some talking points', *Studies in Honour of Ian Maxwell,* 17–25.
Foote, Peter. 1984. *Aurvandilstá. Norse Studies.*
Greimas, A. J. 1966. *Sémantique structurale. Recherche de méthode.*
Greimas, A. J. 1970. *Du Sens. Essais sémiotique.*
Grønbech 1909–12. *Vor folkeæt i oldtiden* I–IV.
Guðmundur Andri Thorsson 1990. 'Grettla', *Skáldskaparmál* I, 100–17.
Gurevich, A. J. 1985. *Categories of Medieval Culture.* [1st Russian ed. 1972]
Harris, Joseph. 1972. 'Genre and Narrative Structure in Some *Íslendinga þættir*', *Scandinavian Studies* 44, 1–27.
Hermann Pálsson. 1971. *Art and Ethics in Hrafnkel's saga.*
Heusler, Andreas. 1911. *Das Strafrecht der Isländersagas.*
Heusler, Andreas. 1912. *Zum isländischen Fehdewesen in der Sturlungenzeit.*
Heusler, Andreas. 1913. *Die Anfänge der isländischen Saga.*
Heusler, Andreas. 1934. *Germanentum. Vom Lebens- und Formgefühl der alten Germanen.*
Heusler, Andreas. 1941. *Die altgermanische Dichtung. Zweite Auflage der neubearbeiteten und vermehrten Ausgabe.* [1st ed. 1923]
Heusler, Andreas. 1943–69. *Kleine Schriften* I–II.
Hume, Kathryn. 1974. 'The Thematic Design of *Grettis saga*', *Journal of English and Germanic Philology* 73, 469–86.
Jóhann S. Hannesson. 1957. *The Sagas of Icelanders (Íslendinga sögur).* Islandica XXXVIII.
Ker, W. P. 1957. *Epic and Romance. Essays on Medieval Literature.* [1st ed. 1896, 2nd edition 1908]
Liestøl, Knut. 1929. *Upphavet til den islendske ættesaga.*
Lindow, John, Lönnroth, Lars and Weber, Gerd Wolfgang (eds.). 1986. *Structure and Meaning in Old Norse Literature. New Approaches to Textual Analysis and Literary Criticism.*
Lönnroth, Lars. 1965. *European Sources of Icelandic Saga-Writing. An Essay Based on Previous Studies.*
Lönnroth, Lars.1976. *Njáls Saga. A Critical Introduction.*
Magerøy, Hallvard. 1957. *Studiar i Bandamanna saga.* Bibliotheca Arnamagnæana XVIII.
Magerøy, Hallvard (ed.). 1981. *Bandamanna saga.*
Maxwell, I. R. 1957–61. 'Pattern in *Njáls saga*', *Saga-Book* XV, 17–47.

Miller, William Ian. 1990. *Bloodtaking and Peacemaking. Feud, Law, and Society in Saga Iceland.*
Mundal, Else. 1977. *Sagadebatt.*
Nordal, Sigurður (ed.). 1913-16. *Orkneyinga saga.*
Nordal, Sigurður. 1914. *Om Olaf den helliges saga. En kritisk undersøgelse.*
Nordal, Sigurður. 1920. *Snorri Sturluson.*
Nordal, Sigurður (ed.). 1923. *Völuspá.*
Nordal, Sigurður. 1940. *Hrafnkatla.* Studia Islandica 7.
Nordal, Sigurður. 1942. *Íslenzk menning* I.
Nordal, Sigurður. 1953. 'Sagalitteraturen'. *Litteraturhistorie B. Norge og Island* [Nordisk kultur VIII:B], 180–273.
Nordal, Sigurður. 1957. *The Historical Element in the Icelandic Family Sagas.* W. P. Ker Memorial Lecture 15.
Ong, Walter J. 1982. *Orality and Literacy. The Technologizing of the Word.*
Propp, Vladimir. 1968. *Morphology of the Folktale.* [1st Russian ed. 1928, 1st English translation 1958]
Röhn, Harmut. 1976. *Untersuchungen zur Zeitgestaltung und Komposition der Íslendingasögur. Analysen Ausgewählter Texte.*
Steblin-Kamenskij, M. I. 1973. *The Saga Mind.* [1st Russian ed. 1971]
van den Toorn, M. 1961. 'Zeit und Tempus in der Saga', *Arkiv för nordisk filologi* 76, 134–52.
Turville-Petre, G. 1953. *Origins of Icelandic Literature.*
Vésteinn Ólason. 1984. 'Bókmenntarýni Sigurðar Nordals', *Tímarit Máls og Menningar* 45, 5–18.
Vésteinn Ólason. 1987. 'Norrøn litteratur som historisk kildemateriale'. *Kilderne til den tidlige middelalders historie. Rapporter til den XX Nordiske Historikerkongres, Reykjavík 1987,* 30–47.

DIANA WHALEY

THE KINGS' SAGAS

Introduction

B ROWSING through the first volume of the *Saga-Book of the Viking Club* (1895–97), one is struck not only by the ingenuity and variety of the articles, which range from 'Whale-Hunting in the Shetlands' to 'The Boar's Head Dinner at Oxford and a Teutonic Sun-God', but also by their enthusiasm—their relish for story, their delight in Northernness and in the remains of Nordic culture in the British Isles. In those days purely philological papers were the exception rather than the rule. Dr Phené, Vice-President of the British Archaeological Society, for instance, gave an account of a horseback 'Ramble in Iceland', in the course of which he visited Reykholt, finding it 'a place savouring . . . of the presence of tourists, for remembrance of the great Saga writer, Snórri [sic] Sturluson' (p. 207); but his own preference was for diving into grassy mounds in the hopes of uncovering a pagan temple. The same volume contains a couple of mentions of *Heimskringla* (pp. 121 and 163), and a copy of *Ágrip* is listed among gifts to the library (p. 4), but otherwise there is little to suggest a vibrant interest in the Kings' Sagas; and indeed the first half-century of *Saga-Book* yields only a handful of articles directly within this area, although there are several passing references.

If, despite the best efforts of Lars Lönnroth (1964, 9–32 and 1975) to counsel us out of it, we persist in the habit of treating the sagas in the now-traditional groups labelled *Íslendingasögur, konungasögur, fornaldarsögur* and so on, we are inevitably led to treat the Sagas of Kings collectively as a close relation of the *Íslendingasögur*, and, almost as inevitably, to treat them as the poor relation—not so much a Cinderella as an ugly sister, old, unshapely and badly made up. As history, the Kings' Sagas have fallen from glory; they are no longer trusted as sources, and historians nowadays tend to prefer social structures and economic trends to lives of kings. As literature, only *Heimskringla* consistently stands comparison with the classic *Íslendingasögur*. But the Kings' Sagas have their moments, such moments as enthralled that intrepid Victorian, Lord Dufferin. This is the prelude to the Battle of Svǫlð in his words, which give a reasonably faithful summary of Snorri Sturluson's account, which in turn depends on Oddr Snorrason's (*Heimskringla* 1941–51, I 353–54; Oddr Snorrason 1932, 198–205). Óláfr Tryggvason and his fleet of seventy ships are approaching the islands behind which their enemies lie in wait:

> Nothing can be more dramatic than the description of the sailing of this gallant fleet— (piloted by the treacherous Earl Sigwald)—within sight of the ambushed Danes and Swedes, who watch from their hiding-place the beautiful procession of hostile vessels,

mistaking each in turn for the 'Long Serpent', and as often undeceived by a new and yet more stately apparition. She appears at length,—her dragon prow glittering in the sunshine,—all canvas spread—her sides bristling with armed men; 'and when they saw her, none spoke,—all knew it to be indeed the "*Serpent*,"—and they went to their ships to arm for the fight.' (1857, 356)

I will be returning to the aesthetic qualities of the Kings' Sagas, and to Lord Dufferin, towards the end of this paper.

The Kings' Sagas have not exactly been neglected, but they have had less attention than the *Íslendingasögur*. Many of them have been very well edited, often with excellent introductions, but there have been few book-length studies, and those there are have rarely reached a wide audience. Hence, in the invaluable *Old Norse–Icelandic Literature: A Critical Guide* edited by Clover and Lindow in 1985, Theodore Andersson's article on the Kings' Sagas occupies forty-one pages, including some ten and a half pages of bibliography, but Carol Clover's treatment of the *Íslendingasögur* is nearly twice as long, and because of the huge volume of critical material, her survey is mainly limited to the last twenty years. Andersson, moreover, having surveyed his field, concludes: 'The charm of kings' saga study is decidedly remote' (1985, 198).

Defining the Kings' Sagas

On the face of it the Kings' Sagas would seem an easy group to define.[1] Sagas are either mainly about kings or not, and we can readily include any sustained prose narratives about individual Norwegian or Danish kings, such as the various sagas about the two king Óláfrs, and any of the multi-reign surveys such as *Fagrskinna* or *Knýtlinga saga*. But some are about jarls not kings (*Hákonar saga Ívarssonar* and the lost *Hlaðajarla saga*), so perhaps *Orkneyinga saga* belongs here too; and what of *Jómsvíkinga saga*, in which Danish monarchs feature largely but not quite centrally, or *Færeyinga saga*, which is often included in the group by the curious logic that it seems really to be an *Íslendingasaga*, except that it is not about Icelanders?

Then we have to consider whether a saga can be in Latin. The first known history of Norwegian kings, the lost work by Sæmundr Sigfússon, seems to have been in Latin. So too were the originals of Oddr Snorrason and Gunnlaugr Leifsson's sagas of Óláfr Tryggvason, although these are lost and beyond direct consideration. But the early Norwegian synoptic histories are difficult. We presumably want to include the vernacular *Ágrip* among the Kings' Sagas, but what about Theodoricus's *Historia de antiquitate regum Norvagiensium* and the anonymous *Historia Norvegiæ*? Although written in Latin, these works are comparable in scope and to some extent in spirit to *Ágrip*, and they cannot be detached from the history of the Kings' Sagas.

Perhaps we should insist on saga-like qualities in our *konungasögur*. Anne Holtsmark limited her treatment of the Kings' Sagas in *Kulturhistorisk leksikon* quite strictly, seeing a purpose to entertain by means of literary artistry as a defining feature which distinguishes Icelandic Sagas of Kings from non-Icelandic chronicles of kings (1964, esp. 42). Others, while acknowledging this distinction, have found it more useful to consider the two groups together.[2] I do not think anyone would claim that there is any self-evidently right way of delimiting the Kings' Sagas, and indeed it is their variety that is one of their greatest strengths.

One aspect of that variety is the way in which, uniquely among the genres of sagas, the *konungasögur* range over all periods of the past. The *fornaldarsögur* and the *samtíðarsögur* are defined chiefly by means of their distance from the events narrated, but in the *konungasögur*, collectively and also within some individual works, all periods are embraced: the remote legendary past, the middle ground of the ninth to earlier twelfth centuries, and the recent or so-called 'contemporary' period, which latter is the subject of the earliest Kings' Saga, *Hryggjarstykki*, and the latest, the now vestigial *Magnúss saga lagabœtis*. These disparities in the distance between the time of events narrated and the time of composition are accompanied by a great diversity of material and handling of material, and this gives the Kings' Sagas a heterogeneity which may make them less neat and comfortable to approach than other branches of saga-literature but which in terms of literary history is a source of interest and strength. The primal soup of tradition—early oral materials inherited from *fróðir menn*, skaldic verse, folk-tale, chronicle, genealogy, hagiography, well-formed *þættir* of skalds at court, and the minute reportage of recent events—not only gives rise to *Heimskringla*, but also profoundly influences the *Íslendingasögur*, not least via the *skáldasögur*.

Heimskringla's place among the Kings' Sagas

Among the Sagas of Kings, *Heimskringla* has always reigned supreme, both because of the political and literary distinction of its author and because it is simply the best. One cannot imagine a crown prince and a prime minister coming together with fifteen thousand others to salute the author of *Ágrip* or the *Legendary saga* as they did to salute Snorri Sturluson and unveil his statue at Reykholt in 1947 (see *Snorrahátíð* 1950). We have the luxury of two standard editions of *Heimskringla* to work from, as well as another newly published, in modernised orthography, and there is the excellent 1941 edition of the *Separate* or *Great saga of Óláfr helgi*. There are four complete English translations of *Heimskringla* as well as several into other languages, and at least half a dozen critical books or collections of essays. Snorri has had his critics. Guðbrandur Vigfússon found Snorri's rendering of the life of Óláfr Tryggvason a 'dull skeleton-like abridgment' (1878, I lxxxiii), and W. P. Ker followed suit, complaining among other things of Snorri's want of consistency in leaving out the moving deaths of Óláfr's dog Vígi and of his queen (which are covered by Adam of Bremen, Oddr Snorrason and the author of *Historia Norvegiæ*), but accepting the story of the sorcerer sent to Iceland by King Haraldr Gormsson in the shape of a whale. About the first episode, Ker asks, 'Was it strict historical judgment, or mere dulness, that left this out' (1908–09, 248), while of the second he says, 'He [Snorri] cannot give himself out, or be accepted as a true, sound rationalist historian. Why did he swallow the whale?' (1908–09, 256). But critical voices are very much in the minority, drowned by a great chorus of acclaim.

As a source of historical information, Snorri's Sagas of Kings have probably been overvalued, as when his *Óláfs saga helga* was labelled the 'Historical saga'. Historians have tended to resort to *Heimskringla* more than to others of the *konungasögur*, seduced by its apparent plausibility into forgetting that so much of Snorri's writing derives directly and probably without any extra information from less reasonable-seeming sources, many of which are still extant.

Snorri probably does deserve his reputation as 'king of saga-writers' (Einar Ól. Sveinsson 1937–38, 73–74). But it cannot be stated too often that *Heimskringla* is a very patchy work, that many of the best moments in it are only slightly improved versions of already powerful scenes in their sources, and that Snorri acquired much of his literary technique from his predecessors. His magisterial control of suspense and viewpoint is learned from Oddr Snorrason and the author of *Færeyinga saga*; the royal speechifying is in imitation of *Sverris saga*, and Snorri's justly famous capacity for presenting more than one view of a character may owe something to the same model. The talent for setting characters in dramatic opposition is shared with the author of *Morkinskinna*, and the distaste for the supernatural and trivial accords with *Fagrskinna*; and so on. So, as W. P. Ker put it, Snorri 'took what he wanted and left them without their due praise' (1908–09, 250).

The only sensible response to all this is not to start denigrating *Heimskringla* on principle, but to continue to recognise that it is not in every respect superior to its peers, and while admiring it, to guard against exaggerating the personal contribution of Snorri Sturluson, great though that is. The corollory is that more attention could be given to the other Kings' Sagas. Many have been well re-edited in the last decade or so: *Ágrip* and *Fagrskinna*, *Bǫglunga saga*, *Hákonar saga Hákonarsonar*, the *Legendary saga* and *Óláfs saga Tryggvasonar in mesta*. *Hulda* is in progress. There has been important work on the genesis of works such as *Fagrskinna* (e.g. Jakobsen 1970), the *Hulda–Hrokkinskinna* compilation (Louis-Jensen 1977), *Sverris saga* (e.g. Blöndal 1982), *Skjǫldunga saga* and *Hryggjarstykki* (Bjarni Guðnason 1963 and 1978).

But on the whole, critical works on Kings' Sagas other than *Heimskringla* are scarce, and certainly fuller scrutinies of works such as Oddr Snorrason's saga,

Morkinskinna and *Fagrskinna* would be enjoyable and revealing; possibly also the Sagas of Kings in *Flateyjarbók* and other late compilations, however derivative they may be. Accordingly, the remainder of this paper represents an attempt to address some issues within the Kings' Sagas without giving *Heimskringla* more than its fair share of attention.

Five issues

The highlights of the Kings' Sagas are mainly battles—so much so that one of them, *Fagrskinna*, has been dubbed a 'battle saga', *orustusaga* (Bjarni Aðalbjarnarson, ed., *Heimskringla* 1941–51, I xviii). But these sagas have themselves also been something of a battle-ground, or at least the scene of lively debate. In what follows I will be separating out five aspects of the Kings' Sagas, which, although not unique to this genre, are importantly characteristic of it, and which have been the object of scholarly striving, and sometimes of scholarly strife. Although, in reality, there is a great deal of overlap between the five issues, they will provide a convenient framework for reviewing developments in scholarship over the past century. They are: (i) Earliness; (ii) Norwegian connections; (iii) Clerical influences; (iv) Literary affiliations; (v) Historical basis.

(i) *Earliness.* If the Kings' Sagas begin with Sæmundr's history, or with Ari's *Konunga ævi*, both now lost, we are in the first quarter of the twelfth century. If they begin with *Hryggjarstykki*, we are in the middle of the twelfth century. Even if we exclude these works on the grounds that they are not now directly extant, we can trace the composition of the Kings' Sagas back into the twelfth century, with the Norwegian synoptics and Oddr Snorrason's *Óláfs saga Tryggvasonar*.

There has been significant new thought on the dating of the so-called *Oldest saga of Óláfr helgi*, which I will return to later in a wider context. In another major development, Bjarni Guðnason's work on *Hryggjarstykki* suggests a date somewhat earlier than it had customarily been assigned to, around 1150, so earning it the proud title '*Fyrsta sagan*' (1978).[3]

On the whole, though, the Kings' Sagas are quite accurately datable and therefore not subject to scholarly fashion on this point, so that we can still reckon, as a hundred years ago, that the main period of activity was *c.*1160–*c.*1230, especially the second half of this period. What has changed, however, is the place of the group in the general chronology of saga-writing. Now that no one believes, as Guðbrandur Vigfússon (1878, I lxviii) and Finnur Jónsson (1920–24, esp. II 266–67) did, that the golden age of the *Íslendingasögur* fell in the late twelfth century and very beginning of the thirteenth, the dating of the best Kings' Sagas and the best *Íslendingasögur* have now reversed positions; and it is now clear that the *konungasögur*, in terms of fresh compositions, were virtually played out by the time *Laxdæla saga* and *Njáls saga* were written. The positive side of this, as far as the Kings' Sagas are concerned, is that they can be seen as having had a fundamental and formative role in the development of saga-writing generally. Heusler, for instance (1914, 66), suggested that the writing down of the Kings' Sagas opened the way for the *Íslendingasögur* and *fornaldarsögur* to be committed to vellum. Nordal saw the history of saga-writing as progressing in a great arch from dry scholarship to wild fantasy, with the classic equipoise of the *Íslendingasögur* at the zenith and the *konungasögur* on the ascendant path, and with *Egils saga* as the essential link between the two groups (e.g. 1920, 128–30; 1953, 251). This view may now appear too elegant to be real, and it has been disturbed at least by the re-dating of some of the *Íslendingasögur*, including Jónas Kristjánsson's proposal that *Egils saga* may be later than formerly thought (1977, 470–71); but there is still room for seeing certain of the *kongungasögur* among the influences on the *Íslendingasögur*, especially on those with a shared interest in tales of Icelandic skalds at the Norwegian court—*Egils saga, Hallfreðar saga* and *Fóstbrœðra saga* (see e.g. Olsen 1965, 70; Jónas Kristjánsson 1972, 164–65).

(ii) *The Norwegian connection*.[4] Within the running Nordic debate over the true homelands of certain poetic and prose texts and their manuscripts (usefully reviewed in Magerøy 1965), the problem of weighing up the possible Norwegian contribution to the development of the Kings' Sagas is an interesting challenge. Nearly all the main characters in nearly all the Kings' Sagas are Norwegian—a fact so obvious that it is seldom mentioned. Is it possible that some of the grand gestures of word and deed in the sagas were actually performed by the men to whom they are attributed? Unlikely, I admit, but perhaps worth leaving open as a possibility. Similarly, even if we do not nowadays believe that the sagas are faithful records of detailed oral narratives which sprang up soon after the events, and hence really Norwegian sagas,[5] Norwegians must surely have handed their traditions to Icelanders in at least a semi-coherent narrative form. And even in the thirteenth century there may have been a residue of local material from Scandinavia still available for use by Icelandic authors. This is extremely difficult to identify and quantify, but good arguments have been advanced for Snorri Sturluson's use of traditions gathered in Trøndelag and the surrounding regions, and from Tønsberg and Västergötland.[6]

Moving rapidly on to slightly more secure ground, most of the skalds before AD 1000 were Norwegian, and they bring us closer to the events than anything else in the sagas. And when we reach the literary stage, there is substantial Norwegian involvement, by authors, scribes and patrons, in the development of the Kings' Saga, sufficient perhaps to invite the question whether sagas have to be Icelandic.

Among the earliest of the surveys of kings, at least three were produced in Norway, and probably by Norwegians: the vernacular *Ágrip*,[7] and two Latin works, Theodoricus's *Historia de Antiquitate Regum Norwagiensium* and the

Historia Norwegiæ. (Theodoricus also mentions a now lost, but probably Norwegian, *Catalogus Regum Norwagiensium.*) The interrelations of these three texts and the degree to which they are indebted to Icelandic oral or written tradition (other than the 'ancient poems' of Icelanders acknowledged by Theodoricus in his prologue) have been debated in great detail, but inconclusively.[8] More certain is the case of the so-called *Legendary saga of Óláfr helgi* (*Helgisagan*) which, although it derives from the Icelandic *Oldest saga*, contains interpolations from two Norwegian works and only survives in a Norwegian manuscript (Jónas Kristjánsson 1976, 293).

Whatever the truth about the early Norwegian historians' debt to Icelandic tradition, influence in the opposite direction is beyond dispute. Oddr Snorrason, for instance, 'evidently knew and used Theodoricus' (Jónas Kristjánsson 1988, 157), and Snorri in *Heimskringla* occasionally incorporates passages more or less verbatim from *Ágrip*, as does the author of *Fagrskinna*. All the Icelandic sagas of Óláfr helgi were served, directly or indirectly, by Latin accounts of miracles which were set down in Niðaróss (Trondheim), home of the saint-king's shrine. Niðaróss in the days of Archbishop Eysteinn (1161–88) is an obvious base for historiographical and hagiographical effort; indeed Theodoricus dedicated his book to Eysteinn, and evidently drew on his *Acta Sancti Olavi* (Turville-Petre 1953, 171).

Norwegian royal patronage also doubtless played a part in the emergence of the Kings' Sagas, but the importance of this is not easy to assess. Not all would necessarily agree with the attractive view voiced by Anne Holtsmark that the Kings' Sagas in a sense take the place of skaldic encomia from the mid-twelfth century onwards (1964, 42), and even *Sverris saga*, despite the claim of its prologue that it was supervised by Sverrir himself, does not seem as ingratiating as might be expected (see Andersson 1985, 224 and 226, and references there).

A few decades later the court of Hákon Hákonarson (1217–63), firmly associated with works such as *Tristrams saga*, *Mǫttuls saga* and *Konungs skuggsjá*, as well as with Sturla Þórðarson's saga of Hákon himself, may well have encouraged the writing of sagas about earlier kings of Norway by Icelanders or possibly Norwegians. The strongest case can be made for *Fagrskinna*, which not merely incorporates narrative materials of Norwegian origin, but was probably composed for a Norwegian patron, and possibly by a Norwegian.[9] *Fagrskinna* may indeed have been the '*konungatal*' read to King Hákon Hákonarson on his death-bed. *Heimskringla*, meanwhile, hardly reads like a royal command performance, any more than its author fulfilled his early promise as a royal sycophant; but most of the main extant manuscripts have known early links with Norway, and it seems likely that some or all of these, together with other Kings' Saga manuscripts, were produced for the Norwegian market during Iceland's subjection to Norwegian rule, *c.*1262–1380 (see Stefán Karlsson 1979).

However strong the Norwegian links, the fact remains that even if sagas do not by definition have to be Icelandic, the great majority of the Kings' Sagas are fairly and squarely so.[10] Their authors, therefore, each with his individual perspective shaped by local or familial affiliations, religious and political preferences, present us with a rich variety of Icelandic perceptions of the Scandinavian past, which have not yet been explored to the full (although Andersson 1985, 224–27 gives a useful lead in the direction of synthesis).

(iii) *Clerical influences*. The clerical status of authors to some extent goes hand in hand with the use of the Latin language, and with influence from the mainstreams of Latin historiography and hagiography. Theodoricus is an extreme example: a monk who appears to have studied abroad, perhaps at S. Victoire in Paris (Turville-Petre 1953, 171 n., citing O. A. Johnsen). Among his sources and models were the lost *Translatio Sancti Olavi*, a *Catalogus Regum Norwagiensium*, Latin histories by French authors, and works by Pliny, Lucan, Sallust and Horace, and the Church Fathers. His contemporary, the author of *Historia Norvegiæ*, knew and used the work of Adam of Bremen. In Iceland, Gunnlaugr Leifsson was a monk at the Benedictine monastery of Þingeyrar, the best Latinist of his generation, and author of a life of Bishop Jón Ǫgmundarson of Hólar. Styrmir Kárason, author of a *Lífssaga Óláfs helga* and friend of Snorri Sturluson, was prior of the Augustinian community on Viðey. In fact Snorri himself is exceptional in being the only identified author of Kings' Sagas who was fairly definitely not in holy orders, and who cannot be demonstrated to be directly indebted to any writings in Latin.[11] The sophistication of Snorri's intellectual background is now better appreciated than formerly, thanks especially to Margaret Clunies Ross's work on *Snorra Edda* (1987) and Sverrir Tómasson's work on prologues (1988), but the extent of Snorri's direct knowledge of Latin, long a point of disagreement, has only recently been discussed head-on, in an illuminating paper by Anthony Faulkes (1993).

Clerical training equipped men for literary endeavour, and ecclesiastical direction and the monastic life encouraged mutual influence and corporate enterprise among clerical writers, as has already been seen in connection with the see of Niðaróss. In Iceland, Þingeyrar is the school most often mentioned in relation to the Kings' Sagas, with the sagas of Óláfr Tryggvason by Oddr Snorrason and Gunnlaugr Leifsson among its most famous products. But the role of these two distinctly hagiographical works, 'full of exaggeration and supernatural intervention' as Jónas Kristjánsson puts it (1988, 157), is debatable. Jónas himself sees their role as significant: 'They are the first sagas that deal with the distant past and have roots both in native oral tradition and in foreign literature: they point the way forward to Snorri Sturluson and the anonymous authors of the sagas of Icelanders' (1988, 159). Theodore Andersson, on the other hand, has suggested that 'they represented an eccentric school of saga writing and should not be taken as the point of departure for the later tradition' (1985, 213).

Certainly there are reasons to think that these two works are not necessarily representative even of the whole 'Þingeyrar school'. Among the other works associated with these same two writers, *Eymundar saga* and *Merlínússpá* have a markedly different character, as has *Sverris saga*, partially the work of the Þingeyrar abbot Karl Jónsson.[12] The variety of the Þingeyrar productions reminds us that clerical authorship is far from synonymous with 'clerical style'. Further, the pre-eminence of Þingeyrar as an ancient home of the writing of Kings' Sagas (Nordal (ed.), *Egils saga* 1933, lxviii, and 1953, 199–200) is open to challenge, for, as Andersson argues in a recent paper (1993, following Kválen 1925), Munkaþverá may well have been the focus for the writing of sagas, including *Morkinskinna*, which emphasised human character and political conflict and hence paved the way for the author of *Heimskringla*.

Another old scenario which now appears too straightforward is that which envisaged a gradual separation of clerical from secular culture in Iceland, culminating in the secular classics of the thirteenth century. Nordal pointed out that around 1200 original native literature was still very much in the minority in relation to foreign literature, Latin or translated (1953, 208), and reckoned that the years around 1220 were a watershed, after which clerical influence was in retreat (1953, 225). This view has now given way to a much more complex picture, which recognises the heterogeneity of clerical productions and the difficulty of pinning down 'clerical' or 'learned style' (Jónas Kristjánsson 1981) or defining the boundary between clerical and secular activity. Lars Lönnroth has asserted that contemporary authors and audiences did not make a real distinction between native and foreign writings, and emphasised the co-operation between laymen and clerics in the production of literature (1964, 33–42), rather as Anglo-Saxonists have eroded the notion of a great divide between monastery and mead-hall in England after the conversion (Wormald 1978). The clean distinction between two streams of historical writing, one clerical, with a strong legendary tinge, and the other a more realistic attempt to write about contemporary or past rulers, is blurred from the very outset by the *passio*-like nature of *Hryggjarstykki*, emphasised by Bjarni Guðnason (1978). Theodore Andersson therefore has some justification in writing: 'There is now no reason to believe that the history of the Kings' Sagas entails the gradual freeing of native talent from the confining traditions of the Church. Most of the first narrative efforts in the vernacular (*Orkneyinga saga*, *Færeyinga saga*, *Jómsvíkinga saga*, *Morkinskinna*) are as secular as Snorri's work' (1985, 213). But even if Andersson is right that the sagas of Óláfr Tryggvason by Oddr Snorrason and Gunnlaugr Leifsson are not the mainstream but a minor tributary, we cannot ignore them, or *Ágrip*, the *Legendary Saga* and Styrmir, and perhaps there is now a danger of underrating the clerical input where earlier scholarship overrated it.

(iv) *Textual affiliations*. Even in the days when talk of the possible oral roots of saga-writing was more in vogue, the Kings' Sagas were recognised as exceptionally 'literary' in their make-up, deriving their material chiefly from written sources, and handling it in ways characteristic more of written than oral culture (e.g. Heusler 1914, 66). This, coupled with the fact that some of them can be assigned fairly certain authorship, dates and/or provenance, opens up rich possibilities for tracing lines of literary-historical development. The extreme complexity of the literary links is shown, for instance, in the stemma proposed by Fidjestøl for the works containing skaldic verse (1982, 10). It is not surprising, then, that what we might call the complex intertextuality of these sagas has given rise to some extremely weighty and detailed investigations, especially of the earlier stages in the tradition, by Bjarni Aðalbjarnarson (1937), Siegfried Beyschlag (1950) and Svend Ellehøj (1966). I suspect that those who have read these books from cover to cover are a small and heroic minority—none of them was reviewed in *Saga-Book*. But in fact, whether the Kings' Sagas are viewed as historical sources, as literature, or as something in between, any evaluation of them will almost inevitably involve considering where the authors or compilers got their materials, and what they did with them, or will want to discover what is the co-operative product of a process of accretion, and what is unique to a particular work. The books by Hallvard Lie on the style of *Heimskringla* (1937) and by James Knirk on oratory in the Kings' Sagas (1981), for instance, would be greatly impoverished without their comparative dimension, and this kind of 'applied' source study tends to reach a wider readership than the 'pure' variety.

Perhaps one reason why the 'pure' work on literary affiliations can seem remote and disheartening is that much of it has been more concerned with what is not there than with what is—with speculation about the contents of Sæmundr's postulated history or Ari's lost *Konunga ævi*, or with reconstructing the original, lost version of *Morkinskinna* rather than appreciating the one we have. This approach seems to be less fashionable now than formerly, at least as far as it concerns works for which there is no direct evidence at all. Finnur Jónsson postulated early sagas of individual kings including Magnús góði and Haraldr Sigurðarson as models for the relevant parts of *Morkinskinna* and hence for *Heimskringla* (1920–24, II 622–23, 628, n. 3), and as recently as 1967 de Vries considered it almost self-evident ('fast selbstverständlich') that such biographies must have existed (1964–67, II 281); but even so patient a scholar as Jónas Kristjánsson is willing to lay these phantoms to rest: 'Since any that may have existed have disappeared, it is safer to leave them out of the picture' (1988, 160; see further Andersson 1985, 218–19).

And of course we know that the picture will never be complete. Scholars of integrity and prodigious stamina will sift all the evidence and reach quite different conclusions about literary links; many lost written stages will never be found; and the contribution of oral tradition, despite the valiant efforts of scholars like Beyschlag, can never be fully defined, so that works such as Oddr Snorrason's *Óláfs saga Tryggvasonar* or *Morkinskinna*, whose sources are not easily pinned down, are left in dignified neglect (Andersson 1985, 218).

On the other hand, real progress can be made and has been made, especially concerning the sagas about Óláfr Haraldsson inn helgi. For most of this century the consensus was that an intermediate stage lay between the *Oldest* and *Legendary* sagas of Óláfr helgi—the so-called *Middle saga*, now lost, which had been characterised by interpolations from *Ágrip* and *Fóstbrœðra saga*.[13] Then in 1972, in the course of his reappraisal of *Fóstbrœðra saga*, Jónas Kristjánsson brought off a wonderful coup by relieving us of the *Middle Saga* (1972, esp. 156–63 and 223).

Views of the '*Oldest saga*' have also been radically revised. The eight fragments taken by Gustav Storm as belonging to it have been reduced to seven (de Vries 1967, 240 n. 17) and then to six (Louis-Jensen 1970 and Jónas Kristjánsson 1972). The two rejected fragments, in AM 325 IVa 4o, are now believed to belong to a separate collection of Óláfr miracles, so that we have returned to the position taken by Árni Magnússon, who labelled them *Ex miraculis Sancti Olavi* (quoted in Kålund 1889–94, I 554). Without the last two, Arnamagnæan, fragments, the *Oldest saga* no longer appears so hagiographical as formerly, or so old, since the evidence for dating it in the third quarter of the twelfth century was mainly to be found in the so-called seventh fragment. It is now considered more likely to be a product of the years around 1200, so that it must relinquish its claim to be 'the oldest saga known to us, and probably the first ever written' (Turville-Petre 1953, 190). This also opens up the possibility that the sagas of Óláfr Tryggvason may predate those about Óláfr helgi, or be contemporary with them, rather than being a response to them, although of course the cult of Óláfr helgi in Norway, and the early writings associated with it, presumably predated that of his namesake in Iceland. Another related development is that the *Oldest* and *Legendary sagas*, whose close kinship has always been recognised, are now seen almost as texts of one and the same work (Jónas Kristjánsson 1976, 292–93 and 1988, 160).

The sources for the *konungasögur* of Snorri Sturluson received thorough and sensible scrutiny from Gustav Storm in 1873, and surprisingly little has been added on the subject since then, except for some excellent introductions to editions and translations. The view that Snorri's *Separate saga of Óláfr helgi* predates *Heimskringla* has been generally accepted (Nordal 1914, anticipated by others; summary in Whaley 1991, 54–55). The question of the sources of Snorri's *Óláfs saga helga*, however, remains unsatisfactorily open, and Thorkil Damsgaard

Olsen may have been right when he said that Snorri's *Separate Óláfs saga* depended on the same sources as the *Legendary saga*, but with such a rich admixture of material from oral and written tradition, and the author's imagination, that it would be a desperate undertaking to try to discover what the sources were (1965, 67). It is usually asserted that Styrmir Kárason's *Lífssaga Óláfs helga* must have been a major source, if not the major source, for Snorri's *Óláfs saga* (e.g. Bjarni Aðalbarnarson, ed., *Heimskringla* 1941–51, II ix). But the scraps from Styrmir preserved in *Flateyjarbók* and elsewhere are so different from Snorri's usual taste that it seems very unlikely that Styrmir's work was a major source, except of course that it can be argued that this is precisely why they are left over, Snorri having already used the parts that were congenial to him. Another difficulty is the number of stages postulated within a short space of time, given the later dating of the *Oldest saga*, if it has to turn into the *Legendary saga* (in Norway) and influence Styrmir before he in turn influences Snorri, presumably in the mid 1220s. Such a chronology is possible, but tight. I confess that I personally warm to the suggestion of Anne Heinrichs (which, so far as I know, she has not argued in detail) that Styrmir's saga did not really exist in any fixed and unitary form (1976, esp. 18; *Legendary saga* 1982, 12–13).

Apart from the light it throws on individual sagas, the chief value of source study is the insight it gives into the chronology and development of saga-writing, and this kind of investigation will doubtless continue to flourish, even if the confidently deterministic approach of older scholars has been challenged by a sense of variety and chance mutation at work, as expressed by Andersson when he claims, 'There is nothing in Icelandic literature from 1150 to 1200 that leads inevitably to Snorri' (1985, 216). In any case there is at least one major leap of development still to be explained: the fusion of detailed individual biography (of the two Óláfrs, or of Sverrir, for instance) with the rapid surveys of longer tracts of time. Depth and breadth come together for the first time in *Morkinskinna*, and there were plentiful structural models of both to stimulate the venture, but we still cannot answer the question where the materials for it came from. On a yet broader front, we are still a long way from having a definitive account of the place of the Kings' Sagas in the development of saga-writing as a whole.

(v) *Historical basis*. More than any other genre, the Sagas of Kings are founded upon historical events—events which seem to have some basis in actuality and are of more than personal consequence. Several of them have prologues; they incorporate the evidence of major skaldic poems which we still take to be probably genuine; and in general they appear more seriously concerned with sifting evidence than the *Íslendingasögur*, for instance.[14] They also seem to express a collective will to provide comprehensive coverage of large spans of history. Thus *Sverris saga*, *Bǫglunga saga*, *Hákonar saga Hákonarsonar* and *Magnúss saga lagabœtis* form a continuum; and *Morkinskinna* may have been composed to fill the gap between *Óláfs saga helga* and *Sverris saga*.[15] All these characteristics suggest that the authors of the Kings' Sagas at least wanted to give the impression of striving to inform, to present historical truth, however they understood that. The historical element in the *konungasögur* is undoubtedly part of their attraction; it provides historians with a great wealth of information, however much they protest about its unreliability, and it should suggest that these works are to be read, each on its own terms, but always as something rather different from the *Íslendingasögur*.

In sixteenth-century Scandinavia the Kings' Sagas were treasured by humanistic scholars first and foremost for their historical interest, and, as Else Mundal has emphasised (1977, 9–12), this had profound consequences for the criticism not just of the *konungasögur* but also of the *Íslendingasögur* and *fornaldarsögur*, which were sought out with the same zeal for information about the Nordic past and treated, along with the *konungasögur*, as historical documents. Belief in the historicity of various sorts of sagas was sustained by the assumption that narratives of events had been passed more or less unchanged down the generations by popular oral tradition. The great 'saga-debate' began when scholars started to question these assumptions. In this sense, the post-medieval study of the *konungasögur* influenced the study of other sagas, just as the writing of the *konungasögur* influenced saga-writing generally.

The battle over the historicity of the Kings' Sagas has produced what is probably the most spectacular reversal of all in scholarly positions, and at times it has generated real fighting talk, as when Finnur Jónsson declared: 'The historical trustworthiness of the sagas—however grandiose that sounds—I will maintain and defend until I am forced to lay down my pen' (my translation).[16] Perhaps it would not be a gross overstatement to say that in the nineteenth century the *konungasögur* were taken as reliable until they were proved unreliable, whereas now the opposite principle holds sway. As a specific example, P. E. Müller in the early nineteenth century thought that the more dialogue a saga contained the more likely it was to be trustworthy (so Magerøy 1965, 96), whereas Knut Liestøl, speaking of *Sturlunga saga* and the *Íslendingasögur* in 1930 (88–89) asserted that the reverse was true.

Although historians such as P. A. Munch, writing his monumental history of Norway in the 1850s, were well aware that there were contradictions and unlikelihoods in the saga accounts of early Norwegian history, there was a general willingness, in default of any better evidence, to accept them as true in broad outline. His account of the Jómsvíking battle at Hjǫrungavágr, for instance, is almost nothing but a tissue of quotations from the sagas (1852–63, I 2, 114–22). Early this century, however, scholars such as Lauritz Weibull, Moltke Moe and Halvdan Koht turned their attention to *Heimskringla* and other Kings' Sagas, and not only uncovered specific factual errors but more importantly realised that the narratives were often shaped by international folk-tale or by ideological templates derived from more recent Norwegian history. To illustrate, Weibull not only questioned details about the Jómsvíkingar but disputed their very existence (1911, 178–95). Halvdan Koht saw *Historia Norvegiæ*'s famous image of Óláfr helgi as the once and future king, *rex perpetuus Norvegiæ*, and the corresponding prophecy of his eternal reign in the *Legendary saga*, as a propagandist invention inspired by archiepiscopal policy in Niðaróss after 1163 (1914, 382).

There are various ways in which historians could respond to the ground being cut from under their feet in this way. One is to proceed as before, but with greater caution. It is difficult to write a history of medieval Norway without referring to works such as *Ágrip*, *Fagrskinna* or *Heimskringla*, and with the appropriate caveats it seems perfectly reasonable to cite their witness, however second-hand it may be.

Another response to the loss of trust in the *konungasögur* as historical documents is to appreciate them instead for what they are: twelfth- or thirteenth-century views of the past, which can give us a profound insight into the mental world of the author and his contemporaries (e. g. de Vries 1964–67, II 295, speaking of *Heimskringla*). The issues raised by the events in the Kings' Sagas are, after all, on the same grand scale as the events themselves: such things as the evolution of the Norwegian nation-state and its conversion to Christianity; the balance of power within Scandinavia; the rule of law and the nature of true kingship.

Investigation of the ideology of the *konungasögur* is certainly an area with promise for growth, and the few sorties in this direction have been invigorating. They began with the skirmish between Koht (1914 and 1954–56) and Paasche (1922) as to whether there were any consistent ideological tendencies in *Heimskringla*, and they culminate in Sverre Bagge's recent book, *Society and Politics in Snorri Sturluson's Heimskringla*, whose purpose is 'to reconstruct his [Snorri's] general ideas of society and political behaviour' (1991, 5). In the hands of someone less careful than Bagge, however, this kind of study could be a rather risky venture. It should ideally be founded on a clear notion as to how much freedom a saga-writer had—from the influence of sources or of historical actuality—to select or slant his materials in particular directions; but this freedom is very difficult to gauge.

Yet another option is to write off *Heimskringla* and other Kings' Sagas as any kind of history, and rehabilitate them as literature; to apply to them Hayden White's dictum, 'When a great work of historiography or philosophy of history has become outdated, it is *reborn* into art' (1975, 67; his italics). This may sound very new and liberating, and although it is not new (for scholars of the early Enlightenment period already revalued the *Íslendingasögur* and Eddaic poems in this way; see Mundal 1977, 18), it is liberating. Studies like James Knirk's book *Oratory in the Kings' Sagas* (1981) or Marianne Kalinke's article on the saga of

Sigurðr Jórsalafari in *Morkinskinna* (1984) are to be welcomed, and certainly a great deal remains to be said about the Kings' Sagas from the literary point of view: about the shaping of individual narrative episodes or the structure of whole sagas, the portrayal of character, diction and style, and so on. However, it would again be naive to think that we can leave the question of historicity behind, for even if we know that the *konungasögur* are not factually reliable, we cannot ignore the likelihood that their authors felt themselves bound to preserve ancient traditions, indeed to write history, however partisan it might be, however much attended by supernatural happenings, heroic gestures and improbable utterances. The writers of the Kings' Sagas may therefore have been less free, and less motivated, than the authors of the *Íslendingasögur* to produce elegant and imaginatively compelling narratives.

Finally, one of the greatest challenges in this area still to be met is to establish how the *konungasögur* relate to other medieval European historiography. It has been suggested, for instance, that Snorri might have known the works of Henry of Huntingdon and William of Malmesbury (Moberg 1987, 56–60 and 78–79), but this could be investigated further, and although Sverre Bagge's work (1990 and 1991) again makes strides in relation to *Heimskringla*, it would be interesting to see a broader discussion of the question how far the authors of the *konungasögur* resemble their continental contemporaries in terms of their aims, their choice of material or their style.

Summary and envoy

To review the ground covered so far: I began by characterising the Kings' Sagas rather uncharitably as old, ugly, unshapely and badly made up. They are certainly a very amorphous category, in which saga is flanked by, and at some points fuses with, hagiography and historiography, and in which the interests of imparting information or pressing a partisan line may override aesthetic considerations. However, the variety of these sagas, together with their relatively early date, turns out to be a positive advantage: the diverse materials and styles of writing are interesting in themselves, and they mature and merge in *Heimskringla*, as well, presumably, as influencing the development of the *Íslendingasögur*. Their mainly Norwegian subject-matter and the influence of Norwegian protagonists and skalds, patrons, authors and scribes makes them more deserving than any other branch of the sagas of the old title 'Old Norse sagas' in its newer sense of 'Old Norwegian sagas'. Clerical influence is also more demonstrable here than in most varieties of saga, although still in some ways elusive.

The literary relations of the Kings' Sagas, and their place in the development of saga-writing generally, have always preoccupied scholars, and will surely continue to do so. Certainly, some large questions of literary history remain to be answered. We seem to have blurred the simple elegance of the evolutionary model proposed by Sigurður Nordal, in which dry historical scholarship matures into art, literature frees itself from clerical constraints, and Sagas of Icelanders are heirs to Sagas of Kings; but we have not overturned it altogether.

The historical or quasi-historical content of the Kings' Sagas is part of their fascination, and if they have ceased to be treasured as historical sources, they are still at least the noble containers in which most of the skaldic encomiastic poetry is preserved.[17] New ways of appreciating them as historiography or literature have opened up, and much is still to be explored. We have not exhausted the potential for considering what medieval Icelandic authors thought they were doing—informing, educating, edifying or entertaining, and we have not, in the wake of Steblin-Kamenskij (1973), finished enquiring about the distinction, if there is one, between history and fiction (e.g. Sverrir Tómasson 1988, 189–94).

I am aware that, in addressing very general issues, I have not said very much about the Kings' Sagas themselves, and I would like to end with some simple remarks on the appeal of these sagas.

To modern minds nourished on novels and lyric poetry—to my mind at any rate—the spectacle of a monarch in the ruthless pursuit of political supremacy is less interesting than that of an Icelandic farmer of noble heart and good will caught in a web of circumstance and impelled towards destruction by old-fashioned notions of honour; and few characters in the Kings' Sagas compel our anguished sympathy in the way that a Njáll, a Gísli, a Guðrún or a Kormakr does. If we share the excitement that Victorian readers and travellers such as Lord Dufferin felt in contemplating the 'heroic phantom[s] from Norway's past', that excitement is muted, and it enters into scholarly writings still less than it did in Dufferin's day. Travelling in western Norway, Dufferin wrote of one of those phantoms (1857, 352–53):

> A kingly presence—stately and tall; his shield held high above his head—a broken sword in his right hand. Olaf Tryggvesson! Founder of Nidaros;—that cold Northern Sea has rolled for many centuries above your noble head, and yet not chilled the battle heat upon your brow.

And later:

> Who shall say how much of modern heroism may owe its laurels to that first throb of fiery sympathy which young hearts feel at the relation of deeds such as Olaf Tryggvesson's?

We may be too grown-up, too sane and too professional to join in the boyish hero-worship engaged in by some Victorians. But our perception of questionable motives behind much of the heroic behaviour does not disfigure the picture, it just darkens its colours, and we may still appreciate the scope that the royal subject-matter and grand scale of the Kings' Sagas gave their authors for the portrayal of individual character and for the depiction of grand events—bold exploits on the distant shores of Ireland, the Mediterranean or the Holy Land, the movements of great fleets and armies, the deliberations of assemblies, or scenes of doom-laden kings fighting to the death amid huge armies. As Shakespeare knew, there are few sights more stirring than the fall of kings, 'for within the hollow crown keeps death his court'. Three kings and two jarls meet at Svǫlð; a king dies and a saint is born at Stiklastaðir; the Wends are routed at Hlýrskógsheiðr by the young king Magnús Óláfsson, with supernatural aid from his saintly father, while the bells of Niðaróss, five hundred miles away to the north, echo across the battlefield.[18] Only a king could vow to Christianise Norway or die in the attempt, or declare: 'A king is for fame, not for long life (*Til frægðar skal konung hafa, en ekki til langlífis*)';[19] and even a Kjartan or a Bolli could not match the glamour of Sigurðr Jórsalafari. Against the background of large political and military manoeuvrings, the quieter and more subtle moments gain in poignancy: Óláfr Haraldsson rests his head on Finnr Árnason's lap before taking up arms at Stiklastaðir; Hákon Aðalsteinsfóstri makes painful compromises between religious faith and political expediency.[20] And perhaps because there is no class distinction in Icelandic saga-writing—no *stilus grandiloquus* in the Sagas of Kings to alienate by its pomposity—the scenes portrayed, both the grandiose and the homely, retain their appeal, and will doubtless continue to do so for at least another hundred years.

NOTES

[1] See Nordal 1953, 180 for a summary of the traditional groupings of sagas (1953, 180). Surveys of the Kings' Sagas, with or without explicit discussion of the definition of the genre, include Jón Helgason 1934, 137–63, de Vries 1964–67, II 233–314, Olsen 1965, Schier 1970, 9–33, Andersson 1985, and Jónas Kristjánsson 1988, 147–78.

[2] Among them Thorkil Damsgaard Olsen (1965), whose title is 'Kongekrøniker og Kongesagaer'.

[3] This dating is not entirely new. W. P. Ker, for instance, put Eiríkr Oddsson *c*.1150, adding that he was 'thought by some to be the first author in the characteristic Icelandic style' (1908–09, 250).

[4] For the sake of brevity and simplicity, I am, with apologies, leaving out of account Sven Aggesøn's *Brevis Historia Regum Dacie* and the *Historia Danorum* of Saxo Grammaticus, and their connections with Icelandic tradition. A survey of these and other works of Danish historiography, Latin and vernacular, is given by Brix, 1943, 3–24. Also regrettably beyond the scope of this paper are the *þættir* about Icelanders at the Norwegian court which are either preserved independently or incorporated into lives of kings in works such as *Morkinskinna* and *Flateyjarbók*. A useful introduction is Bjarni Guðnason 1976.

[5] Rudolf Keyser even believed that sagas had been written down in Norway, and only later copied in Iceland, but this view was generally rejected by his contemporaries (Magerøy 1965, 97). Toralf Berntsen also argued that Snorri Sturluson must have obtained traditional materials in Norway not only in oral form but also in written narratives comparable with the *Íslendingasögur* (1923, esp. 96–97).

[6] Berntsen 1923, Seip 1954 and Wessén 1952. Magerøy 1965, 99 also refers to Liestøl's work on popular tradition, in which he stresses the usefulness of detailed local knowledge as a sign of genuine Norwegian tradition.

[7] The Ágrip manuscript was in Iceland in the sixteenth century, but the preparation of the vellum looks Norwegian (so Olsen 1965, 69, who lists other manuscripts of Kings' Sagas with Norwegian connections). Bjarni Einarsson considers it most likely that the manuscript was copied in Iceland from a Norwegian exemplar (Ágrip 1984, vi).

[8] See especially Bjarni Aðalbjarnarson 1937, Beyschlag 1950 and Ellehøj 1965; summarised in Andersson 1985, 201–11.

[9] Bjarni Einarsson, ed., Ágrip 1984, cxxvii–cxxxi. Jakobsen 1970, 123: 'Det er mest sannsynlig at forfatteren var nordmann—Trønder'.

[10] So Magerøy 1965, 98: 'Kongesogene er altså ein del av den islandske, ikkje den norske, nasjonallitteraturen'.

[11] The status of Eiríkr Oddsson is not known. Bjarni Guðnason thinks it likely that he received a clerical education, perhaps at Hólar, but that he was not ordained a priest (1978, 140).

[12] It has been suggested that Eiríkr Oddsson also had links of some kind with Þingeyrar (Nordal 1953, 196; Bjarni Guðnason 1978, 146); and Nordal inclined to the surmise that Styrmir was son of Kári Rúnolfsson, abbot of Þingeyrar (1953, 210). Nordal also believed that Heiðarvíga saga might originate from Þingeyrar (Egils saga 1933, lxviii).

[13] Nordal 1914, esp. 201; his view of the evolution of the Óláfr sagas was built on Maurer's. For stemma, see Andersson 1985, 212.

[14] E.g. the Oldest saga with its reference to tœkilig vitni; on this and related matters see Sverrir Tómasson 1975 and 1988.

[15] An opposite kind of co-operation seems to be in evidence when writers avoid what has already been covered. It is likely that Fagrskinna gives such light and unsatisfactory coverage of Stiklastaðir and the career of Óláfr helgi because it had been well documented elsewhere. In a similar way, some manuscripts of Heimskringla lack an Óláfs saga helga, presumably because the writer or patron already owned a copy of Snorri's Separate saga of Óláfr helgi.

[16] 'Sagaernes historiske troværdighed—hvor "stolt" dette end lyder—vil jeg hævde og forsvare, til jeg tvinges til at nedlægge min pen' (1921, 141). Finnur was, it should be said, careful to point out that by 'historical' he meant based on events which actually happened.

[17] Fidjestøl estimates that about 1270 strophes or part-strophes are quoted within the Kings' Sagas (1985, 322).

[18] In Snorri Sturluson's version, Heimskringla 1941–51, I 353–70 (Svǫlð), II 354–94 (Stiklastaðir), and III 41–45 (Hlýrskógsheiðr).

[19] Respectively, Óláfr Tryggvason in Heimskringla 1941–51, I 303, and Magnús berfœttr in III 237.

[20] Heimskringla 1941–51, II 368, and Hákonar saga góða in I, esp. 166–73 and 192–93.

BIBLIOGRAPHY

I *Primary sources*

Adam of Bremen. *Gesta Hammaburgensis Ecclesiæ Pontificum.* 1917. Ed. Bernhard Schmeidler.
Ágrip af Nóregskonunga sǫgum. Fagrskinna—Nóregs konunga tal. 1984. Ed. Bjarni Einarsson. Íslenzk fornrit 29.
Bǫglunga saga I–II. 1988. Ed. Hallvard Magerøy.
Danakonunga sǫgur: Skjǫldunga saga. Knýtlinga saga. Ágrip af sǫgu Danakonunga. 1982. Ed. Bjarni Guðnason. Íslenzk fornrit 35.
Egils saga. 1933. Ed. Sigurður Nordal. Íslenzk fornrit 2.
Færeyinga saga. 1987. Ed. Ólafur Halldórsson.
Fagrskinna: see *Ágrip.*
Flateyjarbók I–III. 1860–68. Ed. Guðbrandur Vigfússon and C. R. Unger.
Hákonar saga Hákonarsonar. 1977. Ed. Marina Mundt. (Also *Rettelser til Hákonar saga Hákonarsonar.* 1982. Ed. James E. Knirk.)
Hákonar saga Ívarssonar. 1952. Ed. Jón Helgason and Jakob Benediktsson.
Heimskringla I–IV. 1893–1901. Ed. Finnur Jónsson. [IV = notes to verses]
Heimskringla I–III. 1941–51. Ed. Bjarni Aðalbjarnarson. Íslenzk fornrit 26–28.
Heimskringla I–III. 1991. Ed. Bergljót S. Kristjánsdóttir *et al.* [III = Lykilbók]
Historia Norvegiæ: in *Monumenta Historica Norvegiæ,* 69–124.
Jómsvíkinga saga. The Saga of the Jomsvikings. 1962. Ed. and trans. N. F. Blake.
Knýtlinga saga: see *Danakonunga sǫgur.*
[*Legendary Saga of Óláfr helgi*:] *Olafs saga hins helga. Die 'Legendarische Saga' über Olaf den Heiligen.* 1982. Ed. and trans. Anne Heinrichs *et al.*
Magnúss saga lagabœtis. 1887. In *Icelandic sagas* II. *Hakonar saga and a fragment of Magnus saga.* Ed. Gudbrand Vigfusson. Rolls Series.
Monumenta Historica Norvegiæ. 1880. Ed. Gustav Storm.
Morkinskinna. 1932. Ed. Finnur Jónsson.
Oddr Snorrason. *Saga Óláfs Tryggvasonar.* 1932. Ed. Finnur Jónsson.
Óláfs saga Tryggvasonar in mesta I–II. 1958–61. Ed. Ólafur Halldórsson.
[*Oldest saga of Óláfr helgi*:] *Otte Brudstykker af den ældste Saga om Olav den Hellige.* 1893. Ed. Gustav Storm.
Orkneyinga saga. 1965. Ed. Finnbogi Guðmundsson. Íslenzk fornrit 34.
[*Separate saga of Óláfr helgi*:] *Saga Óláfs konungs hins helga. Den store saga om Olav den Hellige* I–II. 1941. Ed. Oscar Albert Johnsen and Jón Helgason.
Skjǫldunga saga: see *Danakonunga sǫgur.*
Sverris saga. 1920. Ed. Gustav Indrebø.
Theodricus Monachus. *Historia de Antiquitate Regum Norwagiensium.* In *Monumenta Historica Norvegiæ,* 1–68.

II *Secondary sources*

Andersson, Theodore M. 1985. 'Kings' Sagas (*Konungasögur*)'. In Clover and Lindow 1985, 197–238.
Andersson, Theodore M. 1993. 'Snorri Sturluson and the saga school at Munkaþverá'. In Wolf 1993, 9–25.
Bagge, Sverre. 1990. 'Snorri Sturluson und die europäische Geschichtsschreibung'. *Skandinavistik* 20, 1–19.
Bagge, Sverre. 1991. *Society and Politics in Snorri Sturluson's Heimskringla.*

Berntsen, Toralf. 1923. *Fra sagn til saga: Studier i kongesagaen.*
Beyschlag, Siegfried. 1950. *Konungasögur: Untersuchungen zur Königssaga bis Snorri.*
Bjarni Aðalbjarnarson. 1937. *Om de norske kongers sagaer.*
Bjarni Guðnason. 1963. *Um Skjöldungasögu.*
Bjarni Guðnason. 1976. 'Þættir', *Kulturhistorisk leksikon for nordisk middelalder* XX, cols 405–10.
Bjarni Guðnason. 1978. *Fyrsta sagan.* Studia Islandica 37.
Blöndal, Lárus H. 1982. *Um uppruna Sverrissögu.*
Brix, Hans. 1943. 'Oldtidens og Middelalderens Litteratur i Danmark'. In *Litteraturhistorie A: Danmark, Finland og Sverige.* Ed. Sigurður Nordal. Nordisk Kultur 8A, 3–63.
Clover, Carol J. 1985. 'Icelandic Family Sagas (*Íslendingasögur*)'. In Clover and Lindow 1985, 239–315.
Clover, Carol J. and Lindow, John. 1985. *Old Norse–Icelandic Literature. A Critical Guide.* Islandica XLV.
Clunies Ross, Margaret. 1987. *Skáldskaparmál: Snorri Sturluson's* Ars Poetica *and Medieval Theories of Language.*
Dufferin, Frederick. 1857. *Letters from High Latitudes.*
Einar Ól. Sveinsson. 1937–38. 'The Icelandic Family Sagas and the Period in which their Authors Lived', *Acta Philologica Scandinavica* 12, 71–90.
Ellehøj, Svend. 1965. *Studier over den ældste norrøne historieskrivning.*
Faulkes, Anthony. 1993. 'The sources of Skáldskaparmál: Snorri's intellectual background'. In Wolf 1993, 59–76.
Fidjestøl, Bjarne. 1982. *Det norrøne fyrstediktet.*
Fidjestøl, Bjarne. 1985. 'On a New Edition of Skaldic Poetry', *The Sixth International Saga Conference: Workshop Papers,* 319–31.
Finnur Jónsson. 1920–24. *Den oldnorske og oldislandske litteraturs historie* I–III. 2nd edition.
Finnur Jónsson. 1921. *Norsk-islandske kultur- og sprogforhold i 9. og 10. årh.*
Guðbrandur Vigfússon (ed.). 1878. *Sturlunga saga* I–II.
Heinrichs, Anne. [1976.] 'Episoden als Strukturelemente in der Legendarischen Saga ...' Unpublished paper given at the Third International Saga Conference, Oslo.
Heusler, Andreas. 1914. *Die Anfänge der isländischen Saga.*
Holtsmark, Anne. 1964. 'Kongesaga', *Kulturhistorisk leksikon for nordisk middelalder* IX, cols 41–46.
Jakobsen, Alfred. 1970. 'Om *Fagrskinna*-forfatteren', *Arkiv för nordisk filologi* 85, 88–124.
Jón Helgason. 1934. *Norrøn litteraturhistorie.*
Jónas Kristjánsson. 1972. *Um Fóstbræðrasögu.*
Jónas Kristjánsson. 1976. 'The Legendary Saga'. In *Minjar og Menntir. Afmælisrit helgað Kristjáni Eldjárn.* Ed. Guðni Kolbeinsson et al., 281–93.
Jónas Kristjánsson. 1977. 'Egilssaga og konungasögur'. In *Sjötíu ritgerðir helgaðar Jakobi Benediktssyni.* Ed. Einar G. Pétursson and Jónas Kristjánsson, 449–72.
Jónas Kristjánsson. 1981. 'Learned Style or Saga Style?' In *Speculum Norroenum.* Ed. Ursula Dronke et al., 260–92.
Jónas Kristjánsson. 1988. *Eddas and Sagas.* Trans. Peter Foote.
Kalinke, Marianne E. 1984. '*Sigurðar saga Jórsalafara*: The Fictionalization of Fact in *Morkinskinna*', *Scandinavian Studies* 56, 152–67.
Kålund, Kr. 1889–94. *Katalog over den Arnamagnæanske håndskriftsamling* I–II.
Ker, W. P. 1908–09. 'The Early Historians of Norway', *Saga-Book* 6, 238–65.

Knirk, James E. 1981. *Oratory in the Kings' Sagas.*
Koht, Halvdan. 1914. 'Sagaernes opfatning av vår gamle historie'. [Norwegian] *Historisk Tidsskrift,* Series 5, 2, 379–96.
Koht, Halvdan. 1954–56. 'Tendens i *Heimskringla?*' [Norwegian] *Historisk Tidsskrift* 37, 366–68.
Kválen, Eivind. 1925. *Den eldste norske kongesoga: Morkinskinna og Hryggjarstykki.*
Lie, Hallvard. 1937. *Studier i Heimskringlas stil: Dialogene og talene.*
Liestøl, Knut. 1930. *The Origin of the Icelandic Family Sagas.* Trans. A. G. Jayne.
Louis-Jensen. 1970. '"Syvende og ottende brudstykker". Fragmentet AM 325 IVa 4to.' In *Opuscula* IV, Bibliotheca Arnamagnæana 30, 31–60.
Louis-Jensen. 1977. *Kongesagastudier. Kompilationen Hulda–Hrokkinskinna.*
Lönnroth, Lars. 1964. *Tesen om de två kulturerna.* Scripta Islandica 15 (published 1965), 1–97.
Lönnroth, Lars. 1975. 'The Concept of Genre in Saga Literature', *Scandinavian Studies* 47, 419–26.
Magerøy, Hallvard. 1965. *Norsk-islandske problem.*
Maurer, Konrad. 1867. *Ueber die Ausdrücke: altnordische, altnorwegische und isländische Sprache.* Abhandlungen der königlichen bayerischen Akademie der Wissenschaften XI, 2, 457–706.
Moberg, Ove. 1987. 'Snorre Sturlasson, Knut den store och Olav den hellige', *Saga och sed,* 53–80.
Moe, Moltke. 1926. 'Eventyrlige sagn i vor ældre historie'. In his *Samlede Skrifter.* Ed. Knut Liestøl, II 85–210.
Munch, P. A. 1852–63. *Det norske Folks Historie* I–VIII.
Mundal, Else. 1977. *Sagadebatt.*
Nordal, Sigurður. 1914. *Om Olaf den helliges saga.*
Nordal, Sigurður. 1920. *Snorri Sturluson.* [1973: slightly revised reprint]
Nordal, Sigurður. 1953. 'Sagalitteraturen'. In *Litteraturhistorie* B: *Norge og Island.* Nordisk Kultur VIII:B, 180–273.
Olsen, Thorkil Damsgaard. 1965. 'Kongekrøniker og kongesagaer'. In *Norrøn Fortællekunst.* Ed. Hans Bekker-Nielsen et al., 42–71.
Paasche, Fredrik. 1922. 'Tendens og syn i kongesagaen', *Edda* 17, 1–17.
Schier, Kurt. 1970. *Sagaliteratur.*
Seip, Didrik Arup. 1954. 'Snorre Sturlason og Tønsberg-tradisjon i *Heimskringla*'. In his *Nye studier i norsk språkhistorie,* 153–61.
Snorrahátíð 1947–48. 1950. Gefið út af tilhlutan Snorranefndar.
Steblin-Kamenskij, M. I. 1973. *The Saga Mind.* Trans. Kenneth H. Ober.
Stefán Karlsson. 1979. 'Islandsk bogeksport til Norge i middelalderen', *Maal og minne,* 1–17.
Storm, Gustav. 1873. *Snorre Sturlassöns Historieskrivning. En kritisk Undersögelse.*
Sverrir Tómasson. 1975. 'Tækileg vitni'. In *Afmælisrit Björns Sigfússonar.* Ed. Björn Teitsson et al., 251–87.
Sverrir Tómasson. 1988. *Formálar íslenskra sagnaritara á miðöldum.*
Turville-Petre, G. 1953. *Origins of Icelandic Literature.*
Vries, Jan de. 1964–67. *Altnordische Literaturgeschichte* I–II, 2nd edition.
Weber, Gerd Wolfgang. 1987. 'Intellegere historiam. Typological perspectives of Nordic prehistory (in Snorri, Saxo, Widukind and others)', *Acta Jutlandica* 63, 95–141.
Weibull, Lauritz. 1911. *Kritiska undersökningar i Nordens historia omkring år 1000.*
Wessén, Elias (ed.). 1952. Snorri Sturluson. *Ynglingasaga.*

Whaley, Diana. 1991. *Heimskringla: an Introduction.*
White, Hayden V. 1975. 'Historicism, history and the figurative imagination', *History and Theory* 14, Beiheft: Essays on Historicism, 48–67.
Wolf, Alois (ed.). 1993. *Snorri Sturluson. Kolloquium anläßlich der 750. Wiederkehr seines Todestages.*
Wormald, Patrick. 1978. 'Bede, "Beowulf" and the Conversion of the Anglo-Saxon Aristocracy'. In *Bede and Anglo-Saxon England*. Ed. R. T. Farrell. British Archaeological Reports 46, 32–95.

MICHAEL BARNES

NORSE IN THE BRITISH ISLES

Introduction

I BEGIN by offering a number of quotations. First, on the positions of Norse (synonymous in this article with Scandinavian) and Gaelic in the Western Isles, and particularly Lewis:

> The invasion of the Vikings [in Lewis] amounted to a clearing out of the previous possessors, and the names of the chief features of the country, mountains, rivers, lakes, sea-lochs and capes were all changed (Henderson 1910, 185).
>
> With the exception of some of the island-names themselves, none of the Gaelic place-names in the Isles can be proved to be of pre-Viking date (Fellows-Jensen 1984, 151).
>
> The place-nomenclature in the west of Lewis, then, provides substantial evidence for a continuous Gaelic speaking presence through the Norse settlement period ... From this we can anticipate that language contact between Norse and Gael ranged over several centuries, from the advent of the first Norse settlers up to and beyond the cession of political sovereignty to Scotland in 1266 (Cox 1991, 483).

Second, on the Norse language of Orkney and Shetland, or Norn, as it is often called:

> In several parts of Shetland, especially Foula and the North Isles, the present generation of old people remember their grand-parents speaking a language that they could hardly understand, and which was called Norn or Norse. But it must have been greatly intermixed with Scotch, for many of the old words now dying out and being supplanted by English, are really Scotch, although they are believed by many to be Norn (Jakobsen 1897, 11).
>
> The statement that the Norn died out in the previous century [the nineteenth] must not ... be taken too literally. The process has been a steady and gradual one, which is still continuing even at the present day. One must certainly suppose that even at the beginning of the 18th century the dialect was hard hit, and after that time it seems to have degenerated very rapidly (Jakobsen 1928–32, xix).
>
> ... as long as the Norn was spoken by the Shetlanders 'amongst themselves', it did not deteriorate in the manner thought by some, neither by being inextricably mixed up with Scots, nor by a breakdown of the grammatical system. As far as the available evidence shows, Norn stood firm to the end (Rendboe 1984, 80).

Third, on the result of language contact between Norse and English speakers in the Danelaw:

> ... as it is most unlikely that OE [Old English] and ON [Old Norse] were fully mutually comprehensible, contact forms (Anglo-Danish pidgin) must have been used to some extent in trade and commerce. As the bilingual situation receded, the varieties that remained must have been effectively Anglo-Norse creoles with a tendency in the post-creole situation to restore some of the grammatical distinctions lost in pidginization (Milroy 1984, 11).

The very close similarity between the two languages [Norse and English] makes the emergence of a pidgin language as unlikely on linguistic grounds as it is on social grounds: linguistically, communication could be effected without drastic elimination of linguistic complexities, and socially the need (at least in most places) was for an all-purpose language, not merely for a restricted-purpose minimal language. Creolization is also unlikely on social grounds, and again the languages seem too close linguistically for such an extreme response to communication difficulties (Thomason and Kaufman 1988, 307).

I have chosen these quotations for several reasons. First, to span, as nearly as possible, the hundred years of the Viking Society's existence. Second, to introduce some of the issues pertaining to Norse in the British Isles which have been widely and vigorously debated. Third, to show how greatly views of these issues may differ. The disagreement has various causes. One is increased knowledge: the uncovering of new evidence leads to new interpretations. Another cause is the age-old conflict between the believer and the sceptic. A third is the markedly different extent to which scholars succumb to the blandishments of changing academic fashion. All of this will become apparent in the following survey, which will take the form of brief, critical snapshots of a hundred years of research into the life and death of Norse in England, Ireland, Man, the Hebrides and the Northern Isles. Naturally, given so vast a subject, the range of topics covered and the space devoted to each will have to be severely restricted. I hope nevertheless to be able to mention most of the major issues and to give something of the flavour of the debate.

Before I begin to look at the individual regions of the British Isles, it is perhaps worth making two general points. First, research into the fate of the Norse language in Britain and Ireland by and large reflects the prevailing concerns of historical linguistics at any given time. Up until the middle of this century, for example, the emphasis was almost exclusively on phonology, loan-words and place-names, and the approaches were relatively unhampered by the constraints of definition or of theory. Recent decades have seen a broadening of the scope, a greater willingness to define terms and in some scholars a positive zest for theoretical models against which to evaluate the data. The second point to be made is that the interest of many researchers in the field has not been entirely or sometimes even primarily linguistic. The coming of Norse to the British Isles, its subsequent existence and ultimate demise have not, at least until very recently, featured at all prominently in the literature. The emphasis has instead often been on such questions as the extent of Danish settlement in England or the fate of the pre-Viking Gaelic-speaking population in Man and parts of the Hebrides. Even where the linguistic data are ostensibly the main concern and are not merely brought in to bolster conclusions about the size of Danish armies and the like, Viking settlement patterns usually form the wider context in which they are discussed. A notable exception to this has been the study of Orkney and Shetland Norn. Because of the survival of these branches of Norse until the eighteenth century, attention here has mainly been focused on the question of language shift.

Norse in England

The received wisdom just after the turn of the century on the subject of the Norse language in England was expounded in a much quoted and often praised chapter in Otto Jespersen's *Growth and Structure of the English Language* (1905, 59–83). Jespersen begins by describing the Viking invasions of England. Having set the scene, he goes on—drawing to some extent on Björkman 1900–02—to stress the close kinship and similarity of Norse and English, to discuss at length different categories of Norse loan-words in English and the competition between Norse and native forms, and to suggest that a 'fusion of the two languages' (p. 82) took place. The chapter ends with three brief paragraphs, one on the morphology of the loans, one on contact with Norse as a cause of inflectional simplification in English, and one on Norse syntactic influence. The last of these, despite its speculative character and attribution to Viking-Age Norse of modern Danish constructions, has been quoted with approbation by many later scholars. Jespersen has not been without his critics (cf. in particular Einenkel (1906) and Kirch (1959), who both stress the invalidity of his examples of syntactic influence), but even in the most recent edition of one of the standard histories of the English language (Baugh and Cable 1981, 90–106), it is still substantially his story that is being re-told.

A question of importance to students of the Scandinavian languages, which Jespersen scarcely raises, is: how long did Norse continue to be spoken in England? Later writers tend to show slightly greater interest in the matter, but still often provide no more than a sentence or two in which the conclusions of Ekwall's (1930) and more recently Page's (1971) article on the survival of the Scandinavian language in England are rehearsed. Baugh and Cable (1981, 95) have the following to say: 'While in some places the Scandinavians gave up their language early there were certainly communities in which Danish or Norse remained for some time the usual language'—a conservative enough conclusion, and perhaps the only one for which there is warrant, but its blandness could, one feels, have been tempered by brief discussion of the evidence. For such discussion, Baugh and Cable's readers are directed to the articles by Ekwall and Page. Ekwall begins by arguing in general terms that the survival of Norse in England would have been determined by the number of speakers as a proportion of the population in any given district. He does not think political submission to the English would necessarily have led to the rapid demise of Norse. His examination of the evidence provided by inscriptions, place-names and Norse loan-words in English appears to confirm these initial views, though it is hard to be sure, for he does not present an orderly set of conclusions at the end of the article, but relies rather on the planting of a few stray remarks at different points in his text. In only one case is he unequivocal: the Pennington inscription from Lancashire 'proves that so late as about 1100 a Scandinavian language was spoken in the district even by the upper classes' (p. 24).

In his 1971 article, Page dismembers that part of Ekwall's case which is based on epigraphical sources, and concludes that the epigraphical evidence for the survival of Scandinavian in England is slight. The Pennington inscription, he thinks, could exhibit either corrupt Old Norse or Norse-influenced Old or Middle English: 'From it I would hesitate to argue what language the people of the area spoke in the twelfth century' (p. 172). Page nevertheless stresses that the absence of clear epigraphical evidence of Norse language survival cannot be assumed to indicate an absence of Norse speakers. There are simply insufficient data to determine the matter either way.

Space forbids detailed comment on Ekwall's place-name and loan-word evidence. Suffice it to say that both would benefit from reinterpretation in the light of current knowledge. Many of his linguistic arguments in particular no longer hold, deriving as they do from views about the development of the Scandinavian languages most would now deem invalid. The upshot is that there seems to be very little direct evidence that could help us decide how long Norse survived in England, and we are therefore thrown back on indirect testimony such as the size of the Norse element in later English and on comparison with better-known language contact situations elsewhere.

The extent of Norse influence on English has been widely assumed to indicate prolonged contact between speakers of the two languages (or between speakers of a derivative of Norse and English). About the nature of this contact and its prerequisites, there has been little agreement. To most scholars around the turn of the century, who tended towards a literal interpretation of the sources, the matter was straightforward enough: vast numbers of Scandinavians settled in the eastern half of England and the north-west; they continued to speak Norse for a generation or two, but eventually gave it up in favour of a mixed Anglo-Norse which gradually became more anglicised and was ultimately the source of the influx of Norse elements into English. None of these various assumptions has remained unchallenged. Later scholars have sought to refine them, have questioned their meaning, or totally rejected them. The following points in particular have been made:
(1) There is no incontrovertible evidence that the number of settlers was vast, and a good many indications that it was small. (2) The settlers would have consisted chiefly or only of men and would therefore have taken English-speaking wives who would have taught English to their children; the continuation of Norse speech in England must therefore have been dependent on new waves of settlers.

(3) The term 'mixed' or 'fused' language is by most who use it left undefined; in the absence of a definition, we can have no clear idea what is envisaged. (4) In the light of current socio-linguistic models, the results of Norse-English linguistic contact are only explicable on the assumption that a pidgin developed that was subsequently creolised. (5) There is no warrant whatsoever for the belief that a pidgin or creole developed in Viking-Age England, and by definition, therefore, no justification for talk of a 'mixed' or 'fused' language.

Of these five points, the second is the most easily dealt with in that, unlike the others, it is a matter of pure speculation and raises no theoretical issues. The following seems a fair assessment of the arguments (Hansen 1984, 81):

> This entire discussion is of little avail; we are dealing with sociolinguistic subtleties which cannot be reconstructed by means of the borrowings. Besides, it was not necessarily decisive whether Danes married other Danes or married into English families. More important is the relative status of the two languages outside the family ... and if Scandinavian was a high-prestige language for a couple of generations, the nationality of the Danish soldiers' wives is of minor importance.

The mention of high prestige leads naturally to the debate about numbers. Are the Norse settlers to be numbered in tens of thousands, as originally believed, or in a few hundreds, as argued at one time by Sawyer (see the review of the controversy in Fellows Jensen 1975)? The principal argument against a very small settlement has been the extent of Norse influence on English, but this has been countered by pointing to Weinreich's statement (1953, 92): 'Even for extensive word transferring, large numbers of bilingual speakers need not be involved and the relative size of the groups is not necessarily a factor.' The higher or even aristocratic social status of the Norse settlers is sufficient explanation for the borrowing, it is suggested. Argument and counter-argument here form part of a historical rather than a linguistic debate, which is perhaps why Weinreich's words of caution, taken out of context, have been elevated almost to the status of an axiom (Kisbye 1982a, 50). It is certainly possible, given the right circumstances, for a minority to exercise linguistic influence on a majority, but were the circumstances in Viking-Age England right? The linguistic evidence, such as it is, tends to suggest they were not. Norman French—indubitably a high-prestige minority language in England—left its mark on areas of life such as government, administration, culture and fashion; Norse influence, on the other hand, seems for the most part to have been restricted to basic, everyday vocabulary. Historically, too, there are difficulties. Whatever the status of the Danish and Norwegian settlers in their homeland (and this is uncertain), it remains to be demonstrated that they enjoyed higher prestige in England than the natives. For those primarily interested in Scandinavian linguistic history, the numbers question is in any case largely a red herring. Norse speech, for whatever reason, clearly enjoyed sufficient prestige for a sufficiently long period to exercise widespread influence on English.

It is with the nature and process of this influence that recent discussion on Norse-English language contact and the fate of Norse in England has been concerned. Kisbye (1982a; 1982b), arguing without the benefit, or burden as some might see it, of a general theoretical model, reaches the following conclusions. (1) There was a degree of mutual comprehensibility between speakers of Norse and English. (2) The settlers and their descendants did not constitute an upper class. (3) Norse lasted into the eleventh century in England and an Anglo-Norse mixed language was still in existence in some parts of the country as late as the early twelfth century. (4) Anglo-Norse arose primarily through the efforts of the settlers to speak English. (5) Norse influence caused or helped on its way the inflectional simplification of English. (6) The influence of Norse on English was of enormous dimensions. The arguments that accompany these conclusions vary in quality and extent. Mutual comprehensibility is supported by a demonstration of far-reaching structural and lexical similarities between Norse and English. Against the notion that the settlers enjoyed upper-class status, detailed arguments are adduced along the lines of the point made above about the nature of Norse loans in English. The Anglo-Norse mixed language is little more than an article of faith, but is said to make an appearance in some of the inscriptions discussed in particular in Page 1971 (see above). The origin of Anglo-Norse in settlers' attempts to speak English is offered as the most reasonable explanation of the data, while the effects of Norse influence in causing or assisting the simplification of the English inflectional system, as well as the massive extent of the influence, are taken as more or less axiomatic.

Less sanguine than Kisbye is Hansen (1984). Her conclusions at the end of a wide-ranging, though somewhat rambling and occasionally turgid article are that everything is uncertain (p. 88):

> Whatever the result of the contact between English and Scandinavian is called and whatever models we try to fit the borrowings into, it is impossible to make inferences about the causes. There are too many unknown quantities. Therefore we mainly find ourselves compelled to guessing, though some hypotheses are of course more valid than others.

In much the same style she goes on to suggest widespread bilingualism, among both Norse and English speakers, as a cause of Norse influence on English. Like Kisbye, she does not find that any particular prestige can have attached to the Norse settlers or their speech, and she therefore concludes that there must have been a large number of settlers 'to ensure the necessary, long survival of the Scandinavian language in England, which is compatible with the theory of secondary immigrants' (p. 89). As an alternative explanation to bilingualism she suggests the extensive transference of vocabulary as a result of language death— a phenomenon that has been noted elsewhere:

At the time when they [the borrowings] first emerged, that is 1200–1400, there was no standard English owing to the Normal [sic] French influence . . . and this weakened position may have facilitated the acceptance into the various ME dialects of Scandinavian words introduced during the last stages of the language shift (p. 88).

The full theoretical implications of the Anglo-Norse mixed language so widely touted in the literature are given a thorough airing in Hines 1991. The observable data, he suggests, point to a mixture on at least two levels (p. 415):

. . . a level of basilectal, restricted and utilitarian language produced by a shift in Old English targeted upon Scandinavian or containing the residue of the atrophy of Scandinavian under English dominance, and a higher level in which English is the dominant, lexifier language but within which Scandinavian items also carry definitive status.

Hines's argument, as I understand it, is that the language of the first-generation Scandinavian settlers had higher prestige than English and therefore became a target language for English speakers when the need arose for communication between the two groups. This explains, among other things, why items of basic Norse vocabulary were carried into English: if English had been the target language, one would have expected its basic vocabulary to have been the first element mastered. The form of speech that arose in these circumstances probably fulfilled the criteria for a 'model pidgin' (p. 408). Not long after the initial settlement, however, perhaps as early as in the second generation, a change set in. A desire arose among the Scandinavians to distance themselves from their sordid past and to adapt to the higher and more stable Anglo-Saxon culture. The product of this attitudinal shift was a process of Anglo-Scandinavian acculturation, thoughtful and deliberate, one of whose manifestations, if not the most visible, was the establishment of a higher-level form of Anglo-Scandinavian speech, which served to make the settlers feel more at home in their new surroundings while still emphasising their separate identity. (Though Hines does not himself make the point, it might be that the English loans in Scandinavian discussed by Hofmann (1955, 21–148) occurred as part of such a process.)

Hines's paper is closely argued, and both evidence and theoretical models are adduced at relevant points. He does not jump aboard the pidginisation and creolisation bandwagon which has been rolling with increasing velocity in recent years, but is content to give it an encouraging wave as it passes (p. 420):

The value of the term [creole] lies not in summarizing the details of the history of Scandinavian English language mixing, but in locating analogous data and associated theory. From this the usual cross fertilization of case-study and general understanding can proceed.

Whether one is convinced by the scenario Hines sketches is another matter. Scarcity of evidence is a problem, and there is at least one aspect of the question to which he gives little consideration: the degree of mutual comprehensibility between Norse and English. The talk in the first of the above quotations from his paper of 'the residue of the atrophy of Scandinavian under English dominance' is a reference to the following notion (cf. Hines 1991, 406): because Norse and English were fundamentally so similar, resistance to the loss of the former was probably weaker than might otherwise have been expected; as Norse was gradually worn down, the bulk of what remained will have been basic vocabulary which, because of the kinship of the two languages, was easily preserved in a final amalgam of the dominant and subordinate forms of speech. Hines does not actually recommend this idea, but it is not dismissed either and seems to feature as an alternative to his pidginisation hypothesis (cf. the above quotation from p. 415 of his paper). It is legitimate to wonder, I think (in spite of the fact that definitions of pidginisation do not appear to require a specified level of dissimilarity for the process to take place), whether the conditions for the development of a basic system of communication would have existed where the languages in contact were as similar as it is suggested Norse and English were. Of course, Hines may have reasoned as follows: either they were not similar—in which case a pidgin must have been the answer—or they were similar—which will have obviated the need for a pidgin and facilitated the retention of basic Norse vocabulary in English as Norse died out as an autonomous language. However, these two hypotheses are never discussed as alternatives, so it is hard for the reader to judge their precise status in the overall analysis. Difficult though it is, the question of the degree of mutual comprehensibility between Norse and English does, I think, require serious discussion, not least because it has loomed so large in the debate about Norse-English language contact in the Danelaw and elsewhere in England.

In the same year as Hines gave his paper, Thomason and Kaufman published *Language Contact, Creolization, and Genetic Linguistics* (1988), which contains as one of a number of case studies a section entitled 'English and other coastal Germanic languages, or why English is not a mixed language' (pp. 263–342). This deals in part with the influence of French on Middle English, but is in the main a detailed study of the process and effects of language contact between English and Norse. As the title of the section suggests, the two authors do not believe that English and Norse fused; they are in particular vehemently opposed to theories of creolisation, partly because such theories do not in their view accord with the observable facts and partly because of an innate scepticism about claims to have found the Holy Grail.

> In spite of the relatively large number of grammatical elements of Norse origin in Norsified ME, their effect on English structure was almost trivial. Thirty-eight of the fifty-seven traits [that the authors deem to be indicative of Norse influence], or 67 percent, are mere phonological variants of what English had had in the first place. It is as though Norsification largely reflects a fad whereby an English speaker would parade his knowledge of Norse while speaking English (p. 298).

We . . . acknowledge . . . that overarching models that use a small number of axioms and try to explain practically everything annoy us. We dislike reductionism (ad absurdum). We are splitters, not lumpers. The purpose of this book is to introduce some *subtlety* into the thoughts and words of historical linguists (p. 328).

Thomason and Kaufman's contribution is to the debate about the development of English. Detailed argumentation is brought to bear not just to show that Middle English is not a mixed language, but also to demonstrate the geographical route by which the Norse element, which the authors believe originally existed in its most widespread form in Midland English, ultimately spread to all dialects. This concentration on the fate of English allows Thomason and Kaufman rather a free hand in their treatment of Norse. To begin with, it permits them to ignore most of the recent and some of the earlier debate not only about the effects of contact between Norse and English, but also about the size of the Scandinavian settlement in England. Thus the names of Ekwall, Fellows-Jensen, Hansen, Kisbye and Page—to mention but a few—are missing from their bibliography, and Sawyer is offered as the principal historical authority ('Sawyer's [1971 edition of *The Age of the Vikings*] is the most up-to-date analysis of the archeological and historical data on the Viking raids on and settlement of parts of Britain, and will be taken as essentially the latest word for the purposes of this study' (p. 360)). The authors' reluctance to delve too deep into the Scandinavian element of the equation has consequences for their presentation. Most noticeable is the vagueness they display about what might have happened when speakers of Norse and English came into regular contact with each other—a vagueness which stands in stark contrast, for example, to Hines's carefully sketched scenario. What we are offered is a number of contradictory or improbable statements which stand more or less bereft of supporting documentation. On p. 267 it is suggested that Norse 'probably lasted no more than two generations after 955', while on p. 282 the authors say they are 'convinced that Norse was largely or entirely absorbed by English in the Danelaw by A.D. 1100'; a map (p. 337) depicting 'the demise of Norse' in different areas of England gives dates ranging from 920 to 1160. 'An intense contact situation' between Norse and English led, we are told, to 'category (3) [heavy] borrowing or considerable influence through shift, or (more likely) both', although, to take account of Sawyer's view that the number of settlers was small, it is also suggested that the 'pre-existing close typological fit' between the two languages might have permitted heavy borrowing with less intensive contact (p. 281). Whatever the truth of any (or none) of this, 'Norsified English arose at a time when Norse was still spoken but going out of use in its area' (p. 284), for 'in many ways Norse influence on English was a kind of prestige borrowing that took little effort to implement' (p. 303).

I would not want these quotations, which I think amply illustrate the deficiencies of Thomason and Kaufman's treatment of Norse, to be taken as typical of the work as a whole. On the wider theoretical questions, and on the development from Old to Middle English the authors exhibit a higher level of competence and float a number of interesting ideas. The contention in particular, well supported by evidence, that the change from synthetic to analytic structure in English began before Norse influence became relevant, coincides neatly with the recent demonstration by Ringgaard (1986) that simplification of the Common Scandinavian inflectional system was well under way in parts of Denmark before the onset of Middle Low German influence in that country.

A great deal more could be said on the subject of Norse in England, but it is time now to turn to the Q-Celtic-speaking areas in the west of the British Isles.

Norse in Ireland, Man and the Hebrides

As far as is known, Norse settlers in Ireland were for the most part concentrated in a small number of towns, notably Dublin, while in Man and the northern Hebrides they appear for a time to have become the dominant element in the population, if not to have driven out the earlier inhabitants altogether. Only in part commensurate with this picture, we find that Norse influence on Irish is small and that there are very few place-names in Ireland of Norse origin, that Manx vocabulary has no more than a scattering of Norse loans although Norse place-names in the island are plentiful, and that the northern Hebrides, especially Lewis, show considerable Norse influence, even, if we are to believe certain scholars, on the level of phonology.

To cover with anything like the care I accorded to the situation in England even part of the debate that has surrounded the rise and fall of Norse in the Q-Celtic-speaking areas of the British Isles would lead too far in the present context. I must therefore pass by such theories as the one (which enjoyed some popularity in the early years of this century) that Norse saga-writing began in Ireland—a theory which presupposes not only a highly developed literary culture, but also a sufficiently stable linguistic situation and a language prestigious enough to support such a culture. Norse *was* written in Ireland—we now have some thirteen runic inscriptions from that country (the majority from Dublin), virtually all of which appear to be in a kind of Norse, but it is a far cry from these laconic, sometimes incomprehensible messages to the lengthy sagas envisaged by, for example, Bugge (1908). What I would like principally to do in the following is to stress the similarity and the differences I perceive between the debates about Norse in the Q-Celtic areas and Norse in England, and to offer a few comments of my own.

Once again, it cannot fail to strike those whose primary interest lies in the Scandinavian field how little interest the majority of scholars discussing Norse–Celtic language contact in Ireland, Man and the Hebrides have shown in the fate of Norse. Just as was the case with England, attention has focused on the usefulness of the linguistic evidence as historical source material and on the extent of Norse influence on the indigenous language. One difference can, however, be observed: there has been less talk of pidgins and creoles in the Celtic context, although in fact, because of the wide linguistic gap between Q-Celtic and Norse, one would imagine that the islands of the west provided more fertile ground than England for the development of basic contact languages. Indeed, such a language is just what Marstrander (1915) seems to be describing when he says of the notorious Gall–Ghoídhil (p. 8):

> At de i stor utstrækning har været bilingve ligger i navnet og i sakens natur. At ordforraad, syntaks og fraseologi er blandet sammen, kan man ta for givet. ('That they were to a large extent bilingual is clear from the name [Gall–Ghoídhil] and really goes without saying. That vocabulary, syntax and phraseology were mixed [Norse and Irish], can be assumed as a matter of course.')

But then, the sophisticated terminology of sociolinguistics was not available in 1915.

It is with Marstrander's book (which, exceptionally, does evince some interest in Norse) that serious investigation into the linguistic effects of the Scandinavian presence in Ireland can be said to begin. Although in the years since it appeared the work has been shown to have many inadequacies, there has been no attempt at a full-scale revaluation of the material that forms its subject-matter. Indeed, later studies often do little more than chew over various of the details, approving some of Marstrander's findings and condemning others (cf. e.g. Greene 1976). This means that the dominant themes in discussion of the contact between Norse and Irish have been phonology and loan-words, although place-names have also featured (e.g. Oftedal 1976). Jackson (1962) shows awareness of the need to distinguish between loan-words and structure in the discussion of Norse influence on the Celtic languages, but in the case of Irish, at least, he finds evidence of structural influence to be lacking. Regarding the survival of Norse speech in Ireland, most writers consider that it lasted in Dublin and certain other towns until shortly after the Norman invasions began in the 1160s, its final demise perhaps coming early in the thirteenth century. The reasons for this judgement are historical rather than linguistic—the self-contained nature of many of the Viking centres—but it has also been shown that most of the small number of Norse place-names to be found in Ireland passed directly from Norse into English.

Perhaps the reason relatively little has been written about Norse–Irish linguistic contact lies in the paucity of the sources—although lack of evidence is seldom a barrier to the voicing of scholarly opinion. I cannot help wondering, however, whether the application of new methods and modes of thought to such little evidence as there is might not help us to a better understanding of the linguistic consequences of the Norse invasions of Ireland.

In comparison with Ireland, the Isle of Man offers a rich harvest to the seeker after Norse: a wealth of place-names and between thirty and forty runic inscriptions, though Norse loan-words in Manx are few. Here as elsewhere, the debate has centred on the nature and extent of the Scandinavian settlement, and the linguistic evidence has been used in support of differing interpretations of Manx history in the Viking and early Middle Ages. Recently it has been claimed that the place-name evidence in particular suggests that Man was largely, if not wholly, Norse speaking in the period 900–1300, or, in the most conservative terms in which the argument has been couched: 'If, during these centuries, Man is to be considered a predominantly Gaelic-speaking kingdom under Norse rule, the evidence for this must be sought elsewhere than in the place-names' (Gelling 1970–71, 138; cf. also Gelling 1978). Against this it has been argued that the totality of the evidence, archaeological, historical, literary and linguistic, points to the widespread survival of Gaelic, certainly among the peasant population, and probably at a higher social level too, during a period of dominance by a small Norse aristocracy (Megaw 1978). To the extent that a consensus has now been reached, it is that the Norse settlement was considerable and involved all levels of society rather than just a small ruling class, but that Gaelic did continue to be spoken side-by-side with Norse (Fellows Jensen 1978; 1983; Gelling 1991). I concur in this conclusion, and therefore reckon with a long period of Norse–Gaelic contact on Man.

Not all who have discussed the linguistic evidence have had a historical agenda. It is true that Marstrander's great monograph on the Norse settlement of Man (1932b), although written by a philologist and containing much linguistic material, was (as he himself admits, p. 340) primarily historical in its intention, but in parallel with the wider debate which this work in part initiated there has, to take just one example, been intermittent discussion of the likelihood of Celtic influence on the language of the Manx runic inscriptions (Olsen 1909; Seip 1930; Page 1983)—a discussion characterised in equal measure by its clear linguistic concerns and its inconclusiveness. In part arising from the perceived intermixture of Norse and Gaelic in the Manx inscriptions is the assumption that behind it must lie an intermixture of the two populations (Marstrander 1932b, 51; Megaw 1978, 276–78), and the concomitant assumption of widespread bilingualism (Megaw 1978, 288). Oddly enough, though, in the light of the apparent breakdown of the Norse inflectional system in at least one of the inscriptions, no one seems to have proposed pidginisation and creolisation as alternatives to bilingualism. Perhaps, as in the case of Irish, this is because later Manx Gaelic shows no effects of such a development.

The date at which Norse finally became extinct on Man has been the subject of differing estimates. Marstrander (1932b, 49) thought some time in the fifteenth century likely, and in this he was followed by Gelling (1970–71, 174), but the demonstration that one of the principal sources on which they based their conclusions is about a hundred years older than was originally thought has led to a revision of this estimate: Gelling (1978, 257) now offers a conservative 'some time after 1300', Megaw (1978, 279) 'within a generation or two of the end of the native dynasty—that is, soon after 1300'.

Investigation of Norse in the Hebrides echoes the Manx debate to the extent that much interest has focused on the question of the continuity of Gaelic speech in the areas of densest Norse settlement. Three of my initial quotations deal with this issue, starting with Henderson's somewhat simplistic assumption that the changing of the names of 'the chief features of the country' implies 'a clearing out of the previous possessors', continuing with Fellows-Jensen's contention that virtually none of the Gaelic place-names in the Isles can be shown to be pre-Viking and ending up with Cox's counter-claim that a substantial body of place-names in the west of Lewis do appear to pre-date the Norse settlement. Cox's conclusion, which is clearly significant, is based on phonological and morphological features in a group of nearly 3,000 names he collected over an area of about 150 square kilometres. Cox further considers that his evidence supports the notion of a gradually developing bilingualism, though perhaps only on a limited scale (1991, 484–90), and he believes that collection and study of all the relevant material will ultimately reveal 'evidence for what we might call Hebridean Norse, the variety of Old Norse spoken in the Hebrides' (p. 489).

Borgstrøm, in his purely linguistic study (1974) of Norse–Gaelic contact in the Hebrides (in which he picked up the thread from Marstrander 1932a) had some years earlier argued the odd and in its presuppositions opposite case (from Cox) that although the relative paucity of Norse loan-words in Scottish Gaelic indicated a lack of Gaelic–Norse bilingualism, Norse had nevertheless exercised considerable phonological influence on Gaelic, imparting preaspiration to a variety of dialects and a south-west Norwegian pitch pattern to that of Lewis. He explains this unexpected development in terms of a sudden language shift (p. 102):

> When the mutual isolation of the two linguistic groups ended, new generations of Norse children learnt Gaelic in a correct native form, only occasionally carrying over some sub-phonemic features or other habits of speech from their first language.

Irrespective of the correctness or otherwise of Borgstrøm's belief in such phonological influence, he does seem, albeit incidentally, to have put his finger on a paradox: a massive Norse settlement and a Norse speech community lasting for several centuries, but only marginal or uncertain influence on spoken or written Gaelic to show for it. His explanation is lack of significant linguistic contact. Yet in the case of Man, where a similar historical development is assumed and its impact on the indigenous language appears no greater, it has been argued by some that bilingualism was widespread. Here, a solution to the paradox might be the alleged re-settlement of the island in the late Middle Ages by Gaelic speakers from Galloway and elsewhere (cf. Gelling 1991, 146–47; it should be remembered, though, that Galloway was reputedly the home of the linguistically mixed Gall–Ghoídhil), but evidence for such re-settlement is lacking. (A similar influx of Gaelic speakers into Lewis—equally unsusceptible of proof—appears an unavoidable assumption, one might add, for those who believe that this part of the Hebrides became entirely Norse speaking during the Viking Age.) It is clear that we are dealing here with matters of the utmost uncertainty. Even the size of the Norse loan-word element in Lewis Gaelic and Gaelic as a whole seems as yet poorly documented (cf. Christiansen 1938; Oftedal 1962b; Cox 1991, 490, 492–93).

With evidence so scarce, it is hardly surprising that views about the length of time for which Norse persisted as a spoken language in the Hebrides should have the appearance of guesswork (see, however, Cox 1991, 479). 'Probably in the 13th or 14th century' is Borgstrøm's seemingly intuitive estimate of the period in which Norse was finally superseded by Gaelic (1974, 91), while survival into the early fifteenth century is mooted as a possibility by Oftedal (1962a, 48), who in an article published in the same year nevertheless offers the more conservative suggestion that Norse influence on Gaelic language and culture 'may have continued long after 1266' (Oftedal 1962b, 118).

Norse in Caithness, Orkney and Shetland

As we have seen, it is the *arrival* of Norse in England, Ireland, Man and the Hebrides—and the extent of the subsequent contact between speakers of Norse and the indigenous languages—that has fired the scholarly imagination. With Caithness, Orkney and Shetland it is different. Here interest has centred on the *demise* of Scandinavian speech. This is understandable in the light of the historical and linguistic circumstances. However long the indigenous language or languages of Caithness and the Northern Isles survived the Viking settlement, Norse seems rapidly to have become dominant, and sooner or later to have become the native idiom of the whole area, extinguishing more or less without trace such tongues as may have been spoken there earlier. Nothing is therefore to be learnt about language contact, loan-words, pidgins, creoles and the like from Viking-Age or early medieval Caithness, Orkney or Shetland. Such interest as has been evinced in the linguistic situation in northernmost Britain during this period has instead revolved around the type of Scandinavian speech the settlers brought with them and the extent to which features characteristic of developing Shetlandic, Orcadian and Caithness Norse can be observed in the relatively plentiful written sources from the region. Results in both cases have been meagre. There is a consensus that some variety of western Norwegian must have been the dominant strain, but disagreement over whether the input was primarily from the north-west or the south-west of Norway (Barnes 1984, 34–35). Few, if any, specifically Caithness or island features can be found in the runic inscriptions or the Latin-alphabet documents from the region: the most significant collection of inscriptions—those from Maeshowe in Orkney—seem largely, if not entirely, to have been carved by visitors to the islands (Barnes 1991a), while Scandinavian writing in the Latin alphabet mirrors faithfully the development of the written language in Norway.

Given such a comprehensive lack of exciting data, it is hardly surprising that scholars concerned with the Norse of Caithness, Orkney and Shetland should have turned their attention to the period after c.1350, when the language entered a period of competition with Scots. It has been customary to refer to the Norse of this period as Norn (from *norrœnn* 'Norwegian, Norse', or *norrœna* 'Norwegian, Norse language'), a term first recorded in 1485 or thereabouts; that is a custom I shall observe here.

Knowledge of Norn comes from loan-words in Scots or English, of which well over 10,000 have been recorded, from a few texts written down or published in the seventeenth and eighteenth centuries, while Norn was probably still a living language, and from odd verses, sayings and snatches of conversation collected in the late nineteenth century some time after the last native speaker had gone to the grave. (Discussion of these sources together with references can be found in Barnes 1991b. In the following I shall concentrate entirely on Orkney and Shetland Norn; for the Caithness variety, which died out much earlier, possibly in the fourteenth or fifteenth centuries, I refer the reader to Thorsen 1954.)

The study of Orkney and Shetland Norn until recently had concentrated on collection and documentation (best exemplified by Hægstad 1900, Jakobsen 1928–32, and Marwick 1929). To the extent that opinions were expressed about the manner in which Norn succumbed to Scots, they reflected a general belief in a gradual shift between about 1600 and 1850, accomplished at least in part by the steady infusion of Norn with Scots vocabulary and grammar—a process which, it seems to have been thought, led ultimately to an amalgamation of the two languages. The unusually large Norn substratum to be found in Orkney and Shetland Scots was seen as the remains of the Norn share in this mixed language. In its purest form the Scots–Norn fusion hypothesis is probably to be found in Flom 1928–29.

It was not until 1984 that a challenge was made to the prevailing view of post-Reformation linguistic development in Orkney and Shetland. In an article with the intriguing title 'How "worn out" or "corrupted" was Shetland Norn in its final stage?'—'worn out' and 'corrupted' being descriptions applied to Orkney and Shetland Norn by earlier, mainly eighteenth-century writers—Laurits Rendboe made the plausible claim that 'worn out' means not 'decayed', but 'dropped out of fashion', and he went on to argue that as long as Norn continued to be used by native speakers it survived in pure form, unadulterated by Scots pronunciation, grammar or lexicon. According to Rendboe, there can be no question of a gradual intermixture of the two languages in Shetland. All the evidence points to the conclusion (reproduced in one of my initial quotations) that 'Norn stood firm to the end'.

Against this, it seems to me, rather romantic view of the demise of Norn, I have argued (1989; 1991b): (a) that such data as we have in no way warrant Rendboe's conclusion; and (b) that the shift from Norn to Scots in both Orkney and Shetland should be viewed in the light of political and social developments in the islands in the sixteenth to eighteenth centuries and in the context of the increasing body of knowledge about language death. In particular I commended to Rendboe's attention Nancy Dorian's splendid and seminal study of the death of East Sutherland Gaelic (1981). This work describes with admirable clarity and in great detail the loss of functions and the structural erosion that are affecting another language of northern Britain as it reaches the end of its struggle against English encroachment. The difficulty, of course, is to know whether the changes that Dorian observed in the dying Gaelic dialect of eastern Sutherland are general tendencies or specific to that particular situation. Many of the changes, it is true, seem also to characterise other languages in decline (cf. Dressler and Wodak-Leodolter 1977; Rindler-Schjerve 1989), but it would be unwise to attempt a reconstruction of the death of Norn in Orkney and Shetland on the basis of linguistic parallels alone. That is where study of the political and social developments in the relevant period comes in. Such study may, as I have suggested, be expected to uncover useful supporting evidence. It should go hand in hand with more thorough analysis of the linguistic sources—not only of the Norn fragments that have survived, but also of certain writings in Scots. Brian Smith has recently pointed out to me that there were several attempts as early as around 1800 to reproduce Shetland dialect (i.e. the form of Scots then used in the islands) and that the differences between these and the dialect texts of today are so small as to make plausible the contention that a settled linguistic situation pertained before the beginning of the nineteenth century. This could indicate, he thinks, that the language shift in Shetland took place somewhat earlier than the late seventeenth-early eighteenth-century date which has normally been proposed.

Whatever view we take of the way or ways in which Scots supplanted Norn in the Northern Isles and the dates at which the shift took place, we can all agree that much work remains to be done. This unoriginal if not uninspiring conclusion clearly applies with equal force to the other instances of Scandinavian language death in the British Isles on which I have touched, but in the case of Orkney and Shetland the relative nearness of the events perhaps holds out greater hope that such work will produce tangible results.

Concluding remarks

In this paper, I have approached the subject 'Norse in the British Isles' from a linguistic and from a Scandinavian point of view. My principal concerns have been the coming of Scandinavian speech to Britain and Ireland, its interaction with the different indigenous languages, the length of time for which it survived and the manner of its demise. About most of these matters our knowledge is poor, as I have shown, and in many areas lack of evidence seems likely to ensure that it remains so. We can employ new theories and models as they become available, but these will hardly be sufficient to overcome the chronic shortage of data. A vacuum such as this is clearly what inspires the enunciation of diametrically opposed views like those I quoted at the outset. As so often in life, certainty comes in inverse proportion to knowledge.

Since, in spite of my gloomy prognostications, scholars are likely to continue to work in the field, I will end by entering a plea (a) for clear definitions and a rigorous adherence to definitions once given, and (b) for the judicious use of theories and models coupled with the cultivation of a healthy scepticism towards the claims that are made concerning their explanatory powers.

The need for clear definitions is adequately illustrated by the many assertions about the date at which Norse died out in different parts of the British Isles. Such assertions can only be properly understood if we know precisely what we mean when we say that a language has died. It is widely held, for example, that for Manx Gaelic the end came with the passing away of Ned Maddrell on 27 December 1974 (e.g. Thomson 1984, 257; Broderick 1991, 63-64), since he was the last native speaker. But is the death of the last native speaker what is meant by those who speak of the demise of Norse in Man shortly after 1300 or in the fifteenth century? The 'mixed language' is another problem area. Definitions of 'creole' vary widely (Hines 1991, 420), but creoles, under different definitions, are at least entities which have been shown to exist. Most who talk of mixed languages or the like do not appear to have any clear conception of the creature they are describing, largely, I suppose, because true language fusion is a very sparsely documented process indeed. The development in Orkney and Shetland apparently envisaged by some, according to which Norn gradually adopted more and more Scots features until it became more Scots than Norn, is, as far as I know, without parallel.

The problem with theories and models in the present context is one that bedevils historical linguistics in general: the uncertainty involved in basing conclusions about what happened in a given linguistic situation on the results of analogous situations elsewhere. Lack of evidence may force one to suggest that what has been documented for other languages at other times has been replicated in one's own case study, but in adopting such a solution one must never forget that language is a human activity—and human activity is, in the final analysis, unpredictable.

BIBLIOGRAPHY

Barnes, Michael. 1984. 'Norn', *Scripta Islandica* 35, 23–42.
Barnes, Michael P. 1989. 'The death of Norn'. In: (Heinrich Beck ed.) *Germanische Rest- und Trümmersprachen*, 21–43.
Barnes, Michael P. 1991a. 'Norwegian, Norn, Icelandic or West Norse? The language of the Maeshowe inscriptions'. In: (John Ole Askedal, Harald Bjorvand and Eyvind Fjeld Halvorsen eds.) *Festskrift til Ottar Grønvik*, 70–87.
Barnes, Michael P. 1991b. 'Reflections on the structure and the demise of Orkney and Shetland Norn'. In: (P. Sture Ureland and George Broderick eds.) *Language Contact in the British Isles*, 429–60.
Baugh, Albert C. and Cable, Thomas. 1981. *A History of the English Language* (3rd ed.).
Björkman, Erik. 1900–02. *Scandinavian Loan-Words in Middle English*.
Borgstrøm, Carl Hj. 1974. 'On the influence of Norse on Scottish Gaelic', *Lochlann* 6 (*Norsk tidsskrift for sprogvidenskap*, suppl. vol. 11), 91–103.
Broderick, George. 1991. 'The decline and death of Manx Gaelic'. In: (P. Sture Ureland and George Broderick eds.) *Language Contact in the British Isles*, 63–125.
Bugge, Sophus. 1908. *Norsk Sagafortælling og Sagaskrivning i Irland*.
Christiansen, Reidar Th. 1938. 'Sudrøy-norn', *Maal og minne*, 1–27.
Cox, Richard A. V. 1991. 'Norse–Gaelic contact in the west of Lewis: The place-name evidence'. In: (P. Sture Ureland and George Broderick eds.) *Language Contact in the British Isles*, 479–94.
Dorian, Nancy C. 1981. *Language Death*.
Dressler, Wolfgang and Wodak-Leodolter, Ruth (eds.). 1977. *Language Death* (*International Journal of the Sociology of Language* 12).
Einenkel, Eugen. 1906. 'Die dänischen Elemente in der Syntax der englischen Sprache', *Anglia* 29, 120–28.
Ekwall, Eilert. 1930. 'How long did the Scandinavian language survive in England?' In: *A Grammatical Miscellany Offered to Otto Jespersen . . .*, 17–30.
Fellows Jensen, Gillian. 1975. 'The Vikings in England: A review', *Anglo-Saxon England* 4, 181–206.
Fellows Jensen, Gillian. 1978. 'The Manx place-name debate: A view from Copenhagen'. In: (Peter Davey ed.) *Man and Environment in the Isle of Man* 2 (*British Archaeological Reports* (British Series) 54(ii)), 315–18.
Fellows-Jensen, Gillian. 1983. 'Scandinavian settlement in the Isle of Man and northwest England: The place-name evidence'. In: (Christine Fell *et al.* eds.) *The Viking Age in the Isle of Man*, 37–52.
Fellows-Jensen, Gillian. 1984. 'Viking settlement in the Northern and Western Isles—The place-name evidence as seen from Denmark and the Danelaw'. In: (Alexander Fenton and Hermann Pálsson eds.) *The Northern and Western Isles in the Viking World*, 148–68.
Flom, George T. 1928–29. 'The transition from Norse to Lowland Scotch in Shetland, 1600–1850', *Saga-Book* 10, 145–64.
Gelling, Margaret. 1970–71. 'The place-names of the Isle of Man', *The Journal of the Manx Museum* 7, 130–39, 168–75.
Gelling, Margaret. 1978. 'Norse and Gaelic in medieval Man: The place-name evidence'. In: (Peter Davey ed.) *Man and Environment in the Isle of Man* 2 (*British Archaeological Reports* (British Series) 54(ii)), 251–64.

Gelling, Margaret. 1991. 'The place-names of the Isle of Man'. In: (P. Sture Ureland and George Broderick eds.) *Language Contact in the British Isles*, 141–55.
Greene, David. 1976. 'The influence of Scandinavian on Irish'. In: (Bo Almqvist and David Greene eds.) *Proceedings of the Seventh Viking Congress*, 75–82.
Hansen, Bente Hyldegaard. 1984. 'The historical implications of the Scandinavian linguistic element in English: A theoretical evaluation', *Nowele* 4, 53–95.
Henderson, George. 1910. *The Norse Influence on Celtic Scotland*.
Hines, John. 1991. 'Scandinavian English: A creole in context'. In: (P. Sture Ureland and George Broderick eds.) *Language Contact in the British Isles*, 403–27.
Hofmann, Dietrich. 1955. *Nordisch–englische Lehnbeziehungen der Wikingerzeit* (Bibliotheca Arnamagnæana 14).
Hægstad, Marius. 1900. *Hildinakvadet*.
Jackson, Kenneth H. 1962. 'The Celtic languages during the Viking period'. In: *Proceedings of the International Congress of Celtic Studies*, 3–11.
Jakobsen, Jakob. 1897. *The Dialect and Place Names of Shetland*.
Jakobsen, Jakob. 1928–32. *An Etymological Dictionary of the Norn Language in Shetland*.
Jespersen, Otto. 1905. *Growth and Structure of the English Language*.
Kirch, Max S. 1959. 'Scandinavian influence on English syntax', *Publications of The-Modern-Language-Association-of-America* 74, 503–10.
Kisbye, Torben. 1982a. 'Danelagen—sprogstruktur, befolkningsstruktur'. In: (Hans Bekker-Nielsen and Hans Frede Nielsen eds.) *Nordboer i Danelagen*, 43–66.
Kisbye, Torben. 1982b. *Vikingerne i England—sproglige spor*.
Marstrander, Carl J. S. 1915. *Bidrag til det norske sprogs historie i Irland*.
Marstrander, Carl J. S. 1932a. 'Okklusiver og substrater', *Norsk tidsskrift for sprogvidenskap* 5, 258–314.
Marstrander, Carl J. S. 1932b. 'Det norske landnåm på Man', *Norsk tidsskrift for sprogvidenskap* 6, 40–386.
Marwick, Hugh. 1929. *The Orkney Norn*.
Megaw, Basil. 1978. 'Norseman and native in the Kingdom of the Isles: A re-assessment of the Manx evidence'. In: (Peter Davey ed.) *Man and Environment in the Isle of Man 2 (British Archaeological Reports* (British Series) 54(ii)), 265–314.
Milroy, J. 1984. 'The history of English in the British Isles'. In: (Peter Trudgill ed.) *Language in the British Isles*, 5–31.
Oftedal, Magne. l962a. 'Norse place-names in Celtic Scotland'. In: *Proceedings of the International Congress of Celtic Studies*, 43–50.
Oftedal, Magne. 1962b. 'On the frequency of Norse loanwords in Scottish Gaelic', *Scottish Gaelic Studies* 9, 116–27.
Oftedal, Magne. 1976. 'Scandinavian place-names in Ireland'. In: (Bo Almqvist and David Greene eds.) *Proceedings of the Seventh Viking Congress*, 125–33.
Olsen, Magnus. 1909. 'Om sproget i de manske runeindskrifter', *Forhandlinger i Videnskabsselskabet i Christiania* 1909, No. 1.
Page, R. I. 1971. 'How long did the Scandinavian language survive in England? The epigraphical evidence'. In: (Peter Clemoes and Kathleen Hughes eds.) *England before the Conquest*, 165–81.
Page, R. I. 1983. 'The Manx rune-stones'. In: (Christine Fell *et al.* eds.) *The Viking Age in the Isle of Man*, 133–46.
Rendboe, Laurits. 1984. 'How "worn out" or "corrupted" was Shetland Norn in its final stage?', *Nowele* 3, 53–88.

Rindler-Schjerve, Rosita. 1989. 'Sprachverschiebung und Sprachtod: Funktionelle und strukturelle Aspekte'. In: (Heinrich Beck ed.) *Germanische Rest- und Trümmersprachen*, 1–14.
Ringgaard, K. 1986. 'Flektionssystemets forenkling og middelnedertysk', *Arkiv för nordisk filologi* 101, 173–83.
Sawyer, P. H. 1971. *The Age of the Vikings*.
Seip, Didrik Arup. 1930. 'Norske paralleller til de uregelmessige fleksjonsformer i manske og irske runeinnskrifter', *Norsk tidsskrift for sprogvidenskap* 4, 401–04.
Thomason, Sarah Grey and Kaufman, Terrence. 1988. *Language Contact, Creolization, and Genetic Linguistics*.
Thomson, R. L. 1984. 'The history of the Celtic languages in the British Isles'. In: (Peter Trudgill ed.) *Language in the British Isles*, 241–58.
Thorsen, Per. 1954. 'The third Norn dialect—that of Caithness'. In: (W. Douglas Simpson ed.) *The Viking Congress. Lerwick, July 1950*, 230–38.
Weinreich, Uriel. 1953. *Languages in Contact*.

CHRISTINE FELL

NORSE STUDIES: THEN, NOW AND HEREAFTER

THIS title is not of my choosing. I do recall agreeing to give a lecture on this or some such subject. That it appears under this head I suppose to be the fault or virtue of Professor Peter Foote, and I started doing what Professor Foote instructed when I was his postgraduate student virtually a third of a century ago. This clearly demonstrates, as we today celebrate the centenary of the Viking Society for Northern Research, what powerful influences have been at work in the last third of that century in the shaping of Norse Studies Now and Hereafter. I will however start with the Then, that dim, forgotten past before the Enlightenment of Professor Foote's era.

Historians are only just beginning to recognise the dangers inherent in periodisation and nowhere is periodisation more curious than in our fossilised and arbitrary division of European chronology into the three ages: Classical Antiquity, Medieval and Modern. We who work in the humanities have lived with this division for so long we can forget how odd it seems to the non-specialist. A few years ago, arguing on Nottingham University Senate for the importance of retaining a Chair of Modern Literature, it was some time before I realised that to my scientist colleagues I appeared to be arguing for a Chair of Late Twentieth Century Literature.

Following Denys Hay's exposition on 'Flavio Biondo and the Middle Ages', we attribute to Biondo (1392–1463) the dubious distinction of being the first scholar to have a concept of the Middle Ages, though his term was *media tempestatis*. Other Italian writers stumbling uncertainly among similar phrases lit on *medium ævum* in 1604. The NED surprisingly has no citations for the 'Middle Age' or 'Ages' before the mid-eighteenth century, none for 'medieval' before the nineteenth, where a remarkably large number are from Ruskin's *Lamps of architecture*. Presumably the Latin rather than the Anglicised form was preferred. It must be one of the greatest con-tricks of all time. One thoughtful historian decided that circa 1000 years had elapsed since the fall of Rome at the hands of the Goths (AD 476) and so now was a new dawn. Evidently throughout Europe people and nations rushed to change their thinking and their plumbing overnight in order to turn from 'Medieval' into 'Renaissance' man.

At any rate the period covered by the term Old Norse studies in theory stops when these so-called Middle Ages also come to an end, though in practice since sagas continued to be copied by hand, editors of sagas continue to use post-medieval material in preparing their editions. The period of Norse Studies may by some scholars be defined more narrowly yet according to which scholar is presenting the evidence and what the evidence is. Since publishers (not to mention sponsors of exhibitions) currently consider 'Viking', for example, more of a buzz word than 'Norse', the Viking Age gets into many a book or onto the dust-jacket where its scholarly credentials are distinctly unsound.

But Norse Studies may also be defined by region, or by discipline. The last of these may now mean the study of historical event, language in text or surviving as place-name, literature in the widest sense, artefact and excavation. Geographically we may follow wherever the Vikings led, or, if we engage in source criticism, whatever led to them. Or we may confine ourselves to country, province, town or trade route. My survey of the way in which these studies have developed will inevitably be selective in its use of data and arbitrary in its generalisations.

Part of the mythology brought about by periodisation, especially in the division between 'medieval' and 'modern', is the assumption that it is only with the new learning of the sixteenth century that we began serious studies of the early period. The pace and range of scholarship may have changed but the assumption is open to challenge. In this country we can cite King Alfred as the first Norse scholar of distinction. Janet Bately does not attribute to Alfred the writing of the Old English *Orosius*, but the words *Ohthere sæde his hlaforde Ælfrede cyninge* suggest that it was Alfred's own probing questions that prompted detailed information from Ohthere on Norwegian geography, demography, economy, philology and trade. The *Anglo-Saxon Chronicle* is a record made for posterity and on it has been based the writing of history about Viking raids and invasions in England ever since. Not all subsequent historians have known it as a primary source. But the early Norman chroniclers used it at first hand and then their work was used in turn by later chroniclers. The 'tremulous Worcester hand' that glosses so many Old English manuscripts is that of a thirteenth-century historian and philologist teaching himself a language in order to read primary vernacular sources.

However, a number of events in the late fifteenth and sixteenth centuries contributed to an intensification of historical research, some of them European, some peculiarly English. By peculiarly English I mean, of course, Henry VIII, by European the change from script to print, perhaps more significant long-term for the development and diffusion of scholarship than any so-called Renaissance and Reformation. (Current political double-talk about the 'reform' of the universities, induces thoughtfulness about the balance of meaning and propaganda in such terminology.) But in England it was that act of vandalism, the dissolution of the monasteries, that gave impetus to the private collector, the private library, the independent, secular scholar. It is not always easy to divorce Anglo-Saxon and Norse studies in any discussion that involves either links between Germanic cultures or the Viking presence in Anglo-Saxon England, but it might be fair to say that among Tudor scholars the concentration of Matthew Parker and his circle was exclusively on the Anglo-Saxon material. In the early seventeenth century it

NORSE STUDIES: THEN, NOW AND HEREAFTER 87

was Sir Henry Spelman and the Dutch scholar Richard Verstegan who recognised and re-introduced the Norse dimension. It is not, to Spelman, of interest in its own right, merely a part of the early history of England.

When he refers to Danes in his general prose they feature as the villains against whom Alfred fought. But Spelman recognises their impact on both English law and English language. He is in correspondence with the major Scandinavian scholars of his day and discusses etymologies in his letters to Ole Worm. In his *Glossarium Archaiologicum*, first published 1627, he does not recognise 'law' as a Norse word, but certainly recognises *lahslit* as *vox Danica*, *husting* as *forum Danis*, and in discussing *dreng* can inform us that the Danish still have a class of people whom they call *dreng* in the singular, *drenge* in the plural.

Verstegan's interest also is very much with language and culture, not merely with the sequence of historical events. In *A Restitution of Decayed Intelligence In Antiquitie, concerning the most noble and renowned English Nation* published in 1605 he has sections on 'The Antiquitie and Proprietie of the Ancient English Toung', 'The Etymologies of our Saxon proper names', 'Of the Surnames of our Ancient Families'. He is however concerned on the one hand to minimise the influence of both Danish and Norman, and on the other hand, to stress their relationship, thus on both counts emphasising Englishness. He has read Olaus Magnus and can look at linguistic cognates with occasional accuracy. Writing of the word *konungr/cyning* he says 'Wee Englishmen have abridged it into one sillable and so made it *king* and the Danes and Swedians have made it *kong*.' On the other hand I fear our place-name experts would not be happy with his comments on what we know as the Norse settlement indicator *by*.

> In this termination many of our ancient surnames do end, as first for example *Willoughby*, the surname of honorable and woorshipfull families, also *Kirkby*, *Holtby* and many others: the particle *by* serving to express neer unto what thing of note the resydence of such a familie was, when this their surname first began; as beeing neer unto some noted *willow tree*, or by a *Churche*, or by a *wood*, for *holt* in our language is otherwise *wood*.

Knowledge of the Scandinavian part in the settlement of the British Isles was never lost, and it seems likely that knowledge of the cultural, linguistic and national links between the various Germanic peoples was not lost either. But it is not until Sheringham's *De Anglorum Gentis Origine*, published 1670, that Britain re-acquires knowledge of Norse and Icelandic literature. I say re-acquires with some diffidence for it is hard to separate Old Norse and Old English literary traditions in post-Conquest, multi-racial, multi-lingual Britain. Certainly there is clear indication in the work of William of Malmesbury that he knew some names and stories that otherwise feature only in Icelandic saga. The Norse runic futhark is used not only in epigraphy but appears in post-Conquest manuscripts, most notably Oxford St John's 17, but not only there. The Outer Isles continue to speak Norn, and to ballads in Norn I shall return. And I may as well here mention my conviction that the Gawain poet's extraordinary obsession with and control of form owes a good deal more to the art of the skald than any other poetic tradition. But, as Verstegan and Spelman would say, all these traditions had merged into 'Englishness'—apart from the survival of independent cultures in the islands. Sheringham starts again, looking at Scandinavian literature and related antiquities as a separate study.

He is extremely well-read in contemporary Scandinavian scholarship, particularly influenced by the work of Ole Worm. There being in that period no adequate English translations for words such as 'runic' and 'skald', and indeed no Latin equivalent either, he adopts Scandinavianised Latin for such terms as he cannot translate. He is interested in runes, interested in Norse mythology, interested in Eddic poetry and presents whole chunks of *Hávamál* both in Old Norse and translated into Latin. For those in the seventeenth century who did not have direct access to Scandinavian authors, Sheringham is the first English writer to alert his readers to this range of material, and to quote Old Norse texts at length. Following close on Sheringham is Aylett Sammes whose *Britannia Antiqua Illustrata or the Antiquities of Ancient Britain derived from the Phoenicians* was published in 1676.

There is a short enough space between the two publications of Sheringham and Sammes, but since Sheringham writes in Latin and Sammes writes in English their contributions are different. To Sheringham belongs the credit of being the first writer to publish Old Norse literature in England, to Sammes the double credits of Anglicising certain Norse words (some of which we retain) and of translating Old Norse literature not into Latin but into English, and colloquial English at that, not stilted translationese. Sammes's introduction of Norse words into English in fact ante-dates the NED on a number of items. The NED offers Sir Walter Scott's use in his novel *The Pirate* for the first appearance of *berserk* and continues with Emerson's stunning contribution 'Out of terrible Druids and Berserkers come at last Alfred and Shakespeare'. By the time the NED's first Supplement was published English had developed the adverb 'berserkly', illustrated by two examples, (1) *The Economist* in 1963 claiming a policy as 'berserkly dangerous'; (2) a novel of 1967, 'The headlamps illuminated a tree which seemed to be leaping berserkly towards her'. This is a perfect example of a word introduced as a technical term because it was deemed untranslatable which has gone on to have a semantic life of its own. But it was Sammes in 1676 who introduced the word from Old Norse (or rather from his reading of contemporary Scandinavian scholarship) and he introduced it in its precise Norse sense. Some of the words he tries to naturalise fade again out of the language, for example the Old Norse term for goddesses, *dísir*, which had no popular future ahead of it. The history of *scald* and *scaldic* is more interesting.

Today only scholars use the terms *skald/skaldic*, and whether they choose the spelling *c* or *k* will depend on the accident of their training and the consciousness of their preferences. The *c* spelling of course goes back to Sheringham and his sources because when one Latinises a barbarian word with a *k* in it one must replace the *k* by a civilised roman *c*. Sheringham and Sammes both adopt the word though remain in a good deal of doubt about its grammatical forms. The NED's first citation is a century later, from Percy's *Five Pieces of Runic Poetry*. I have dealt in other places with the reinvention and rubbish in the use of the terms 'rune' and 'runic' and will leave that one out of my discussions here.

The uncertainty about grammar allows Sammes three forms of the plural, *scaldri*, *scaldi* and *scalders* and we find briefly that two forms of the singular surface in English, *scald* and *scalder*. The NED entry says austerely under *skald*:

> Usually applied to Norwegian and Icelandic poets of the Viking period, but often without any clear idea of their function and the character of their work.

Sammes himself is fairly clear about the nature of skalds, or skaldic poetry and of kennings, as indeed was Sheringham, though I find Sammes of a more engaging and questioning turn of mind. Thus Sammes:

> The *Scaldi* were commonly of the chief Blood of their Country, oftentimes of the Kings Councel and his attendance in War, that with their own eyes they might be witness of great Actions, and not taking them upon trust, might be better able with truth to deliver them to Posterity. Those things which in the Verses of the Ancients we find wrapt up in Fables, shew only the genius of the Authors, who accounted it a piece of Art to hide plain truths under the shadow of words, by which colours as a pleasant bait they sought to recommend their works to the Reader.

Sammes continues with an exposition of the nature of kennings, though not under that name, and again his grammar is, not surprisingly, uncertain. His sources varied in their transliteration of ð and þ, so here begins in England the double form Odin/Othin. Like others before and after him Sammes is happy with the identification of Woden and Óðinn. On skaldic poetry he tells us that 'from its sweetness of its running it was called *Odins miod* that is Odins mead'. On weapons 'a sword by the Scaldri is called *Othin edur*, Wodens fire', and, one I particularly like, *skurtur Odin* rendered 'Wodens doublet'.

Post-Sammes the word *scald* in its variety of forms enjoyed a vogue among the literati and for some time the precision with which seventeenth and twentieth century scholars endeavour to use it was totally lost. Warton in his *History of English Poetry* of 1774 kindly tells us, 'In the place of their old scalders, a new rank of poets arose called Gleemen or Harpers'; Finlay in 1808 refers to 'Skaldic remains preserved in the Edda'. But everyone's favourite reading on the subject must be Edward Jerningham's *The Rise and Progress of the Scandinavian Poetry Part the First*:

> 'Ye glowing masters of the Scaldic song
> Still other pow'rful gifts to you belong:
> The lofty pine that meets the mountain gale,
> Th' expanding oak that crowns the lowly vale,

> Shall as your fingers touch the furrow'd rind,
> Display the treasures of the musing mind:
> There by the voice of whisp'ring nature call'd,
> In future times shall stand the youthful Scald,
> There shall he meditate the Runic store,
> There woo the science of the tuneful lore;
> . . .
> Enough—the pow'r I now bestow enjoy,
> In Virtue's cause the forceful harp employ:
> Go forth, ye glorious conquerors of the mind,
> Achieve the hallow'd task to you assigned:
> Applaud the valiant, and the base controul,
> Disturb, exalt, enchant the human soul.'
> Thus to his minstrels spoke the awful pow'r—
> The conscious Scalds avow the' inspiring hour:
> And now dividing into many a band,
> Strew their wild poetry o'er all the land.

The romantic image of the north, found in the poetry of Wordsworth and Coleridge, blended with a concept of poetry inspired by the grandeur of nature and of such poetry as a moral force, is clear enough in the above quotation from Jerningham, more fully realised in Southey. For Amos Cottle's incompetent translation of the poetic Edda (1797) Southey wrote an introductory poem:

> Wild the Runic faith
> And wild the realms where Scandinavian Chiefs
> And Scalds arose, and hence the Scalds' strong verse
> Partook the savage wildness. And methinks
> Amid such scenes as these, the Poet's soul
> Might best attain full growth.

'Such scenes as these' are then predictably identified as a landscape of pine-covered rocks, mountain forests, lakes and beech trees.

Edith Batho, former student of W. P. Ker at London University was, I think, the first to point out that it was Sir Walter Scott who had the firmest grasp on the realities of Norse life or Viking life or indeed of the medieval period in general. He disparages his own light reading of works at which 'taste may blush and frown, and sober reason mock' but those works appear to include such medieval romances as now figure on a university's English department syllabus. His own thoroughly light-hearted frivolity *Harold the Dauntless* contains much sentiment appropriate to its day and its audience. But the account of the conversion of Harold's heathen father I consider to be the most penetrating brief summary I know of the likely pragmatic realities of the Viking Age in England. The old heathen in question, responding to the Bishop of Durham's admonitions on the welfare of his soul, says simply:

> Give me broad lands on the Wear and the Tyne
> My faith I will leave and I'll cleave unto thine.

Scott's novel *The Pirate* is a stern indictment of the romantic folly of viewing Viking raids as in some way more splendid, more admirable than the ruffianly piracy of any other period. And it is Scott who pursued not only secondary sources but Old Norse originals. In his abstract of *Eyrbyggja saga* he shows again the acuteness of his scholarly perception in his comments on Snorri Sturluson:

> That such a character . . . should have risen so high in such an early period, argues the preference which the Icelanders already assigned to mental superiority over the rude attributes of strength and courage, and furnishes another proof of the early civilization of this extraordinary commonwealth.

For evidence of continuity rather than renaissance of Norse literature Scott has one magnificent footnote to *The Pirate*, the reliability of which I leave to others to determine. Thomas Gray's poems, published in 1768 included *The Fatal Sisters* based on a Latin version of *Darraðarljóð*. Gray's sources have been extensively analysed, and there is no conclusive evidence that he knew any Old Norse. But his poems, real poems not just tranlationese, enjoyed considerable popularity. Scott's footnote, appearing some forty years after Gray's publication, reads:

> Near the conclusion of this chapter it is noticed that the old Norwegian sagas were preserved and often repeated by the fishermen of Orkney and [Sh]etland while that language was not quite forgotten. Mr Baikie of Tankerness, a most respectable inhabitant of Kirkwall, and an Orkney proprietor, assured me of the following curious fact.
>
> A clergyman, who was not long deceased, remembered well when some remnants of the Norse were still spoken in the island called North Ronaldshaw. When Gray's Ode, entitled 'The Fatal Sisters' was first published, or at least first reached that remote island, the reverend gentleman had the well-judged curiosity to read it to some of the old persons of the isle, as a poem which regarded the history of their own country. They listened with great attention to the preliminary stanzas:-
>
>> Now the storm begins to lour,
>> Haste the loom of hell prepare
>> Iron sleet of arrowy shower
>> Hurtles in the darken'd air.
>
> But when they had heard a verse or two more, they interrupted the reader, telling him they knew the song well in the Norse language, and had often sung it to him when he asked them for an old song. They called it the Magicians or the Enchantresses. It would have been singular news to the elegant translator, when executing his version from the text of Bartholine, to have learned that the Norse original was still preserved by tradition in a remote corner of the British dominions.

Throughout the Victorian period scholarly and literary interest in the north increases, and is presented in history, in editions of texts, novel or poetry with varying degrees of accuracy. Tennyson gets more hooked on Arthur and the Celtic twilight than the Norse, but Matthew Arnold offered in 1855 an epic on the death of Balder. I was deeply moved to find in my mother's copy of Arnold, written with the fine nib of the map-pen she used when young, the sage comment on *Balder dead*: 'This is also Homeric in tone, even though the subject is taken from the

Norse mythology' followed by the elegiac apology 'This poem will only be read by the few.' I fear she was right. She then added a marginal note in which she simply bracketed three names Balder, Samson, Achilles, and it took me several seconds to get the point. A pity Dumézil was not equally laconic!

One thing we note among the skalds and others still in literary vogue in this period is the prevailing and recurring myth that the Vikings drank mead/ale/wine (take your choice) out of the skulls of their enemies. It is now so well-known that this belief arose out of a mistranslation of a kenning that it is hard to see why it remained so long uncorrected. As an exercise for pure amusement I thought I would excavate some of the more bizarre examples. Sammes and Sheringham take their text of the death-song of Ragnar from Ole Worm but whereas Sheringham presents his material in a straightforward manner Sammes finds it funny and gives us a burlesque version:

> They believed that after death they were to go into Wodens hall, and there drink Ale with him, and his Companions, in the Skulls of their Enemies. To this end they imagined a certain goddess called Dyser, employed by Woden, to convey the souls of the Valiant into his drunken Paradice. And methinks I see the Danish king Lothbrock, in his Fur-Leather Breeches (for so his name importeth) in as good Verses as Ale could inspire, hugging himself with the hopes of Full-Pots in the World to come.

Two stanzas of the death-song are given in runes (copied of course from Worm) and translated. I quote only the first:

> We have stood true to Snick and Snee
> And now I laugh to think
> In Wodens Hall there Benches be,
> Where we may sit and drink.
> There we shall tope our bellies-full
> Of Nappy-Ale in full-brim'd Skull.

The error was not Sammes, but that of his source, and no one in England knew enough of Norse or of the kenning habit to correct it. Thomas Penrose writing *The Carousal of Odin* in 1775 begins:

> Fill the honeyed bev'rage high
> Fill the Sculls, 'tis ODIN's cry:

and a little later tells us:

> The feast begins, the Scull goes round

which always sounds to me irresistibly like a comment on the morning after. Byron, being Byronic as who shall blame him, in his poem on a drinking cup made out of a skull, offers the happy thought:

> And when at last our brains are gone
> What nobler substitute than wine?

Lestley (1793) sees deprivation of a well-filled skull as Odin's punishment for crime (my italics):

> Know thou feeble Child of Dust
> Odin's brave and Odin's just;
> From the Golden Hall I come
> To pronounce thy fatal doom:
> *Never* shalt *thou* pass the scull
> Of rich Metheglin deep and full.

In the Victorian era Matthew Arnold, being, as my mother observed, Homeric in his treatment of northern myth, is not content with a plain undecorated skull, certainly not one filled with anything so vulgar as Sammes's 'nappy ale':

> And on the tables stood the untasted meats
> And in the horns and gold-rimm'd skulls the wine.

Yet Arnold had clearly not read his latest guide to Northern Antiquities. As I. A. Blackwell judiciously says in the Preface to his 1847 reissue of Percy's translation of Mallet, the original publication was at a time when the most important documents bearing on the period were but imperfectly known. One of his revisions occurs in the description of 'the religion which prevailed in the north' and it is no surprise to find ourselves once again reading the death-words of Ragnar:

> Accordingly King Ragnar Lodbrok, when he was going to die, far from uttering groans, or forming complaints, expressed his joy by these verses. 'We are cut to pieces with swords; but this fills me with joy when I think of the feast that is preparing for me in Odin's palace. Quickly, quickly seated in the splendid habitation of the gods, we shall drink beer out of curved horns'.

Blackwell's footnote is worth quoting at length:

> We have substituted 'curved horns' for 'the skulls of our enemies;' Finn Magnusen and Professor Rask having shown that this is the true meaning of the original passage, literally 'soon shall we drink ale out of the curved branches of the skull' ie of an animal, a figurative expression employed by the Scald to indicate the usual drinking horns, and that Olaus Wormius, Bartholin and other writers of that period whom our author has followed were totally mistaken in rendering it 'ex concavis crateribus craniorum . . . It is this mistake that has given rise to the erroneous notion, that the heroes of Valhalla drank their ale out of the skulls of those they had slain in battle . . . We think that a daily dinner consisting solely of boiled pork, washed down with ale and an occasional draught of mead, was bad enough in all conscience, without making skulls serve for drinking cups. — Ed.

What must make the strongest impression on those of us who work in Norse studies today is, if one can disregard the more extreme absurdities, how one-sided all this is. The image of the North is coming through a fairly slight range of skaldic and Eddic poetry, and of course through mixtures of fact and nonsense on runes, on mythology, on 'barbarian' customs from widely read secondary syntheses such as Mallet. Genuine historical and editorial work is going on alongside these extravagances, but popular image either lags far behind scholarship, or uses scholarship for its own fantasies. The superb philologist George Hickes, working from the edition of Verelius, transcribed and translated into English in 1705 'The

Waking of Angantyr' from *Hervarar saga*. His rendering is not bad except for the transformation of bones rotting in an ant-hill into 'so may you all be within your ribs as a thing that is hanged up to putrifie among insects'. But the melodrama of the tale induced many a dreadful translation. Poor Hervor had to conform to inappropriate stereotypes, in one version not even allowed to get back safely to her ship, but perishing in the burial mound 'while flames amid her ringlets play'. After Scott's sensible abstract of *Eyrbyggja saga* we have to wait for Icelandic prose to make its impact on the English imagination, which it slowly does. The sober world of *Íslendinga sögur* does eventually take over from the wild world of runic bards.

Nevertheless the imagination of the Victorians often seems limited by its own conditioning, and as any feminist critic knows it is hard to get behind Victorian automatic assumptions about appropriate roles for men and women, as also views about ethnic superiority and 'the white man's burden'. This sometimes comes over most clearly in the children's books of the period. In Wray Hunt's *The voyage to Vineland*, Viking culture meets Maya in a confrontation which sounds like, but is not intended to be, a caricature of the Kiplingesque view of the British in India.

I quote one incident only. A Maya slavegirl is rescued from a cruel owner by Rolf the Viking leader. Rolf took the child to 'be petted and consoled by the fierce Vikings who would kill a thousand men in open fight without a qualm, but drew the line at such torment of children . . . Rolf was sick of the stupid superstition of the people, and of their senseless cruelties. "I think", he cried, "that these folk are not of our human race at all. They have no manhood or womanhood in them, but are worse than wolves and bears." The Vikings nodded agreement, "Let us get away", they cried, "back to our own clean lands in the North, where men are men and women are women."'

The dimension that has been totally lacking so far is the visual. When the Anglo-Saxons looked at Vikings the image that dominated their vocabulary was sea-faring. True, they sometimes refer to Vikings as heathens or even slaughter-wolves, often as 'Danes', though 'Danes' is rarely precise and obviously used of invaders from any part of Scandinavia. But four common words are *flotman*, *sæman*, *sceigðman*, and *æscman*. The first two are etymologically transparent, not apparently pejorative, and synonymous, since Old English *flot* is 'water deep enough to float a ship on'. Old English *sceigð* is borrowed from Old Norse, but the compound *sceigðman* for the chap who arrives in a *sceigð* is an Anglo-Saxon invention. I do not want here to go over the linguistic complexities of *æsc*, *æscman* and *æschere*, but independent Old English words or loans, they are used *only* of the Vikings from the ninth century onwards. Another Old Norse word for a ship, *knǫrr*, is Anglicised as *cnearr*. But though those who copied historical records, like Camden, continued to mention the Vikings as raiders from the sea, it is not really until archaeologists discovered the great Gokstad and Oseberg ships in 1880 and 1904 respectively that the Vikings as sea-goers recaptured the imagination.

The serious discipline of philology goes back to Hickes, but archaeology is a comparative newcomer. We do not have to go back very far to see what improbable or anachronistic visual impressions earlier periods produced of Anglo-Saxon or Viking ships, weapons, dress, buildings and the like. Together with a more sophisticated approach to art-history this has been one of the major developments of the twentieth century. But one of archaeology's difficulties has been that historians like to use it as a hand-maid rather than a partner. Philology has had similar trials. I recall a promotions committee at Nottingham where a historian who shall be nameless said of a colleague in the English Department who shall be nameless that he had 'a remarkable grasp of history for a man of letters'.

The pattern, which obviously I simplify, goes something like this: in the first instance, the very first instance, scholars, or annalists, or chroniclers, endeavour to get the record straight, to report events. At a later date some historians are still trying to get the record straight but viewing it from a greater distance they look at a variety of documents and endeavour to extrapolate actual occurrence from partial and prejudiced accounts. At this stage they may start looking at other sources than documentary record, at coins, at epigraphy, even at poetry or saga. Yet it becomes apparent that no historian can master all the disciplines, can control all the materials. Scholars in different areas of history become specialists, become archaeologists, runologists, numismatists, even literary critics. The historian, still viewing herself or more probably himself as the synthesiser, believes that he can use the findings of all these disciplines whereas in fact, in areas where he does not control the methodology it is unwise to deploy the results. A few of us, recognising these dangers, established a quarter of a century ago a group of interdisciplinary scholars to ensure that the next time Peter Sawyer published *The Age of the Vikings* we savaged it in draft rather than in reviews. The distinguished historian Henry Loyn was one of this group. It did not prevent him from bringing out *The Vikings in Britain* without asking for a word of advice from philologist or archaeologist, and therefore making a thorough balls-up, if I may use that technical term, of philological and archaeological evidence.

We are in a perilous situation. All of us are constantly approached by publishers for more glossy books, preferably with the word 'Viking' somewhere in the title. Yet no historian can control the vernacular sources nor indeed any data other than Latin record: the archaeologist cannot read texts, Latin or vernacular, except in translation: the philologist, like myself, has to ask constant questions of others to make sure that word and thing (in translating descriptions of objects) have some relation. I once asked a professor of French how he felt about relying on translation. He assured me that wherever he knew a language he knew also translation was totally unreliable: wherever he did not know a language he found translations perfectly adequate.

We are all in the same blinkered situation. On the one hand we plunge ever more deeply into our own specialisms. On the other hand we emerge from them to be greeted by demands for overall syntheses which we are ever less qualified to produce. This should be the situation which the Viking Society aims to rectify in future programmes and developments not only in itself but in its relation to the relevant disciplines throughout UK Universities. It is a society for Northern Research and Northern Research has shifted as fashions change and as those who run the Society define the term. But we do in Britain have something unique to offer in this field. In Scandinavia Norse Studies have naturally enough evolved in departments of Scandinavian Studies as they have in one or two places in Britain: in America as in Germany, Old Norse is studied within departments of German. Anglo-Saxonists in the USA are, by and large, as profoundly ignorant of the Norse dimension as Matthew Parker of blessed memory. And equally many Norse scholars are ignorant of the Anglo-Saxon dimension. This is not deeply significant in all areas of Norse studies. But in this country much fruitful scholarship has come out of the fact that Old Norse language and literature is read in departments of English and read alongside the language and literature of the Anglo-Saxons. In so far as we look at vernacular languages side by side, as we look at Norse influence on English, and, because English missionaries went to Norway and Iceland, at English influence on Norse; in so far as we look at Vikings in England, whether at their historical impact or their traces in the sculpture, the epigraphy, the jewellery, the laws and the language, there is much to be said for an educational tradition which encourages students and scholars to investigate Anglo-Saxon and Viking links and parallels. It is not the only way of approaching Vikings or Norse Studies but it is a way practised seriously only in this country and worth preserving.

The other tradition that is useful and important particularly in the present educational climate in this country (I do not speak for others) is that the Viking Society like the Viking Congress has existed to promote interdisciplinary awareness. I do not say either has always succeeded in this, for I have clear memories of some Viking Congresses where wicked philologists snuck out to the nearest source of beer while the archaeologists were lecturing, and even those upright and virtuous characters the archaeologists did not attend *every* lecture on manuscript minutiae. But interdisciplinary studies are both academically desirable and at present politically encouraged. It has been said, possibly by the quondam librarian of Corpus Christi College, Cambridge, that the stress is too often on the inter and not enough on the discipline. He may be right. But for all that, I was taught in an English department where the only facts I was ever told about the Anglo-Saxon and Icelandic texts I read were grammatical ones—'Kindly note, Miss Fell, that that *-an* ending is a weakened dative plural'—and it was not until I joined the Viking Society that I knew there were such artefacts as Viking ships, or swords or even runes. I would not have known a pseudo-penannular brooch if it had been handed to me on a dinner-plate, and I certainly would not have known that academic studies existed which would enable me to discover whether such an object was Viking, Anglo-Saxon, Pictish or Indonesian.

It is in the hope that such ignorance may be a matter of the Then rather than the Now of Norse studies that we at Nottingham as elsewhere now have interdisciplinary undergraduate and postgraduate courses in Viking studies where students may learn a little of the range of scholarly methodologies that give us a picture of a culture, a context within which individual academic disciplines work, the way in which those individual disciplines contribute to a holistic view.

The other aspect of our studies that is Then, Now and must be Hereafter is international co-operation. Again the extent to which this is or has been present has fluctuated through the centuries. But anyone who has read the learned and long correspondence between Henry Spelman and Ole Worm (not to mention the record of what Ohthere said to his *hlaford Ælfred cyning*) knows that such co-operation has a long and distinguished history. As we use other disciplines and must at least know something of their methodologies, so we use the work of scholars in parallel disciplines and other countries. Anglo-Saxon runologists need to know intimately the work of Scandinavian runologists and vice versa. If we use Norse mythological material to interpret Anglo-Saxon paganism it is not enough simply to have read the primary texts (or, as sometimes happens, a generalised summary). We must know the latest work in Scandinavia on those texts, the scholarship on the manuscripts, not merely the syntheses. We are actually quite good at this at the moment, perhaps more in some disciplines than others, and it is particularly welcome to see so many of our friends from Scandinavia here at this Centenary Symposium. I merely stress the importance of its continuation where we are good at it, its fuller implementation where we are—I will not say 'bad', merely 'less good'.

Since Professor Foote included Hereafter in my title he clearly has faith in my visionary and prophetic powers. But I do not know what else to say about Hereafter. I have already quoted Byron in this paper and his view of the future is one that has always appealed to me:

> I say the future is a serious matter:
> And so, for God's sake, hock and soda-water.

Or, looking at the present higher education scenario, something stronger than hock might be needed. It is hard with the existing government returned to power to retain belief in a salaried academic future for those of us in esoteric disciplines, or in the survival of time for serious research. The writing of more Jorvik scripts may even be thrust upon us. We are already aware that the private scholar is again with us, the brilliant young academics working in banks or insurance offices, engaged in serious research evenings and weekends. Research and teaching instead of being mutually beneficial become the objects of separate University

Funding Council exercises, and I strongly suspect the hidden agenda behind the abolition of the binary line was in order to prevent university teachers from claiming in future that their research is essential to their teaching role. How far we can make change, or of course 'reform', work for us rather than against us remains to be seen.

If I may end on an exhortatory note, I think it essential that we do two things: firstly as far as possible that we use change wherever we can in the interests of our scholarship, that we look to ways of making, for example, modularisation give us frequent full-semester sabbaticals, that we look for international funding of international and interdisciplinary co-operation. Many of us are already committed to this way of thinking and engaged in these activities. In my view they are a necessary condition for survival. Secondly, though there is room for the private scholar there is no room in universities now for the amateur. The media image of our profession is deeply injurious to us, we are 'whingeing dons living in ivory towers set in groves of academe'. Where do journalists get their language? And what the media feeds them on, politicians and the public appear to devour with unseemly greed. We must not only be committed to being professionals but to being seen as professionals. I confess to being unsure how we are to achieve it, but I consider this, too, essential for our survival.

Doubtless in another Hereafter in whatever Valhalla awaits us we shall be deemed in scholarship as in other walks of life to have left undone those things which we ought to have done and to have done those things which we ought not to have done, and it may well be that there is no health in us. But I at least shall take comfort from the words of my favourite author (other than Byron), Saki:

> Not that I ever indulge in despair about the Future; there have always been men who have gone about despairing of the Future, and when the Future arrives it says nice, superior things about their having acted according to their lights. It is dreadful to think that other people's grandchildren may one day rise up and call one amiable.

BIBLIOGRAPHY AND ABBREVIATIONS

Arnold, Matthew. 1908. *Poetical Works* [annotated copy ex libris G. M. Fell].
Bately, Janet (ed.). 1980. *The Old English Orosius.*
Batho, Edith C. 1929. 'Sir Walter Scott and the Sagas: Some Notes', *Modern Language Review* 24, 409–15.
Blackwell, I. A. 1847. *Northern Antiquities translated from the French of M. Mallet by Bishop Percy,* new ed.
Cottle, Amos. 1797. *Icelandic Poetry, or the Edda of Saemund translated into English verse.*
Earle, John and Plummer, Charles. 1892. *Two of the Saxon Chronicles Parallel.*
Hay, Denys. 1959. 'Flavio Biondo and the Middle Ages', *Proceedings of the British Academy* 97–127.
Hay, Denys. 1977. *Annalists and Historians.*

Hickes, George. 1703–5. *Linguarum Veterum Septentrionalium Thesaurus.*
Hunt, Wray. [n.d.] *The voyage to Vineland.*
Jerningham, Edward. 1784. *The Rise and Progress of the Scandinavian Poetry. A Poem in Two Parts.*
Mallet, Paul Henri. See Blackwell 1847.
NED = *A new English dictionary on historical principles.* 1884–1928.
Omberg, Margaret. 1976. *Scandinavian Themes in English Poetry, 1760-1800.*
Penrose, Thomas. 1775. *Flights of Fancy.*
Robinson, Fred. C. 1984. 'Medieval, the Middle Ages', *Speculum* 59, 745–56.
Sammes, Aylett. 1676. *Britannia Antiqua Illustrata.*
Sheringham, Robert. 1670. *De Anglorum Gentis Origine Disceptatio.*
Spelman, Henry. 1687. *Glossarium Archaiologicum.*
Tolkien, Christopher (ed. and trans.). 1960. *The saga of King Heidrek the Wise.*
Verstegen, Richard. 1605. *Restitution of Decayed Intelligence.*

BJARNE FIDJESTØL

PAGAN BELIEFS AND CHRISTIAN IMPACT: THE CONTRIBUTION OF SCALDIC STUDIES

I

THE impact of Christianity is difficult to measure. If I were asked whether Norway is now a Christian country, I would be rather embarrassed how to answer. I would have to search for some tangible criterion of a country's being Christian, perhaps the habit of bell-ringing from church towers on Sunday mornings. Bell-ringing in my country is performed by mechanical means, the ropes untouched by human hand, and most people have more or less forgotten the significance of it. Still, according to this heuristic criterion, Norway is a Christian country and the United Kingdom even more so.

In scaldic poetry there is no bell-ringing, but nevertheless some resonance from the scalds' faith or *siðr* may be heard in their language and poetic figures. In order to find something that can be measured, I shall not in the first instance talk about the ideas of their poetry, but of the more unconscious level of their poetic diction. There is an attempt at unveiling the religion of the scalds by means of counting the religious references in their language in Jan de Vries's famous study *De skaldenkenningen met mythologischen inhoud* (1934). In this book he noted the occurrence of mythological names in scaldic poetry, and he found a rapid decline coinciding with the introduction of Christianity—as was to be expected—but more interestingly he observed a new increase in the second half of the twelfth century, which he interpreted as a mythological renaissance (de Vries 1934, 9, 53). From these findings de Vries drew important conclusions for the history of Eddaic poetry, conclusions beyond the scope of this paper. But first and foremost they relate to the religious history of the scaldic art, showing the heathen 'bell-ringing' first fading away and then growing stronger again.

The increase detected by de Vries in the second half of the twelfth century is not very marked, and it may be questioned whether it is statistically significant. Since it coincides, however, with a well-documented interest in the past, attested by the prose histories and historical poetry of the period, it is hardly unexpected. De Vries's material is too heterogeneous, however, to tell us very much about the real attitudes of the scalds. Since the scalds sometimes chose to treat matter from the past which included heathen mythology, they inevitably had to use a mythological vocabulary, but little is known about their real attitudes towards it. What is needed for this purpose is a text corpus where other factors as far as possible are kept constant, so that the development in the use of mythological kennings can be studied in isolation. In particular the choice of subject-matter should not be allowed to interfere with the statistics. This, of course, is the ideal situation of the laboratory which we cannot expect to obtain in real life. In the well-established corpus of scaldic poetry addressed to princes, however, we come fairly close to this ideal. This is a conservative genre covering nearly four centuries of Nordic history before and after the introduction of Christianity, and its main themes and diction remain remarkably little changed down the centuries. It therefore offers an eminently level playing-field for the study of minor changes and longitudinal developments.

I have therefore made an effort to rework de Vries's study, but unlike him I have restricted the scope to the corpus of court poetry, a genre covering a long period, which because of its relationship to political history had the best possible conditions of transmission.[1]

In this corpus I have noted all occurrences of names of divine beings in kennings, and kennings only,[2] and after having counted the total number of kennings, I have calculated the percentage of kennings containing a mythological allusion, distributed in spans of 25 years apiece. De Vries calculated the frequency of mythological allusions in relation to stanzas, but following a sensible suggestion of Stefán Einarsson (1936), I have given the frequency in relation to the total number of kennings.

The results of my calculations may be tabulated as follows.

Period	Corpus number	Stanzas	Kenn.	Myth.k.	Myth.k.%
–949	1–3	26.25	60	7	11.66
950–974	4–7	22.50	70	18	25.71
975–999	8–17	56.50	199	57	28.64
1000–1024	18–26, 30–31	109.75	197	19	9.64
1025–1049	27–29, 32–39, 43–44	129.00	168	16	9.52
1050–1074	40–42, 45–60	146.75	162	16	9.87
1075–1099		•	•	•	•
1100–1124	61–67, 74, 76–77	81.25	104	6	5.76
1125–1149	68–69, 75, 78–79	54.75	36	1	2.77
1150–1174	70–71, 73, 80–81	28.75	50	1	2.00
1175–1199	82–83	3.00	5	0	0.00
1200–1224	84–86	104.50	288	31	10.76
1225–1249	87–89	12.50	19	2	10.52
1250–1274	90–95	96.25	180	9	5.00
		Σ 871.75	Σ 1538	Σ 183	11.90

BAR CHART

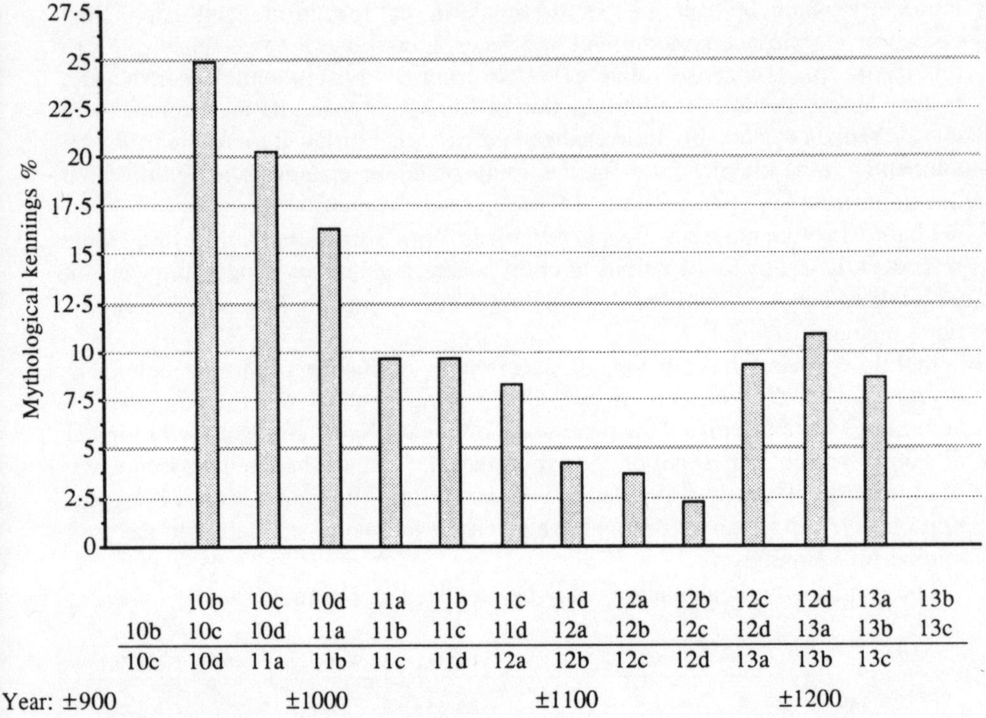

The bar chart shows the percentage of kennings containing a mythological allusion, calculated as a 'moving average' for three-quarters of a century. The percentages found in column 6 of the table, which represent the numbers actually occurring in the stanzas for each separate period, have thus been replaced by the average of the figures for three adjacent periods. The purpose of this operation is to even out the impact of the greatly varying number of stanzas transmitted from each period; see column three in the table. The figures under the bar chart represent centuries and the letters quarter-centuries; thus for example 10b means the period 925–949 (though in this particular case it includes everything prior to 950).

My result is less striking than that of de Vries, but in my opinion both the reliability and the validity of the statistics are greater. The graph shows a rapid decrease in mythological allusions in the kennings in these poems, from 25% in the latter half of the 10th century to 2–3% in the latter half of the 12th century, but then there is a notable increase, obviously due to the 'renaissance' of Snorri Sturluson and his nephews. The important difference from de Vries's results is that there is no trace whatsoever of a twelfth-century renaissance.

II

The perhaps rather trivial conclusion to be drawn from these statistics is thus that, judged by their use of mythological kennings, the court poets were in the course of time thoroughly converted to Christianity. The statistical decrease in their use of mythological kennings is a rather crude index of their attitude towards religion, however, and I should like to supplement the purely statistical view of court poetry by a second examination of the same material, highlighting the usually brief statements of religious content which occur sporadically in it. These short statements correspond to 'die eingeklammerte Floskel' in the terminology of Wolfgang Lange, and to a certain extent to 'Aussage in der Randzone des Gedichts' (Lange 1958, 31–42; cf. also the material and discussion in Edwards 1982–83). By examining the content of these statements the nature of the change of religion may be described rather more closely, and it may be possible to detect continuity as well as renewal.

Scaldic style is known to be highly repetitious and so are these short statements. In fact, the greater part of them turns out to be clearly divisible into no more than three groups—the first expressing the idea that the prince is carrying out the will of the gods or of God, the second containing intercession for the prince, and the third expressing ideas on the king's position as intermediary between God and the people.

(1) *At mun banda*

The first item, which I have found some 16 times in my corpus, may be labelled *at mun banda*—'at the will of the gods'.[3] This is a quotation from a poem by Eyjólfr dáðaskáld on Eiríkr blóðøx, which occurs in the *stef* of the *drápa*, in a sufficiently prominent position to provide the name for the whole poem—*Bandadrápa*:

> Dregr land at mun banda
> Eiríkr und sik . . .
> . . . ok ræðr síðan
> jarl goðvǫrðu hjarli.

Eiríkr conquers the land to the pleasure of the gods (*or* at their will), and thereafter he rules over the god-protected country.

The king acts so to speak on behalf of the gods, and they protect his realm.

In a poem addressed to Eiríkr's son, Haraldr gráfeldr, this idea is developed, so that the king almost appears as an incarnation of the divinity: 'Sigtýr himself was in the sea warrior; the gods governed him'.

According to the sagas, Eiríkr blóðøx and his sons were Christian, but evidently only superficially so. The scalds treated them as good heathens, as the quotation from *Bandadrápa* demonstrates. How far back into heathen antiquity the idea expressed in *Bandadrápa* reached cannot be decided, but it clearly survived the conversion to Christianity, apparently unchanged. Sigvatr Þórðarson has the same motive in its briefest possible form, *Goð vildi svá*, and Þórleifr jarlsskáld used it in a markedly Christian context in a poem to Sveinn tjúguskegg:

> Opt með œrnri giptu
> ǫðlings himins rǫðla
> Jóta gramr en ítri
> Englandi rauð branda.

Often with abundant luck from the prince of heaven the glorious king of Jutes reddened swords in England.

In Sigvatr's verse the verb is given in monotheistic singular, which is Christian, but any heathen scald might probably have said the same, putting the verb in the plural. Wolfgang Lange even points to an instance where the same scald uses both plural and singular, namely Þjóðólfr Arnórsson, in his *lausavísa* 13: *Dǫnum vǫru goð grǫm*, and 26: *gengr sem goð vill* (Lange 1958, 32). (*Lausavísur* are not included in the Appendix, since my corpus is confined to the more prestigious and reliable genre of court poems.)

Not only these 'eingeklammerte Floskeln' show an unbroken continuity on both sides of the religious watershed; so does the view of the relationship between the king and his god. In one of the most profoundly heathen poems in the corpus, *Vellekla* by Einarr skálaglamm, in a pair of verses which may have been the *stef* of the *drápa*, Earl Hákon is said to be mightily strengthened by the gods:

> Rammaukin kveðk ríki
> rǫgn Hǫkonar magna.

A similiar expression is used by Sigvatr more *en passant* in the *Erfidrápa* on St Óláfr, where he is talking about his life as a saint in heaven (*Skj.* A I 264; B I 245):

> Jǫfur magnar goð.

From a religious point of view this idea, 'Gott mit uns', is trivial and ubiquitous, far from the profound religious motivation of lordship found in poetry addressed to the earls of Hlaðir, where the ruler may be depicted as the bridegroom of the earth, making it blossom. I presume that is the reason why it could so easily be taken over by the Christian scalds, and in its turn this easy continuity may have contributed to the change of religion. From this point of view, the kings had nothing to lose by adopting the new religion; on the contrary, there was every reason to believe that White Christ was a more powerful ally than the old gods, who had been obsolete for generations in the most prestigious European countries.

The two other groups of brief religious statements in court poems, however, show a more interesting renewal in mentality and ideology.

(2) *Hafi Kristr konungs ǫnd*

The second group consists of brief statements expressing concern for the soul of the prince. In my corpus I have found seven examples, the first of which is from the *Erfidrápa* by Hallfreðr vandræðaskáld on his godfather King Óláfr Tryggvason:

> Kœns hafi Kristr enn hreini
> konungs ǫnd ofar lǫndum!
> May the pure Christ have the king's soul above the earth!

The *klofastef* in *Stúfsdrápa* by Stúfr Þórðarson is very reminiscent of Hallfreðr's verse, and may be an allusion to it, unless perhaps both are reflecting some liturgical formula:

> Hafi ríks þars vel líkar
> vist of aldr med Kristi
> Haralds ǫnd ofar lǫndum!
> May the mighty Haraldr's soul have an eternal gratifying dwelling with Christ above the earth!

In his *Erfidrápa* Sigvatr Þórðarson even prayed for the soul of St Óláfr, obviously unaware that St Augustine had declared that it is offensive to pray for the martyrs (*Injuria est enim, pro martyre orare, Sermo* CLIX 1, *PL* 38, 868).

Particularly zealous in his prayers was Arnórr Þórðarson jarlaskáld. In his poetry the motive is found no fewer than four times, three of which occur in court poetry—the fourth example in a poem to an Icelandic chieftain. (For a discussion of the comparable formula in runic monuments, see Segelberg 1972.)

Old Norse funeral customs as well as literary sources testify to the belief in a life after death among the heathens, and some of *Vǫluspá*'s descriptions of a happy life in the new world are among the parts of this poem that are most reminiscent of Christian ideas. Nevertheless, the Christian doctrine of Heaven and Hell, and in particular the idea that man's eternal fate is dependent upon his religious faith in this life, meant a new outlook on life and death. Preoccupation with a man's inner life, or his soul, is probably one of the most important shifts of mentality brought about by the new religion. To judge by the scaldic sources, however, the only trace of this great human revolution discernible in the first generations of Christian poetry is no more—and no less—than a concern about the dwelling-place of the spirit in the afterworld.

Only around 1100, in Markús Skeggjason's poem in honour of King Eiríkr Sveinsson, the royal founder of the archbishopric of Lund, is concern expressed for the welfare of the soul in this world. The scald says among other things that the king went on pilgrimage in order to heal his inner wounds (str. 12: *mildingr fór of munka veldi móðum fœti sǫl at bœta*; cf. str. 28: *læknask sǫr en iðri*). Expressions like these mark in my opinion a new phase in the process of Christianisation.

(3) *Herr sésk sem goð þengil*

From the point of view of political ideology the third group is the most important. I have labelled it with a phrase from a stanza by Gunnlaugr ormstunga, where the motive first occurs. The *þengill* in question is King Ethelred:

> Herr sésk allr við ǫrva
> Englands sem goð þengil;[4]
> ætt lýtr grams ok gumna
> gunnbráðs Aðalráði.

All the host stands in awe of the generous prince of England as of God; the race of the war-swift king and all the race of men bow to Ethelred.

Sem goð may mean 'as well as God', I presume, but at the same time it means 'as much as God'. At all events, the king is placed in God's vicinity, he is honoured as his representative in the kingdom. Two later scalds, Hallvarðr háreksblesi and Þórarinn loftunga, use nearly identical terms to express the idea that the king, in this case King Canute, protects his land as God protects heaven—God and the king have each their realm, so to speak, and as God's representative on earth, the king is nearer to God than other human beings.

These are the earliest examples of the idea of something like 'king by the grace of God' in Old Norse literature, and it is worth while noticing that, with one relatively untypical exception (no. 5 in the Appendix), all refer to English or Dano-English kings, namely Ethelred and Canute. In his study of English influence on Old Norse poetry Dietrich Hofmann has traced the origin of these ideas in Anglo-Saxon literature (Hofmann 1955, 53–55, 96–97; cf. Lange 1958, 140–43). In embryonic form they contain one of the great themes of medieval political ideology, and it is not possible here to pursue the theme through the history of European kingship. Instead we shall try to follow its development some way in the scaldic poetry on Norwegian kings.

III

In the first instance one is struck by a remarkable restraint in the scalds' use of religious motives for political purposes. The coercive Norwegian mission of the two Óláfrs is often described as a struggle for dominance, in which Christianity was used—or misused—in order to achieve worldly power. And certainly there is no doubt that for these royal zealots their functions as missionaries and as conquerors were not distinct from each other. Success in one field meant success in the other. Nevertheless, it is hard actually to pin-point the political benefit these kings drew from their missionary work in their struggle for power. If political considerations were paramount, it might have been wiser in the first instance not to irritate the Norwegian chieftains by an attack on their religion. After all, Haraldr hárfagri perfectly well succeeded in winning power without having recourse to the

'God who created the sun', to quote the words Snorri Sturluson attributes to this pre-Christian king, and for his son Hákon Aðalsteinsfóstri Christianity was an obvious disadvantage, so that eventually he had to give up his missionary work altogether. I therefore do not think the possibility should be excluded that the two Óláfrs were driven by personal enthusiasm for the religion they had converted to, and perhaps some concern for the 'modernisation' of their country (cf. Wolf 1959, 13).

The quotations from scaldic poems addressed to English kings show that there actually was an ideological potential in Christian ideas of kingship, but in the encomiastic poetry about the two Norwegian militant missionaries there is hardly a trace of it. It is also difficult to see how it could appeal to a nation which was not already largely Christianised.

The significant change occurred only after the death of St Óláfr. The turning-point is *Glælognskviða* by Þórarinn loftunga, a poem on the sanctity of King Óláfr, which has been described as our first hagiographic poem (Lange 1958, 111). There are two particularly striking aspects of this text. Firstly, it was composed at most a couple of years after the king's death, and it demonstrates that the belief in the wonder-working sanctity of the king was already so well established that the scald invites the new king to pray to the saint to grant him his land:

Bið Áleif	To Olaf pray
at unni þér	To eke thy day,
—hann's goðs maðr—	To save thy land
grundar sinnar;	From spoiler's hand.
hann of getr	God's man is he
af goði sjǫlfum	To deal to thee
ár ok frið	Good crops and peace;
ǫllum mǫnnum.	Let not prayer cease.

(Trans. Laing)

As Fredrik Paasche has pointed out (Paasche 1914, 15 [= 1948, 44]; cf. Magerøy 1948, 41), it looks as if the later motive of St Óláfr as *rex perpetuus Norvegiae* is already present.

The second striking point is the fact that the poem is addressed to King Sveinn Álfífuson, the son of King Canute, who reigned in Norway on his behalf after his allies had beaten King Óláfr in the Battle of Stiklastaðir. In the fragments of *Glælognskviða* quoted in the Kings' Sagas very little is said about King Sveinn himself, to whom the poem is addressed, and whom we must expect to have been the primary object of praise. The greater part of the fragment concerns St Óláfr and his miracles. How are we to explain this policy, which produces a poem to King Sveinn, composed by the main scald of his father, but filled with praise of the former leader of the opposing party?

It has been suggested that the scald was inspired by the politics of Sveinn's father in England. According to Erich Hoffmann (1975, 45–46, 81–84) Canute had been active in promoting the worship of St Edmund in England by founding and endowing St Edmund's abbey, notwithstanding the fact that the saint's martyrdom had been caused by Danish invaders and to a certain extent served as a symbol of anti-Danish opposition. King Canute so to speak usurped the ideology and made himself the symbol of the English party. As king of England Canute was now the representative of the same royal institution as St Edmund had belonged to and the advantage to be drawn from this fact outweighed the risk that St Edmund's memory might strengthen the opposition between English and Danes.

Glælognskviða very strongly suggests that something of the kind may have motivated the scald when he composed a poem on St Óláfr in honour of his Danish/English lord. We have seen that Þórarinn had been the scald of King Canute and a probable connection between St Edmundsbury and Niðaróss may be established through the family of Þorkell hávi. Þorkell was earl of East Anglia at the period of the endowment of St Edmund's abbey by the king, and he is mentioned in the sources as one of the principal promoters of this policy (Arnold 1965, 47, 126–27, 341, 344). Now in Trondheim his son Haraldr was the most prominent among the advisers of the young King Sveinn. It is to be noted that Earl Haraldr is referred to in the very same poem, str. 1 (*Þar var jarl fyrst at upphafi*), and he may have suggested the political programme to be followed in it.

However that may be, the only substantial piece of information on King Sveinn in this poem is the significant fact that he had now taken his seat in Þrándheimr (*hefr sér til sess hagat . . . í Þrándheimi*), where Óláfr had dwelt before he went to Heaven, and where the great king was buried 'alive', i.e. as a saint (*kykvasettr*).

In the cult of saints control of the holy body is of course of paramount importance, and a recent analysis of the development of the city of Trondheim indicates that differing locations of the shrine, in close connection with the developing royal foundations, were a decisive factor in the early medieval history of the town (Christophersen 1992). *Glælognskviða* demonstrates that even at this early period Trondheim was a goal of pilgrims and miracles happened at the king's shrine. The shrine was therefore an object of great value to whoever disposed of it and in the poem the scald entreated the king to take advantage of this position. Possibly one of the reasons for King Sveinn's eventual failure was a certain reluctance on his part to play this card. According to the sagas at least, his powerful mother was rather loath to venerate the Norwegian saint.

The representation of King Óláfr as Norway's eternal king was to be one of the most salient ideological themes in the medieval history of the Norwegian monarchy, as is well known, and from Óláfr's death onwards the cult of the saint became a determining factor in the history of Christendom in Norway as well as in the nation's political development. However, with the exception of the English-influenced *Glælognskviða*, the scalds seem to have been relatively reluctant to assimilate this ideology during most of the eleventh century. This impression may be due to accidental lacunas in the scaldic material. One might also think, however, that among the kings' political advisers other groups than the scalds had the initiative in this respect, e.g. his clergy or political magnates like Earl Haraldr. The scalds may have been more tied to the traditional view of a king's legitimation. But this is mere speculation, of course.

In the *Erfidrápa* of Sigvatr Þórðarson, composed a few years after *Glælognskviða* and during the reign of St Óláfr's son Magnús the Good, Sigvatr confirms that the worship of the saint is well established—he has a golden shrine, mass is celebrated and many miracles are performed: 'I praise the holiness of the king.' But no political exploitation of St Óláfr's sanctity is apparent in Sigvatr's poem, only a moral exhortation to his listeners and himself not to neglect their duties towards the saint.

Sigvatr is also the first to testify to the eclipse of the sun at Stiklastaðir. But in his description of the battle the scald does nothing to conceal the fact that the king had heathens in his army as well as Christians; he just assigned the Christians to a position to the right of the king, which may or may not be a veiled allusion to the Last Judgement.

In the poetry of the reign of Magnús the Good, of which about 85 stanzas are preserved, Christian themes are touched on occasionally, but the fact that Magnús is the royal heir of a holy king is passed over in silence. Referring to Magnús's father in a kenning, instead of using the epithet *inn helgi*, Þjóðólfr Arnórsson describes him as 'the stout': *Áleifs mǫgr . . . ens digra* (*Skj.* A I 364; B I 335).

In a poem in *runhent* addressed to Haraldr harðráði Þjóðólfr mentions that he was the brother of the holy king (*Skj.* A I 368; B I 338–39):

> Jarizleifr of sá
> hvert jǫfri brá
> hófsk hlýri frams
> ens helga grams.

Iarizleif saw in what direction the prince developed. The outstanding holy king's brother came on. (Trans. Faulkes; 1987, 131)

King Óláfr's sanctity is taken for granted, however, and it is by no means focused. In this poem King Haraldr is characterised above all by his membership of the family: he is not only 'brother of the holy king', but 'father of Óláfr [kyrri]' as well, and King Magnús is referred to as *Haralds bróðursonr*. The stanza quoted above concerns another relative, namely Haraldr's father-in-law, King Jaroslav, and the mention of Haraldr's holy brother may be motivated by fact that King Óláfr was well acquainted with Jaroslav. Whether Óláfr is referred to as 'holy' or as 'stout' matters little in this context.

More significant in this connection is a poem in honour of Haraldr's son Óláfr kyrri, the first literate king of Norway, who read the Psalter and wore *drambhosur lerkaðar at beini* ('costly hose laced about the legs'). Óláfr kyrri was contemporary with, and brother-in-law of, King Eiríkr Sveinsson in Denmark, whose eulogy *Hrynhenda* by Markús Skeggjason I have already mentioned as an introduction to the 'high medieval period'. In Steinn Herdísarson's *Óláfsdrápa* we also feel a new spirit permeating literary forms. In this respect it is significant, I think, that the traditional introduction, 'the scald's bid for a hearing', is supplanted by a Christian exordium: 'I call upon the holy lord of heaven (to listen) to my poem, before men, because he is the more glorious.' The scald alludes to the traditional beginning of a scaldic poem, but he emphatically breaks with the tradition.

In this poem the motive from *Glælognskviða*, that the holy king will grant the present king his land, is taken up once more, and this time it is reinforced by the close relationship between the saint and the king (*Skj.* A I 411; B I 381):

Sín óðul mun Sveini
sóknstrangr í Kaupangi,
þars heilagr gramr hvílir,
—hann's ríkr—jǫfurr banna;
ætt sinni mun unna
Áleifr konungr hála
—Úlfs þarfat þar arfi—
alls Nóregs—til kalla.

The warrior king from Trondheim,	From Drontheim town, where in repose
Where his sainted uncle lies,	The holy king defies his foes,
Bravely defends his heritage	Another Olaf will defend
Against the greed of Denmark.	His kingdom from the greedy Svein.
St Olaf gladly granted	King Olaf has both power and right,
Norway to his descendants;	And the Saint's favour in his fight.
No son of Svein of Denmark	The Saint will ne'er his kin forsake
Has any right to claim it.	And let Sveinn Ulfsson Norway take.
(Trans. Magnusson and Pálsson)	(Trans. Laing)

The scald insists that the Norwegian king is the legitimate ruler in the city where the holy king is resting, to the exclusion of another Danish King Sveinn, this time Sveinn Úlfsson, cousin of Sveinn Álfífuson. It is tempting to read this as a kind of polemic against *Glælognskviða*; the political weapons forged by Sveinn Álfífuson's scald are turned against the Danish party, and Óláfr kyrri uses the political and legal advantage of belonging to the family of the saint, as it were invoking his uncle St Óláfr as his 'Spitzenahn'. Nevertheless, the legal notion of *óðal* seems to be no less prominent in the argument than the religious motive of the saintliness of his relative.[5]

IV

In this final section I would like to return to the two principal representatives of the court poetry of the transition period, Hallfreðr vandræðaskáld and Sigvatr Þórðarson, the main scalds of the two missionary Óláfrs.

In his important survey of Old Norse Christian poetry before 1200, Wolfgang Lange (1958) characterised Hallfreðr as 'Typus des dürftig Bekehrten'; according to *Hallfreðar saga*, the hero, during his stay among the heathen Swedes, *blés í kross yfir drykk sínum, áðr hann drakk, en fátt sǫng hann* (*ÍF* VIII, 177). In connection with this, one of the most interesting aspects of Hallfreðr's poetry is the way in which he refers in it to his own conversion. He was compelled to abandon Njǫrðr's kin and pray to Christ, he says (*ÍF* VIII, 159):

verðk ok neyddr frá Njarðar
niðjum Krist at biðja,

and he openly resented the loss of his former faith. However, at the same time he acknowledged the gain, which first and foremost consisted in his close relationship with Óláfr Tryggvason, who consented to be his godfather. Hallfreðr knew what he had done, and there is nothing to indicate that he found the final balance negative. I think that Lange (1958, 38) is quite justified when he argues that 'Hallfreds Christentum heißt Olaf'. On the other hand, Lange did not in my view succeed in finding convincing examples of syncretism in Hallfreðr's poetry. The sad fact that the stanzas addressed to his old rival Gríss are 'av betydligt grov och oaptitlig karaktär' (Noreen 1926, 224; see Lange 1958, 37) is irrelevant to the question of his conversion—after all the scald had not converted to Victorian puritanism. By adding to his *Erfidrápa* on Óláfr Tryggvason a prayer for the king's soul, Hallfreðr was practising his Christianity. Lange thought that the scald had to force himself to this single Christian sentence at the end of his poem (Lange 1958, 37) and that it would have become the Christian poet better to seek comfort in thoughts about God's 'Ratschluß'. But this amounts to begging the question. Intercession for somebody is after all a manifestly Christian act.

Hallfreðr may have been sincere to a greater or lesser extent in his prayer; I do not think that it is possible to know precisely. In the introduction to his study Lange has some very sensible remarks on the inevitability of some kind of syncretism in the assimilation of a new religion. Insofar as the new wine is poured into the bottles of the existing language, the meaning previously invested in religious terms which were reused in a new context must have lingered on some time before the bottles burst. But this view does not legitimate a systematic minimisation of the seriousness of the manifestly Christian statements which are actually to be found in the poetry of the first generation of Christian scalds. Lange accused Paasche of going too far in interpreting Old Norse poetry in the light of medieval Western theology (1958, 25), but one wonders whether Lange himself has not gone too far in reaction to Paasche.

In Hallfreðr's prayer there are no theological subtleties, and it comprises only a tiny part of the total poem (1%). As far as that goes, however, he could just be said to be complying with the Biblical commandment 'when ye pray, use not vain repetitions, as the heathen do: for they think they shall be heard for their much speaking' (Matt. 6: 7). The question of the scald's personal commitment to his own prayer seems in this case not only insoluble, but the very question may be an anachronism.

Lange's general characterisation of Sigvatr Þórðarson's poetry is also worth noting: 'Der Gesamttenor—nicht eigentlich die Themen seiner Dichtung—ist christlich' (Lange 1958, 29). If Hallfreðr was the type of the newly converted, or 'the reluctant Christian', Sigvatr seems remarkably well established in the new faith, as if he had belonged to it for generations. It is of course possible that he had. According to *Skaldatal* his father was the court poet of Sigvaldi jarl, who in Old Norse sources is depicted as a great scoundrel, but who was presumably a Christian all the same, being a subject of the King Haraldr who 'made the Danes Christian'. His scald may well have been Christian too. However that may be, on his journey into heathen Sweden, Sigvatr—unlike Hallfreðr—observed the uncouth manners of the natives with amused curiosity, like a man to whom the heathen religion now seemed rather obsolete.

Of Sigvatr's faith and religious practice we get only glimpses. I have already mentioned that he admonished himself and his listeners to attend to St Óláfr's mass; and he seems to have been particularly attached to the sacrament of baptism. A fragment which is preserved only in Snorri's *Edda*, and which Finnur Jónsson on dubious grounds ascribed to the *Erfidrápa* on King Óláfr (Finnur Jónsson 1920, 295; cf. Fidjestøl 1982, 121), apparently refers to the baptism of Christ in Jordan, and this is the only direct allusion to Biblical history in the known fragments of Sigvatr's poems. (A possible veiled allusion is mentioned below.) A *lausavísa* is devoted to the pleasure the scald took at the baptism of his daughter Tófa, whom the King had honoured by acting as her godfather. In this case a Christian ritual has inspired the scald to a beautiful poetic expression, in his prayer for the king who 'lifted my daughter *home* from heathendom' (*Skj*. A I 268–69; B I 248):

Dróttinn, hjalp þeims dóttur
(dýrr's þinn vili) mína
heim ór heiðnum dómi
hóf ok nafn gaf Tófu;
helt und vatn enn vitri
(varðk þeim feginn harða
morni) mínu barni
móðrakkr Haralds bróðir.

Help Thou, O God, him who—
hallowed be Thy name—from
heathendom redeemed my
daughter and called her Tofa;
Harold's hardy brother
held o'er the font the infant,
grudged not to be her godfather—
glad was I that morning!

(Trans. Hollander)

Sigvatr himself was godfather to King Óláfr's only son, Magnús, and in *lausavísa* 30 there seems to be an allusion to this fact in an obscure context (*Heimskringla, Magnúss saga ins góða* ch. 9; *ÍF* XXVIII, 18–19), and this is probably also the case in *Bersǫglisvísur* 18, where he addresses the young king: . . . *meðal okkar alt's háligt . . . erum, Magnús, vér vegnir; vildak með þér mildum . . . lifa ok deyja*.

Meðal okkar alt's háligt is usually translated 'our relationship is sacred', namely the spiritual relationship which exists between godson and godfather (*LP*, 315). The next line is more difficult to interpret: *erum, Magnús, vér vegnir*. The last word is usually emended to *vægnir*, but perhaps the original reading could be retained and taken to refer to baptism by means of a pun. *Vega* means (1) 'lift up', and (2) 'kill'. The first sense might correspond to *levatio*, the lifting up from the baptismal font, cf. *hefja ór heiðnum dómi*. The second might correspond to a theological interpretation of baptism, according to which it is a symbolic or sacramental death and resurrection. A baptized Christian is thus dead or killed (*veginn*) and yet living. This piece of Pauline theology might lead on to the scald's conclusion where he expressed his wish to *lifa ok deyja* with the generous Magnús.

A possible explanation of Sigvatr's interest in baptism is clearly that it implicitly included him in the royal family, by what for him was a sacred relationship. There are further examples where he treats his relationship to the king in religious language: 'Let Christ punish me with the burning fire if I wanted to be far from the king (namely in the battle)' (*lausavísa* 25, *Skj.* A I 273; B I 252):

> Hafa láti mik heitan
> Hvítakristr at víti
> eld, ef Áleif vildak
> —emk skírr of þat—firrask.

The same suffering is in store for those who betrayed the king for money (*lausavísur* 16–17). In an article in *Maal og Minne* (1975) I have tried to show that Sigvatr here gives an early example of Biblical typology used to promote the king's cause. His betrayers are seen in the image of Judas, which implies, of course, that Óláfr is seen in the image of Christ, whose rule he was about to expand.

The most elaborate triangle God—King—scald is found in two carefully structured stanzas, where the scald says his prayers for the king, *lausavísur* 7–8 (no. 6 might also have been included in the context; *Skj.* A I 267–69; B I 247–48):

> Nú sittu heill, en hallar　　　　　Sit happy in thy hall, O king!
> hér finnumsk meir þinnar　　　 Till I come back and good news bring:
> at, unz ek køm vitja,　　　　　　The scald will bid thee now farewell,
> Áleifr konungr, mála.　　　　　 Till he brings news well worth to tell.
> Skald biðr hins, at haldi　　　　　He wishes to the helmed hero
> hjalmdrífu viðr lífi　　　　　　　Health, and long life, and a full flow
> —endisk leyfð—ok landi　　　　Of honour, riches, and success—
> —lýkk vísu nú—þvísa.　　　　　And, parting, ends his song with this.

Nú eru mælt—en mála	The farewell word is spoken now—
meir kunnum skil fleiri—	The word that to the heart lies nearest,
orð, þaus *oss* of varða	And yet, O king! before I go,
alls mest, konungr, flestra.	One word on what I hold the dearest.
Goð láti þik gæta,	I fain would say, 'O! may God save
geðharðr konungr, jarðar,	To thee, the bravest of the brave,
—víst hefik þann—þvít, þinnar,	The land which is thy right by birth!'
þú ert til borinn—vilja.	This is my dearest wish on earth.
	(Trans. Laing)

Above I have highlighted some of the most conspicuous correspondences between the two stanzas, italicising the semantic parallels and underlining identical or near-identical words in the same verse-position. Sigvatr focuses on his own relation to the king (*skald—konungr—ek—oss*), on his function as scald (*endisk leyfð—lýkk vísu nú*) and as intercessor, first with himself as subject of the sentence and next with God as subject of an optative verb: *Skald biðr hins, at ... Goð láti ...* The scald has in an artistically clever manner used the poetic means of stanza structure in order to give his prayer an elaborate form. I take it as a indication that he took personal interest in his pious undertaking.

The last stroke in my sketch for a religious portrait of Sigvatr scald is in lighter tone, but not necessarily less significant for that reason.

I have already referred to Sigvatr's strenuous journey—or journeys—into Sweden, which he described in an extremely vivid manner in *Austrfararvísur*. The linguistic tenor of this *flokkr* is rather colloquial, and on one occasion, when he had great trouble with a miserable boat, we even learn how the scald was swearing in his bad moments: *taki hlægiskip hauga herr* (*Skj* A I 233; B I 220). Any of us would probably say: 'The devil take ...'—and I think that is almost exactly what Sigvatr meant. *Hauga herr* is a conventional kenning for the *jǫtnar*, who have here been demonised in a Christian interpretation of Norse mythology. Eventually he succeeded in getting over the river, but the way through the great forests was no easier: *Menn veit at mættum meini* (*Skj*. A I 233; B I 221)—'people know that I had problems', it might be translated. The important detail is the singular verb form *veit*, which reveals that it is to be read as a mild oath: 'all the saints know' or something of the kind, cf. expressions like *goð veit* ... According to Fritzner (III 971b), 'Den jevnlige Brug av *veit* i deslige sværgende Udtryk medførte, at det brugtes ogsaa, hvor Ord som betegnede Personen, hvorved man svor, var et Pluralis, istedetfor at svare dertil med Hensyn til Numerus, noget som blev det almindelige ved *menn*: *þat veit menn*'. The occurrence of this piece of bad language in Sigvatr is remarkably early. It is not the language of a fresh convert.

I suspect Sigvatr of having room in his religion also for his humour. In his *Vestrfararvísur* there is a rather ticklish point when he mentions the gifts from King Canute to his fellow-scald Bersi and himself. We have seen what Sigvatr thought about the king's men who sold their lord for money, and now the two scalds might be accused of the same offence. In this stanza (*Skj.* A I 242; B I 227), however, he only comments on King Canute's generosity, complaining that Bersi had got much more than he had. In this connection he somewhat inappropriately (Lange 1958, 32) inserts the commonplace discussed earlier: *ræðr gǫrva ǫllu goð sjálfr.* God himself governs everything—and the scald evidently has to comply with His will. This sounds very pious, but one wonders whether it is not uttered tongue-in-cheek: in the long run God may have looked after Sigvatr by letting him have a worse lot than Bersi this time. (On Sigvatr as a pilgrim to Rome, cf. the interesting remarks in Naumann 1986.)

V

In this contribution I have restricted the scope of investigation to the scaldic court poetry, which in my opinion is a particularly helpful corpus. I do not claim that this corpus is representative of all scaldic poetry. On the contrary, in a general way I think it is probable that heathen elements showed stronger resistance at a greater distance from the missionary kings, but—like Fredrik Paasche—I also find it legitimate to attach particular interest to the ideas of the leading circles of society.

My narrow choice of corpus has been counterbalanced by viewing the material from a variety of perspectives, ranging from a purely statistical evaluation of mythological kennings, through a survey of 'eingeklammerte Floskeln', as Lange calls them, and of one religious/political theme, ending with a closer scrutiny of two main scalds of the period of transition.

My brief conclusion is that the court scalds seem to have been quick to take to the new religion. Real syncretism is hard to detect in their poems, and the scalds of the Norwegian kings are slow to exploit the religion for political ends in any open and obvious way. As far as our corpus can tell us, a Christian royal ideology is manifest in scaldic poems in England already in the days of Ethelred, but particularly in the poetry addressed to King Canute and his son. Only towards 1100 is this theme developed by the scalds of Norwegian kings. At the same time a new concern for the inner life of the human personality also manifests itself.

For the court poets of the first Christian generations the new religion is very much part of their personal relationship with the actively Christian kings, and since they were *hirðmenn* it is natural to think that this relationship was important for their relatively eager reception of the new *siðr*. Loyalty to the king and loyalty to Christ were not to be separated, and the new religion offered strong links by which the scald could be even more closely associated with his king. The court poetry does not give much information on their thoughts about God, but they believed in the reality of Hell and Heaven, and that their life on earth—not least their relation to their Christian king—had consequences for their eternal fate.

APPENDIX: BRIEF STATEMENTS OF RELIGIOUS CONTENT

At mun banda (16 occurrences)

(1) Þórbjǫrn hornklofi:*Glymdrápa*, str. 6 (*Skj.* A I 23; B I 21):

Sá vas gramr . . .	This king was
goðvarðr . . .	protected by the gods.

(2) Glúmr Geirason: *Gráfeldardrápa*, str. 12 (*Skj.* A I 78; B I 68):

Þar vas—þrafna byrjar	There was—the gods
þeim stýrðu goð Beima—	governed this warrior—
sjalfr í sœkialfi	Óðinn himself
sigtýr Atals dýra.	in the sea warrior.

(3–4) Einarr skálaglamm: *Vellekla*, str. 15 and 32 (*Skj.* A I 126, 130; B I 119, 123):

Þeim stýra goð.	The gods guide that man.
Hverr sé if, nema jǫfra	What doubt can there be but that the gods
ættrýri goð stýra?	control the destroyer of the race of princes?
Rammaukin kveðk ríki	I say that the most mighty gods strengthen
rǫgn Hǫ́konar magna.	the authority of Hákon.

(Trans. Hollander)

(5) Þórleifr jarlsskáld: fragment on Sveinn tjúguskegg (*Skj.* A I 141; B I 133):

Opt með œrnri giptu	Often with abundant luck
ǫðlings himins rǫðla	from the prince of heaven
Jóta gramr en ítri	the glorious king of Jutes
Englandi rauð branda.	reddened swords in England.

The authenticity of this fragment may be questioned (cf. Fidjestøl 1982, 101–02).

(6) Tindr Hallkelsson's poem on Earl Hákon is difficult to interpret, but in str. 8 the earl's success is ascribed to the will of the gods (*bǫnd at vildu*) (*Skj.* A I 146; B I 138).

(7) The *klofastef* in *Bandadrápa* by Eyjólfr dáðaskáld (in abbreviated form) (*Skj.* A I 200–02; B I 192):

Dregr land at mun banda	Eiríkr conquers the land
Eiríkr und sik . . .	to the pleasure of the gods
. . . ok rœðr síðan	and thereafter he rules
jarl goðvǫrðu hjarli.	the god-protected country.

(8) Sigvatr Þórðarson: *Erfidrápa* (?—cf. Fidjestøl 1982, 121) on St Óláfr, str. 3 (*Skj.* A I 257; B I 239):

Goð vildi svá.	God willed it thus.

(9) Óttarr svarti: *Hǫfuðlausn*, str. 18 (*Skj.* A I 295; B I 272):

Þik remmir goð miklu	God strengthens you with a great
. . . gagni . . .	victory.

(10) Arnórr Þórðarson jarlaskáld: *Magnússdrápa*, str. 10 (*Skj.* A I 340; B I 313):

... en skipti
skapvǫrðr himins jǫrðu.

The protector of heaven
distributed the land.

(11) Þórleikr fagri: *flokkr* on Sveinn Úlfsson, str. 2 (*Skj.* A I 397; B I 365):

Þar má enn hvárr annan
ǫndu nemr eða lǫndum
... goð valda.

Again God will decide
who takes life or land
from the other.

(12) Haldórr skvaldri: *Útfarardrápa*, str. 6 (*Skj.* A I 487; B I 459):

Yðr tjóði goð.

God helped you.

(13) Haldórr skvaldri: fragment on Haraldr gilli, str. 5 (*Skj.* A I 489; B I 461):

Goðs ráð er þat.

This is God's will.

(14) Þórarinn stuttfeldr: *Stuttfeldardrápa*, str. 2 (*Skj.* A I 490; B I 462):

... við skǫp
hreins goðs.

according to the luck
of the pure God.

(15) Snorri Sturluson: *Háttatal*, str. 12 (*stál*) (*Skj.* A II 55; B II 64):

Harðrǫ́ðum guð jarðar
tyggja lér með tíri.

God grants the hard-ruling king
land and honour.

Vindræfrs jǫfurr gæfu
ǫðlingi skóp ungum.

The king of heaven assigned
good luck to the young king.

(16) Óláfr hvítaskáld: *Hrynhenda* on King Hákon and Earl Skuli, str. 12 (*Skj.* A II 97; B II 108):

Svá vildi guð, framiðr mildi.

The gracious God willed it thus.

Hafi Kristr konungs ǫnd (7 occurrences)

(1) Hallfreðr vandræðaskáld: *Erfidrápa* on Óláfr Tryggvason, str. 29 (*Skj.* A I 166; B I 157):

Kœns hafi Kristr enn hreini
konungs ǫnd ofar lǫndum!

May the pure Christ have
the king's soul above the earth!

(2) Sigvatr Þórðarson: *Erfidrápa* on St Óláfr, str. 22 (*Skj.* A I 264; B I 244):

Feðr Magnúss biðk fagna
flóttskjǫrrum goð dróttin.

I pray to God the Lord that he receive
Magnus's father, who is loath to flee.

(3) Stúfr Þórðarson: *Stúfsdrápa* on Haraldr harðráði, *klofastef* (Stúfr 2/8, 3/8, 6/4) (*Skj.* A I 404–05; B I 373–74):

Hafi ríks þars vel líkar
vist of aldr með Kristi
Haralds ǫnd ofar lǫndum!

May the mighty Haraldr's soul have
an eternal gratifying dwelling
with Christ above the earth!

(4–6) Arnórr Þórðarson jarlaskáld: *Rǫgnvaldsdrápa*, str. 3; *Erfikvæði* on Earl Þórfinnr, str. 24–25 and on Haraldr harðráði, str. 19 (*Skj*. A I 332, 348, 353; B I 306, 321, 326):

Saðr stillir, hjalp snjǫllum, sóltjalda, Rǫgnvaldi!	True ruler of heaven, help valiant Rǫgnvaldr!
. . . inndróttar . . . þeim hjalpi goð geymi!	God help this protector of the bodyguard!
Ættbœti firr ítran allríks, en biðk líkna trúra tyggja, dýrum Torf-Einars goð meinum!	God, free the kin of the mighty Torf-Einarr from all evil! I pray for grace for the glorious prince.
Bœnir hefk fyr beini bragna falls við snjallan Girkja vǫrð ok Garða; gjǫf launak svá jǫfri.	I lift my prayers to the glorious protector of Greece and Garðar for the ruler of men. Thus I reward the king.

(7) Einarr Skúlason: *Haraldsdrápa*, poem in *tøglag* on Haraldr gilli, str. 3 (*Skj*. A I 457; B I 425):

Líkn gefi læknir lofaðr friðrofa heims hafljóma hár lausnari!	May the praised Saviour grant his grace to the noble foe of gold!

Sem guð þengill (5 occurrences)

(1) Gunnlaugr ormstunga: poem on Ethelred, *stef* (*Skj*. A I 194; B I 184):

Herr sésk allr við ǫrva Englands sem goð þengil; ætt lýtr grams ok gumna gunnbráðs Aðalráði.	The whole host fears the generous king of England as God; the family of the warlike king and the race of men bow before Ethelred

(Trans. Foote and Quirk)

(2–3) Hallvarðr háreksblesi: *Knutsdrápa*, str. 7 and 8 (*Skj*. A I 318; B I 294):

Esat und jarðar hǫslu . . . munka valdi mæringr an þú næri.	No famous man under the hazel of the world is closer to the ruler of monks (God) than you.
Knútr verr jǫrð sem ítran alls dróttinn sal fjalla.	Knútr protects his country as the Lord of all (protects) the splendid hall of the mountains (heaven).

(4) Þórarinn loftunga: *Hǫfuðlausn*, *stef* (*Skj*. A I 322; B I 298):

Knútr verr grund sem gætir Grikklands himinríki.	Knútr protects his land as the keeper of Greece (protects) the realm of heaven.

(5) Arnórr Þórðarson jarlaskáld: *Hrynhenda*, str. 19 (*Skj.* A I 337, B I 310):

Eyðendr frák at elska þjóðir	Sure it is that all the people ever,
... grœði lostins goði et næsta	wrecker of the foam-flecked (ships) ...
geima Vals í þessum heimi.	love thee next to God above in heaven.

(Trans. Hollander)

NOTES

[1] I refer to my thesis of 1982, *Det norrøne fyrstediktet*, where I have defined this corpus in detail. I have been criticised for not including poems such as *Ynglingatal* or '*Haraldskvæði*', and though this criticism is not unjustified, the purpose of such exclusions, namely to establish a collection of one genre as homogeneous as possible (cf. Fidjestøl 1982, 179–82), is in the present context an obvious advantage. For the present study I have included nos. 1–95 in the corpus list (Fidjestøl 1982, 170–75). One item has been excluded from it, however, namely '*Øxarflokkr*' by Einarr Skúlason (no. 72). In the original corpus list it was accepted with some doubt (Fidjestøl 1982, 156), and in the present context it can be seen to be too strongly biased, as it more or less amounts to a scaldic exercise in the use of mythological kennings, concentrating on the goddess Freyja.

[2] Most occurrences are proper nouns, but appellatives like *áss* or *regin*, along with kennings for gods, have been included. Names of valkyries are also included, except *hildr* and *gunnr*, which may be common nouns denoting 'war'. Giantesses are not included, partly because it is uncertain to what extent a kenning of the type *trollkvenna byrr* carried heathen connotations. *Gerðr* has been included, however, as an unambiguously mythological figure.

[3] The whole material from my court poetry corpus (cf. note 1) is quoted in the Appendix, with references to Finnur Jónsson's edition (1912–15). Further material from *lausavísur* may be found in Lange 1958, 32. Nos. 1–5 are discussed in Fidjestøl 1991, 117–18, which is an article largely treating similar problems to those in the present article, but concentrating on the heathen period.

[4] It should be noted that *sem goð þengil* is an emendation (by Jón Þorkelsson), accepted by all. The manuscripts have *sem guðs eingill* (Sth. perg. 18, 4to) or *sem guðs þeingils* (AM 557, 4to). Cf. Hofmann 1955, 53.

[5] The argument of *óðal* is also encountered in Sigvatr's stanza on St Óláfr discussed below, and it is a motive in the saga, where the exiled king's duty to recover his *óðal* is presented in a vision as a divine calling (Snorri's *Óláfs saga helga* ch. 188; ÍF XXVII, 340–41).

[6] I think that modern minds often underrate the importance of authority in the acceptance or rejection of a religion and misinterpret its effect as a lack of commitment on the part of the convert. Even St Augustine declared that his belief was dependent on the authority of the church: 'Ich würde dem Evangelium keinen Glauben schenken, wenn mich nicht die Autorität der Kirche dazu bestimmen würde' (quoted from Michael Schmaus, *Die psychologische Trinitätslehre des Hl. Augustinus* (1927), 171).

BIBLIOGRAPHY AND ABBREVIATIONS

Arnold, Thomas (ed.). 1965. *Memorials of St. Edmund's Abbey.* Vol. 1 (Rerum britannicarum medii ævi scriptores 96:1). [Reprint of original edition of 1890]
Christophersen, Axel. 1992. 'Olavskirke, Olavskult og Trondheims tidlige kirketopografi— problem og perspektiver.' In Suphellen, Steinar (ed.). *Kongsmenn og krossmenn. Festskrift til Grethe Authén Blom*, 39–67.
Edwards, Diana C. 1982–83. 'Christian and pagan references in eleventh-century Norse poetry: The case of Arnórr jarlaskáld', *Saga-Book* 21, 34–53.
Faulkes, Anthony (trans.). 1987. Snorri Sturluson. *Edda.*
Fidjestøl, Bjarne. 1975. 'Kongetruskap og gullets makt. Om nokre Bibel-allusjonar hjå Sigvat skald', *Maal og Minne*, 4–11.
Fidjestøl, Bjarne. 1982. *Det norrøne fyrstediktet.*
Fidjestøl, Bjarne. 1991. 'Skaldediktinga og trusskiftet. Med tankar om litterær form som historisk kjelde.' In Steinsland , Gro *et al.* (ed.). *Nordisk hedendom. Et symposium*, 113–31. [Also published in English in *Proceedings of the Seventh Biennal Conference of Teachers of Scandinavian Studies in Great Britain and Northern Ireland 1987*, 58–77]
Finnur Jónsson. 1920. *Den oldnorske og oldislandske litteraturs historie* I. 2nd ed.
Fritzner, Johan. 1886–96. *Ordbog over det gamle norske Sprog* I–III.
Heimskringla. 1941–51. Ed. Bjarni Aðalbjarnarson. ÍF XXVI–XXVIII.
Hoffmann, Erich. 1975. *Die heiligen Könige bei den Angelsachsen und den skandinavischen Völkern. Königsheiliger und Königshaus.*
Hofmann, Dietrich. 1955. *Nordisch–englische Lehnbeziehungen der Wikingerzeit.*
ÍF = *Íslenzk fornrit.* 1933– .
Lange, Wolfgang. 1958. *Studien zur christlichen Dichtung der Nordgermanen 1000–1200.*
LP = Finnur Jónsson. 1931. *Lexicon poeticum antiquæ linguæ septentrionalis. Ordbog over det norsk–islandske skjaldesprog oprindelig forfattet af Sveinbjörn Egilsson.* Revised ed.
Naumann, Hans-Peter. 1986. 'Nordische Kreuzzugsdichtung.' In *Festschrift für Oskar Bandle zum 60. Geburtstag am 11. januar 1986.* Ed. Hans-Peter Naumann (Beiträge zur nordischen Philologie 15), 175–89.
Magerøy, Hallvard. 1948. *Glælognskvida av Toraren Lovtunge.*
Noreen, Erik. 1926. *Den norsk–isländska poesien.*
Paasche, Fredrik. 1914. *Kristendom og kvad. En studie i norrøn middelalder.* [Reprinted in Paasche, Fredrik. 1948. *Hedenskap og kristendom. Studier i norrøn middelalder*]
PL = *Patrologiæ cursus completus. Series Latina.* 1844–64. Ed. J. Migne.
Segelberg, E. 1972. 'God help his soul.' In *Ex Orbe Religionum. Studia Geo Widengren*, 161–76.
Skj. = Finnur Jónsson (ed.). 1912–15. *Den norsk-islandske skjaldedigtning* A I–II ('Tekst efter håndskrifterne'), B I–II ('Rettet tekst'). [Reprinted Copenhagen 1967–73]
Stefán Einarsson. 1936. Review of de Vries 1934 in *Modern Language Notes* 51, 194–95.
Vries, Jan de. 1934. *De skaldenkenningen met mythologischen inhoud.*
Wolf, Alois. 1959. 'Olaf Tryggvason und die Christianisierung des Nordens', *Innsbrucker Beiträge zur Kulturvissenschaft* 6, 9–32.

URSULA DRONKE

PAGAN BELIEFS AND CHRISTIAN IMPACT: THE CONTRIBUTION OF EDDIC STUDIES

TWO Eddic poems are central to the study of pagan and Christian impact in the Norse and Anglo-Celtic world, *Vǫluspá* 'The sibyl's prophecy', and *Rígsþula* 'The rigmarole of Rígr', one a religious, the other a political poem. *Vǫluspá* tells of the cosmic cycle: the birth of the world and the gods is seen to pass into their death, and from that death a fresh world, younger gods, spring. The theological climax of the poem—if I may call it so—is the sacrifice of Baldr. *Rígsþula* tells of the progress of man from Thrall to Earl to King, a progress genetically inspired by a god. I shall concentrate on these two poems.

For *Vǫluspá* we follow the Codex Regius (*c.*1275). Apart from some obvious scribal interference and error, it presents a meticulous text, the closest we shall ever get to that of the original poem. The *Hauksbók* text (*c.*1350) owes its origin to Snorri. He, or a scribe under his direction, altered a text closely similar to that of the Codex Regius, in order to fit certain stanzas where he wanted them in *Gylfaginning*. The variant stanza-sequence in the central section of the poem in the *Hauksbók* text—the most notorious difference from the Codex Regius text (stanzas 21–43)—cannot be shown to have any link with Snorri's interests, but it can be shown to be a distortion of the sequence preserved in the Codex Regius.

Vǫluspá is a unique poem in Norse: unique in its sibylline framework, in its logically ordered sequence of ideas, in its control of sub-themes. In the use of double meaning and hidden meaning it is akin to the subtlest scaldic verse of the tenth century, and the extreme allusiveness of reference to mythological material—material often otherwise unknown to us—indicates an audience deeply versed in pagan legend and, no doubt, fluent in citing it themselves. At the same time there are two pieces of Christian homiletic matter cleverly woven into the poem, the scene of sinners (stanza 39) in the sibyl's vision, plunging through the rivers of death, and the threatening prophecy of the imminent self-destruction of the world through the violence and vice of men: 'Brother will fight brother—they will kill each other' (stanza 44). Neither of these themes of sin have I found in Norse pagan tradition outside *Vǫluspá*.

One could argue that these two Christian motifs represent two interpolations by a Norse Christian poet into a purely pagan *Vǫluspá*, and that it is only by an accident of preservation that we do not have other Norse poems similar to *Vǫluspá*, totally pagan in content. The poetic skills and scope of heathen sibyls might well have developed greatly since 845, when the lady Ota simply 'gave her answers' to a questioning audience at her *séances* on the high altar of Clonmacnoise.

I do not deny these possibilities, but I am led by a few pieces of possible evidence in the text of the poem to argue otherwise. I shall give, first, categorical statements of what I think to be the case, and then attempt to give reasons for them.

Vǫluspá arises from Christian impact on Norse pagan beliefs: without Christianity as an intellectual pace-setter, there would have been no *Vǫluspá* such as we have it. But the poem, though it was designed under Christian intellectual influence, was designed for pagan, not for Christian ends. The poet adapted Christian genres and Christian theological subtleties to give finer articulation to pagan material: to surpass the rough, archaic modes of *Vafþrúðnismál* and *Lokasenna* while preserving their religious inheritance. *Vǫluspá* would originate—I suggest—in the recognition that much of Christian doctrine had its counterpart in Norse: the poet and his circle might be sustained by the conviction that there was no need for a Norseman to adopt Christianity in order to have a religion just as good—a situation adumbrated by Helmut de Boor sixty years ago ('Die religiöse Sprache der Vǫluspá und verwandter Denkmäler', in *Deutsche Islandforschung*, ed. Walther H. Vogt (1930) I, 68–142).

My reasons for these neo-pagan statements lie in the text.

One might suppose that the close of the poem would point to the poem's purpose. Take, for example, stanza 63, the third stanza from the end of the poem. Hœnir probes the future by sacred lottery: he picks out a twig wet with sacrificial blood—a *hlautviðr*. Like a good Norse architect planning a dwelling-place in pagan times, he uses divination to find the most auspicious site (see *Kormáks saga* ch. 2, *Íslenzk fornrit* VIII (1939), 205). Hœnir finds the most suitable site for the dwelling-place of the two sons of the brothers Baldr and Hǫðr to be in the 'wide realm of the winds', that is, in heaven. This is a new location for Norse gods, but one to which the Christian God is well accustomed. We know no son of Hǫðr, but Snorri attributes a son, Forseti, to Baldr. He is a god, we are told in *Grímnismál* stanza 15, 'who puts all dissensions to sleep'. And his dazzling home, Glitnir, roofed with silver and raised on pillars of gold, mirrors the moonlit and sunlit heavens destined for him. Like the Christian God, he will administer justice and peace from above.

But who is Hœnir? Why is the focus upon him here? He is to be identified as the Æsir's high priest of sacrifice, whose task it is to effect all the 'dangerous transitions from death to life', the sacred godfather who sings to awaken life at birth and rebirth. Vedic ritual texts describe very precisely the functions of such a high priest, the 'singer', 'crowing cock', 'bird of the sun', who heralds the dawn (for references and commentary see A. K. Coomaraswamy, 'The sun-kiss', *Journal of the American Oriental Society* LX (1940) 49–51). Hœnir, whose name relates him to the 'crowing cock', gave *óðr* 'the living spirit of the mind' to Askr and Embla, the first twigs of mankind in the old world (*Vǫluspá* stanza 18). In the new world Hœnir presides over the destiny of the sons of the gods who have risen from death and ensures for them life in a limitless heaven. This optimistic close draws upon pagan and Christian concepts.

I suggested that Christian theology had influenced *Vǫluspá*. I would see such influence in the role of Loki in the poem. In *Lokasenna* his role is savage and minatory, played at the front of the stage. In *Vǫluspá* he is in the background, in the shadow of his deeds, until his hostility is open at *Ragnarǫk*. While the gods are still weeping for Baldr's death (stanza 33), the *vǫlva* has a vision of a figure in the underworld, lying in fetters: it is 'recognizable' (*ápekkr*) as that of the malevolent Loki—the one creature who would not weep for Baldr. Why does the poet use this term *ápekkr*? I suggest the term relates to the fact that Loki, when he refused to weep Baldr out of Hel, disguised himself (as a giantess) and called himself Þǫkk, 'Thanks', 'Contented Acceptance'. The *vǫlva*'s term, *ápekkr*, is a play upon Loki's disguise-name, Þǫkk, and upon the fact that he is now no longer disguised, but recognizable. By calling himself Þǫkk, Loki is embodying the 'Thanks', the *Deo gratias* that the Christians give, for the sacrificial death upon which the redemption, the renewal of life after death, depends. Loki has twice committed the *felix culpa* that secures redemption. Baldr had two chances of escaping death, and Loki foiled both of them. He found the mistletoe that could kill him, and he refused to weep him out of Hel. In this Loki is quite unlike the Devil, who sent a dream to Pilate's wife, so that she begged her husband to have 'nothing to do with that just man'. Had she won her plea, Christ would have been uncrucified. In a Carolingian commentary on Matthew 17: 19 (attributed wrongly to Bede: *In Matthaei evangelium expositio*, *Patrologiæ cursus completus. Series Latina*, ed. J. Migne (1844–64), LXXXXII, col. 121) the commentator notes that Satan was terrified that Christ would harrow Hell and make him lose his kingdom of death. On that account he tried to stop the crucifixion, using Pilate's wife as his instrument. Augustine debated anxiously, in considering predestination, what God would have done if Judas had chosen to yield to grace and had refused to betray Christ. God would then have had to find some grace that Judas *would* refuse, so that the crucifixion could take place: it was indispensable.

The elaborate game of Loki and Baldr's death was, I suggest, provoked by this Christian dilemma: the ambiguous trickster Loki becomes almost heroic in his persistence in achieving the necessary death of Baldr—an irony the Norsemen would greatly enjoy. It is sometimes said that the sequence of events in the charade of Baldr's death in *Gylfaginning* is not known from any Norse poem of heathen provenance. This is contradicted by the term *ápekkr*, which refers to the episode of 'Þǫkk the giantess' and by the ambivalent phrasing of *á gengoz eiðar* 'oaths were violated', 'oaths paid for oaths' (stanza 26), where allusion is made to the oaths sworn to spare Baldr, which are effectively cancelled to compensate for the oaths broken in the killing of the giant builder (a structural equivalence no doubt devised by the poet of Vǫluspá). Vǫluspá thus confirms two motifs fundamental to the charade of Baldr's death as related in Gylfaginning: the swearing of oaths to save Baldr from death, and Loki's refusal to weep for him. The charade might well, therefore, be a development of the late heathen period.

I have suggested that Vǫluspá was influenced by Christian genres. The liturgical Cantus Sibyllae, prophesying the end of the world, was introduced into the Church service, in England and elsewhere, from the ninth century onwards, and at least one substantial Latin Sibylline Oracle, the Prophetiae Sibillae Magae, survives from the same period: it is extant in three manuscripts, one of which, dating from the ninth century, can be associated with the area of Tours. The scholarly links between Tours and York were strong: Alcuin of York was abbot of Tours from 794 to 804. It is conceivable that a Latin form of the Sibylline Oracle, as well as that of the Cantus Sibyllae, was known in Anglo-Saxon England.

There are many parallels between Vǫluspá and the Sibylline Oracles, both Latin and Greek, but their more remarkable differences suggest that if the poet of Vǫluspá knew the Christian sibylline mode, s/he remodelled it on the lines of Norse pagan sibylline tradition, in the style of a vǫlva's séance. Nowhere in Latin or Greek sibylline tradition is there an interplay of sibylline voices, as in Vǫluspá, where the vǫlva in the séance—'I'—is informed by a spirit vǫlva—'she'. The Christian sibyl is informed only by God. Nor is the crucifixion of Christ made structurally central to any of the Sibylline Oracles, as the sacrifice of Baldr— blóðogr tívorr—is made central to the structure of Vǫluspá. The vision of the gleaming mistletoe (stanza 31) foretells not only the sacrifice, but the certainty of return. The Sibylline Oracles are more profoundly concerned with the loss of redemption through human sin than with its certainty. By contrast Vǫluspá is an 'Easter poem'.

If any of my suggestions as to the influence Christian thought upon Vǫluspá are at all correct, we have to reckon with a deep absorption of Christian doctrine in a Norse-speaking community, which maintained its own Norse religious traditions in the wider political context of a Christian society.

For Rígsþula the context of composition may not have been very dissimilar from that of Vǫluspá, but there is no evidence whatever of Norse religious partisanship in the poet's behaviour, as there is in Vǫluspá. Rígsþula is a political poem, for which the poet has marshalled only those Norse pagan religious traditions which relate to the structure of society and its politics. He sketches a social history of man and offers a blue-print for ideal kingship.

In order to do this, he employs some of the most archaic material in Indo-European record—to him, no doubt, familiar, old, native stuff—and gives it a modern vitality, that of his own contemporary world. There are the three secular classes, serf, free commoner, nobleman, that we see in the oldest Germanic laws, but they are not presented as a static system which came into being all at the same moment of time, like the Indian classes formed from the cosmic body of Puruṣa, or the Biblical classes from the sons of Noah. In *Rígsþula* the three classes are seen as an evolving family: upon Thrall's ardent, and arduous, labour the prosperity of Churl is based, and upon Churl's prosperity the power of Earl is based. Neither Churl nor Earl is begotten before the class that precedes him has been established. There is a certain economic realism in this, for wealth is based on labour, and rank follows wealth. In Anglo-Danish laws of the early eleventh century it was provided that a *ceorl* could attain the rank of *þegn* if he possessed five hides of land, or a merchant if he made three profitable voyages. The progress of man in *Rígsþula* would seem to reflect just such a society of 'upward social mobility' (for vivid discussion and ample reference see W. G. Runciman, 'Accelerating social mobility: the case of Anglo-Saxon England', *Past and present* CIV (1984) 3–30). Alongside this modernity the poet has maintained the archaic tradition of class colour-symbolism, black for the serf, red for the warrior-farmer, white for the priest-king (see G. Dumézil, 'La Rígsþula et la structure sociale indo-européenne', *Revue de l'histoire des religions* CLIV (1958) 1–9). The poet has not, however, related the symbolic colour to the garments or other trappings of the serf or farmer or aristocrat, as is usual in other records; he has depicted it in the pigmentation of the babies, the first Thrall being black-skinned, the first Churl being ruddy-cheeked and red-haired, the first Earl being shiningly fair. The poet has made these complexions seem naturalistic, in accord with the life each class will lead— muddy or muscular or *sportif*—but that the three-colour schema for the babies was itself older than the poem is shown by the fact that the other motifs in the descriptions of the babies—their different eyes, their swaddling bands—have had to be developed by the poet himself in a tripartite schema for which there is no traditional evidence: only Earl's eyes have ancient authority behind them.

The poet's plan is to show the king as the crown of the three human estates. To this end, he combines two ancient Norse myths, a myth of Heimdallr and a myth of Óðinn. Heimdallr is progenitor of all mankind in its different estates (*Vǫluspá* stanza 1; *Hyndlolióð* stanza 43). His teaching is of procreation. Óðinn is ancestor and patron only of aristocratic houses, of earls and kings (*Hárbarðslióð* stanza 24; *Háleygjatal*). By this conjunction of Heimdallr and Óðinn the poet can make all men 'sons of God' and give to one man only—the highest—'the divine authority to rule'.

For his progenitor god the poet adopts the exotic name *Rígr*, the Irish term for 'king'. The name points to the poem's climax, the establishment of the first king in the Norse world. In his name the union of human and divine will be explicit. Though *Rígr* ensures the conception of the archetypal babies of all three classes, he only acknowledges as son, and gives his name to, one, and that is Earl. He appears to him, teaches him runes, names him *Rígr* and sends him to conquer lands by war. *Rígr iarl*, however, is not the ultimate king. He is outclassed by his youngest son, whose name, *Konr ungr* 'Young Noblekin', foreshadows the future title *konungr*. *Konr ungr* defeats *Rígr iarl* in runic contest and wins from him, as a rightful inheritance, the name of *Rígr*. He now has two royal names, one by human baptism as a scion of noble blood—the Germanic peoples took their kings from the nobility, Tacitus tells us (*Germania* ch. 7)—and one by divine gift: *Rígr Konr ungr*. By so lucidly presenting the *persona geminata* of the ideal king, the poet of *Rígsþula* associates himself with the political ideals of kingship of the tenth and eleventh centuries in the Ottonian courts, Anglo-Saxon England, and Normandy (see E. H. Kantorowicz, *The king's two bodies: a study in mediaeval political theology* (1957), 60–61; C. Carozzi in *Adalbéron de Laon: poème au Roi Robert. Introduction, édition et traduction* (1979), cxix–cxxx).

I have boldly spoken of *Rígr Konr ungr* as the 'crown of the three estates', the 'ideal king' with whom the poem culminates. But this is, of course, a reconstruction, because the end of the poem is lost. The last extant stanza contains part of the speech of an irate crow, who is urging *Konr ungr* to feel envy for the rich Vikings *Danr* and *Danpr*. She hopes, no doubt, that he will take up arms against them and win their lands, that he will follow in the footsteps of his father, *Rígr iarl*.

Snorri Sturluson and Arngrímur Jónsson preserve versions of a Danish legendary genealogy which contain the names *Danr* and *Danpr* and *Rígr* and no doubt relate to the lost ending of *Rígsþula* (see *Ynglinga saga* ch. 17, *Íslenzk fornrit* XXVI (1941), 34–35, where Arngrímur's version is summarized in the notes). Snorri adds that *Rígr* 'was the first to be called *konungr* in the Norse tongue (*á danska tungu*)' and names *Rígr*'s son as *Danpr konungr*. Snorri does not say whom *Rígr* married. Arngrímur gives *Dana* as the name of *Rígr*'s wife, daughter of *Danpr*.

In the light of these two texts, and of the character of Konr ungr portrayed in *Rígsþula*, I would suggest that Konr ungr rejects the crow's warlike plans for attacking Danr and Danpr. However, when she mentions that Danpr has a wise and lovely daughter, Dana, his interest is stirred. Following in his grandfather's footsteps, he approaches Dana's home—where the doors will be wide open—and wins her hand by *ráð* more courtly than that of the archaic old god. Behind this romantic finale lies the pattern of a myth. Rígr Konr ungr creates the first kingdom for himself by exogamy: he weds Denmark as Óðinn wedded Jǫrð. But he brings with him, with the new title, 'King', a cultural revolution. He is not a swashbuckling Viking: he knows the runes of life—*ævinrúnar ok aldrrúnar*—for saving men and blunting swords (stanza 43). He is a giant with the strength of eight men, but he only fights with the power of his mind. Compounded of age-old Norse fictions,

Rígr Konr ungr introduces the modern image of Christ-centred kingship (Kantorowicz, op. cit. ch. 3) to the North.

The evidence of Christian impact upon pagan Norse beliefs in the Eddic verse of *Vǫluspá* and *Rígsþula* is very considerable. The experience of acquaintance with Christian society and religion stimulated a reappraisal of native intellectual ideals on the part of Norsemen and their poets. With their own materials they made their own versions of what they learned from their Christian neighbours. While they were learning, they were also practising, steadily, subtly and flexibly, their own poetic arts. Only these circumstances can, I suggest, explain the depth and brilliance of the poems.

NOTE

These brief pages are drawn from written work on *Vǫluspá* and *Rígsþula* already in press for *The Poetic Edda*, vol. II. I have not, therefore, reproduced here the full documentation. Relevant documentation already published will be found in 'Vǫluspá and sibylline traditions', in *Latin Culture and Medieval Germanic Europe. Proceedings of the First Germania Latina Conference held at the University of Groningen, 26 May 1989* (1992), 3–23, and in 'Eddic poetry as a source for the history of Germanic religion', in *Germanische Religionsgeschichte. Quellen und Quellenprobleme.* Ed. Heinrich Beck, Detlev Ellmers and Kurt Schier (1992), 656–84. References to poems of the Elder Edda are to the edition of Hans Kuhn, *Edda. Die Lieder des Codex Regius nebst verwandten Denkmälern* I, 1962.

ELSE ROESDAHL

PAGAN BELIEFS, CHRISTIAN IMPACT AND ARCHAEOLOGY—A DANISH VIEW

SINCE the manuscripts and the great editions of the Eddas became available to the learned world much thought has been given to pagan Scandinavian beliefs. The dramas of pagan mythology have long fascinated both Scandinavia and the rest of Europe, and for some time—especially during the nineteenth century—the pagan pantheon even produced subjects for great painters.

But historical painting of gods and Vikings, sadly, came to an end, partly because of the development of archaeology as an academic discipline during the second half of the nineteenth century. There were many great discoveries such as the Mammen grave in 1868 and the boat-burials of Gokstad and Oseberg in 1880 and 1904. Contemporary artefacts could now be identified and shown in museums, and painters were much criticized for not being exact in every detail.

Around the turn of the century, however, there seems often to have been a happy relationship between archaeologists dealing with the remains of the late pagan period (graves, pagan symbols, iconography etc.) and Old Norse philologists. Archaeologists, such as Oscar Almgren in 1904, seriously investigated the possibility of interpreting their material (burial-customs for example) against the background of a competent knowledge of Old Norse literature. But as time went on, archaeology became much more concerned with description, typology, dating, function, possible international connections, and, much later, with society, than with religious interpretation. This was partly a result of source-criticism of Old Norse and other medieval texts by the Weibull brothers and others in the early twentieth century, though this criticism was mainly concerned with matters relating to the political history of the Northern countries. A serious blow to the use of Old Norse sources for archaeological interpretation came in 1966 with Olaf Olsen's thesis *Hørg, hov og kirke*. Further, prehistoric archaeologists in Scandinavia who dealt with artefacts of the Viking period generally had very little familiarity with written sources. Anxious to escape criticism, they avoided Old Norse literature; links with philology were broken.

Although this is a reasonably fair general description of the situation in Scandinavia, there were, of course, exceptions. After the inception of the Viking Congresses in 1949, archaeologists at them came to realize that written material might conceivably be useful in the interpretation of archaeological material. Gradually other disciplines in their turn discovered that archaeology could sometimes be helpful to them, not least in relation to such matters as the problems of pagan belief and the conversion.

But on the whole there was little interest in archaeology on the part of students outside this select band, save that nice objects—such as the ferocious animal-head posts from the Oseberg grave, the figure of Freyr from Rällinge, indeed any grave with rich furnishings—were deemed useful illustrations with which to enliven articles and books. There was little effort to co-operate with archaeologists to use material culture as a source for a better understanding of Scandinavian paganism. And paganism, of course, continued to fascinate both the lay and the learned world.

One of the interesting points about archaeological material is that it is contemporary, that more of it is discovered day by day, and that it can be seen and touched. Objects and monuments can be investigated. They are 'real'. But for our purposes they must also 'talk'. They must be described and dated, and then interpreted in relation to our individual studies. And as with written texts they are often susceptible to varied interpretations. The scholar who tries to marry archaeological material to written sources (be they contemporary European, or later Norse or Danish) often gets into trouble, because the texts were written for purposes other than description and explanation of material expressions of pagan beliefs. Hard work in trying to understand each other is necessary before a happy union between archaeology and other disciplines can be brought about and a better understanding of pagan beliefs achieved.

Recent years, however, have seen a great growth in interdisciplinary and international co-operation, both inside and outside formal frameworks. This has opened the eyes of archaeologists and, so it seems, of scholars in some other disciplines to the advantages of using each other's results—and, more importantly, of speaking and working together too (e.g. Steinsland 1986; Sawyer, Sawyer and Wood 1987; Iversen 1991; Steinsland, Drobin, Pentikäinen and Meulengracht Sørensen 1991; Nilsson 1992). This has, for archaeology, resulted in a move towards broader contextual interpretation as a supplement to the usual archaeological methods of describing and dating, finding parallels and plotting distribution patterns.

Much recent work on Scandinavian archaeological material concerned with dating, distribution patterns and cultural identity has also produced a more solid basis on which scholars in different disciplines can work together on pagan beliefs and the conversion. Perhaps the most important innovation has been the use of dendrochronology by which one can date the exact felling-year of a piece of timber used in a construction. One of the most significant dates provided by this method concerns the burial-chamber in the north mound in Jelling: it was, with a high degree of probability, closed in the year 958–59 (Christensen and Krogh 1987). It was undoubtedly here that the last pagan king of Denmark, Gorm, was buried with splendid grave-goods in Denmark's largest burial-mound, following pagan burial-customs. He was buried only a few years before Denmark was declared Christian (which was in about the year 965) by his son, the man who must have been responsible for the pagan burial, and who made Jelling into an enormous dynastic and religious monument park, a true conversion-period monument park. I shall return to Jelling—as this exact year (958–59) provided by dendrochronology gives ample opportunity to investigate very late paganism and very early Christianity in the precise milieu in which decisions were taken. Likewise, other exact dendrochronological dates—such as the dating of the Mammen grave to 970–71 (Andersen 1991), and the dating of Trelleborg and Fyrkat, and their cemeteries, to c.980 (Bonde and Christensen 1982; Christensen and Bonde 1991)—provide totally new possibilities for the understanding of the process of Christianization in Denmark (cf. Roesdahl 1982, 171–83; 1991, 298–300).

Dendrochronology has so far been mainly applied to Viking-Age material in Denmark and south Scandinavia, where oak was abundant. But work in the dendrochronological laboratory at the Danish National Museum has provided dates for some of the main Norwegian royal or aristocratic pagan burials: Oseberg (834), Gokstad and Tune (both c.900–05; Bonde, forthcoming). This is of the utmost interest for students of pagan beliefs, and indeed for nearly all Viking studies.

Normal archaeological work on graves and grave-monuments, which together with symbolic objects such as the Thor's hammers and other miniature tools are the main archaeological sources for paganism, have also resulted in a much better chronological framework for the various types of graves. We can now to some extent trace the development of burial-customs. The seemingly enormous mixture and variation in Scandinavian Viking-Age burial-customs begin to make sense when it is realized that certain burial-types mainly belong to particular regions within Scandinavia and differ from those found elsewhere and at other times. Pagan burials were not the same throughout Scandinavia, nor were they the same throughout the Viking Age, nor did they apply to all strata of society. This is hardly surprising, considering the length of the Viking Age, the enormous extent of Scandinavia and the great social differences within the whole area and period.

Moreover, in interpreting their material, archaeologists have become much more aware that the various Scandinavian regions had different external connections and were influenced by different parts of the world. Norway mainly looked west (and south), Denmark mainly looked south (and west)—and central Sweden turned mainly to the east. This is attested by all manner of archaeological material, including imported objects themselves (e.g. *From Viking to Crusader* 1992, cat. nos. 119–43). We should, therefore, remember that objects and ideas often travel together. The archaeological material of Viking central Sweden is, for example, oriented very much to the east—as has recently been emphasized by the fascinating excavations in Sigtuna (Tesch 1990). Here much eastern European material has been found, including objects from the Kiev region and from the Mediterranean, finds which include such religious symbols as the so-called resurrection eggs from the Kiev region (glazed clay eggs) and pendant crosses of Byzantine type.

PAGAN BELIEFS, CHRISTIAN IMPACT AND ARCHAEOLOGY

Because of these chronological and regional variations, it would be preferable first to apply information from West Norse literature to archaeological material in west and south Scandinavia and vice versa, and not so generally to central Swedish material, although such comparisons may be tempting as the material culture there is so rich and generally the best known to scholars of other disciplines. This is especially true of the Birka material. But many of the ideas present in Viking-Age Birka may well have been semi-Russian, as were the dress and ornaments of some of the people buried there (Hägg 1983).

After this introduction I shall present some selected archaeologically-based topics, the problems of which will only be solved, or fully illuminated, if scholars from more than one discipline work on them—and work *together* on them. The problems raised by modern archaeology in relation to pagan belief and Christian impact nearly always require interdisciplinary co-operation.

Is it possible to relate concepts of death and after-life known from West Norse or Danish sources to certain burial-customs?

Viking-Age burial-customs in Scandinavia are manifold, as are the concepts of death in the written sources. But one male burial-rite, the horsemen's graves of the early to mid-tenth century (the late pagan period), stands out. Such graves are especially well known in Denmark, but also occur in Norway, Iceland and Sweden. These are clearly upper-class graves, often laid down in timbered burial-chambers, the man accompanied by standard grave-goods consisting of riding-equipment (horse, harness, stirrups, spurs), weapons (sword and spear, sometimes an axe, but rarely bow and arrow, which were not upper-class weapons), items of leisure (such as gaming-boards and hunting-dogs), food in containers and various small necessities such as a knife and whetstone. No mail-coat or helmet is known in Denmark; indeed they are only found in one Viking-Age grave at Gjermundbu in southern Norway.

This burial-type is so stereotyped that it probably relates to a distinct social stratum and to specific religious beliefs about an after-life. Could it be that this was related to the idea that dead heroes go to Odin's Valhalla? They would need travel on horse, with food for the journey and the right equipment for the sort of life they would live there, a life of fighting and feasting (mail-coat and helmet being unnecessary and therefore not put in the grave?). In the grand ship-burials, like the Gokstad burial, the ship may have been thought a necessary means of transport for some of the way—it was to a large extent the obvious means of transport for the great chieftains of Viking-Age Scandinavia (Ellmers 1980; Roesdahl 1983; Steinsland 1990a; Näsman 1991).

I can note in passing that the wives of these men also had splendid and stereotyped burials, with waggon-bodies as coffins and fine grave-goods. Very little is known from Old Norse sources about the kind of after-life women were assumed to have had, but judging from the graves it seems to have been comfortable and to have included means of travel—hence the waggon body instead of a whole waggon (e.g. Roesdahl 1982, 169–70; Müller-Wille 1985; Steinsland 1990b).

Was there a late pagan revival just before the introduction of Christianity?

The grandest of the Danish horsemen's burials was probably in the north mound in Jelling and this must have been the grave of King Gorm, the last pagan king of Denmark. As mentioned above, the burial-chamber was almost certainly closed in 958 or 959, that is a maximum of seven years before Denmark was declared a Christian country (according mainly to the Saxon chronicler Widukind). There have been suggestions that this was a Christian burial, partly because of the small silver cup from the chamber, interpreted by some as a Christian chalice (most recently by Capelle 1986), but more convincingly explained as a cup for a rather strong alcoholic drink, *beor* (Fell 1975).

In my opinion there can be no doubt that this burial is pagan, and that the king, Gorm, was buried with splendid pagan ceremony by his son King Harald. Moreover it was very pagan. There is a mound (the biggest in Denmark), there were splendid grave-goods of the sort known from the horsemen's graves, but more of them and of better quality (though little is preserved). The burial is on a royal scale and is clearly a dynastic monument. It is probably also an expression of a late pagan religious and cultural revival, feeding on ancient religious concepts and ancient monument-types and—very interestingly—built at the very same time as the composition of the grand scaldic poems about Valhalla and dead Viking kings in Norway and England, *Eiríksmál* and *Hákonarmál*, *c.*955–65 (Krogh 1983; Roesdahl 1992). The idea of a pagan revival in the last days of paganism has recently been put forward by Gro Steinsland (1990c; 1991a) on a different basis. The burial in the north mound at Jelling seems to support her idea. It is best understood in such a light, and it seems to throw some illumination on two famous poems.

Many attempts have been made to identify pagan cult-places. Recent archaeological excavations have added to the discussion about them. At Borg on Vestvågøy, Lofoten, excavation by Tromsø Museum and University have revealed a chieftain's residence of the eighth–ninth century. Here there were imports from western Europe and the British Isles such as glass vessels, Rhenish pottery and jet jewellery, as well as some gold and silver. Borg was clearly the seat of some local aristocrat, a man like, for example, the roughly contemporary Ohthere from Hålogaland who visited King Alfred of Wessex about 890.

The house at Borg was 83 metres long—the longest Viking-Age building known in Scandinavia. It contained byres and store-rooms, but one room must have been the hall, about 14 metres long and 112 square metres in area. There were unusual fireplaces in the hall. From probably one single posthole came five *guldgubber* (each with a picture of a man and woman embracing each other), which clearly have some religious significance (Stamsø Munch 1991). Steinsland suggests (1990b; 1991b) that they may represent ideas of pagan rulers, the myth of holy marriage between god and giantess whence Norwegian pagan rulers traced their ancestry.

Such an interpretation stresses the importance of the hall at Borg in relation to pagandom. This was probably the very hall where the local aristocrat, the Borg chieftain, celebrated the cult of the region along lines described by Snorri Sturluson (Stamsø Munch 1991; cf. Meulengracht Sørensen 1991). The hall excavated at Borg and the objects found there certainly raise many questions and the evidence has been presented at interdisciplinary symposia; the Borg publication will contain contributions on this topic from scholars of various disciplines.

Recent excavations at Lejre (a place mentioned by Thietmar of Merseburg as a pagan Danish cult-centre, and known from scaldic poetry and histories as an ancient Danish royal seat) have examined a new area. Important archaeological monuments, such as a long ship-setting and rich treasures, have long been known from Lejre, but now an enormous hall has been excavated, 48 metres long and up to 11 metres wide, covering some 500 square metres. It is the largest Viking-Age house known, truly a royal hall. Nothing of religious significance was found during these excavations, but many good quality artefacts were (Christensen 1991). And the existence of this unique building at Lejre, of all places, adds weight to the idea of Lejre as an important cult-centre, with close connections with the king. It is possible that full-scale reconstruction of this hall of all halls will be built by the architect Holger Schmidt.

My last examples of archaeological finds related to pagan cults comprise some small metal human heads with horned head-gear of eighth-century date found in Ribe in connection with the seasonal market (there are parallels in Staraja Ladoga, in Uppland and in south-east England). The Ribe examples are particularly interesting, for not only do we have several examples, we also have moulds in which such objects were cast. The Ribe craftsmen obviously mass-produced them. Was this because pagan cult-ceremonies took place during the market season when many people met? (Jensen 1992, 30–34, 50–51; *From Viking to Crusader* 1992, cat. no. 184.)

The problem of possible cult-continuity at the same place from pagan to Christian times was discussed for many years. After the publication of Olaf Olsen's thesis in 1966, however, the matter seemed closed, at least as far as Denmark was concerned. No traces had been found of paganism under medieval churches, and many had been excavated. Churches were not built on top of ancient cult-sites.

Nowadays the picture is not so simple, for the first churches are unlikely to have been placed exactly where the later (still standing) churches were built.

The early churches were undoubtedly built close to the more important farms and villages of their time, but large-scale excavations have now shown that Viking-Age and earlier villages often moved later on, as for example Vorbasse did (Hvass 1984; cf. Roesdahl 1991b, 97–101; *From Viking to Crusader* 1992, 131–33). The earliest churches would be found with villages or farms on their sites in the Conversion period (although none was found in Vorbasse), not in present-day settlements which sometimes go back only to the eleventh or twelfth century. The medieval village might include a church which survives to the present day even if the settlement moved. It has also been shown by excavation that the church site might move too, even if the church remained connected with the original settlement. This means that excavation in existing churches cannot greatly illuminate the problem of cult-continuity (cf. Gräslund 1992).

There are, of course, many other problems concerning pagan beliefs and the gradual introduction of Christianity which can be illuminated by archaeology with interdisciplinary co-operation. One such is the study of changing burial-customs and the establishment of Christian cemeteries and churches during the Conversion period—this has already proved a fruitful area of study and is increasingly being researched (e.g. Roesdahl 1982, 164–83; Gräslund 1991; Jeppesen and Madsen 1991; Näsman 1991; *META* 1992:1–2; Birkedahl and Johansen 1993; also Nielsen 1991, though this work must be used with some care as it contains a number of strange and controversial views). The same is true of syncretism. Awareness of the regional and political variations within Scandinavia is of the utmost importance in this context. In Denmark, for example, there seems to have been a relatively peaceful transition from paganism to Christianity; the Jelling monuments seem to indicate such a policy. Pagan and Christian monuments are side by side. The pagan king Gorm was translated from the burial-mound to a grave in the Christian church which was built between the mounds, where Gorm himself was excavated by Knud Krogh. It has also been demonstrated (using dendrochronological dating) that much of the enormous south mound was constructed after the conversion; it was not finished before the 970s though the ideas connected with mounds must have been basically pagan (Krogh 1983; Christensen and Krogh 1987).

Archaeological sources, supported by written ones, also point increasingly to the tenth and eleventh centuries (the conversion period in Scandinavia) as a period of general turmoil and development, political, social, and artistic. This was the period of many new towns, a new economy (gone was eastern silver), intense international connections (in many directions and on many levels), new ideas of kingship, new artistic ideals, and, we may be sure, social change. This was the period of Scandinavian conversion and probably gives the general background to it. Society was on the move. For archaeological studies in the fields of pagan beliefs and the Christian impact on the North the future, as I see it, lies partly in serious interdisciplinary work and partly in studying the Scandinavian phenomena in a wider context. We might for example consider the near-contemporary conversion of Poland in 966, of Hungary in 975 and of Russia in 988. Not least interesting is the Russian situation, as the burial-customs there (as well as the upper classes themselves) were deeply influenced by Scandinavia, just as central Sweden was influenced by Russia. The earlier conversions of other European countries are also of interest; many similar mechanisms seem to have been at work during their conversions even if the chronology is not the same. The introduction of Christianity often seems to have activated parallel expressions and reactions.

BIBLIOGRAPHY

Almgren, Oscar. 1904. 'Vikingatidens grafskick i verkligheten och i den fornnordiska litteraturen'. In *Nordiska Studier tillegnade Adolf Noreen*, 309–46.
Andersen, Harald. 1991. 'Dendrokronologisk datering af Mammengraven'. In *Mammen. Grav, kunst og samfund i vikingetid*. Ed. M. Iversen, 43–44.
Birkedahl, Peter and Johansen, Erik. 1993. 'Nikolajbjerget', *Skalk* 1993, 3–8.
Bonde, Niels. Forthcoming. Article in *Antiquity*.
Bonde, Niels and Christensen, Kjeld. 1982. 'Trelleborgs alder. Dendrokronologisk datering', *Aarbøger for nordisk Oldkyndighed og Historie*, 111–52.
Capelle, Torsten. 1986. 'Zum Silberkelch von Jelling', *Acta Archaeologica* 55 (1984), 199–200.
Christensen, Tom. 1991. *Lejre—syn og sagn*.
Christensen, Kjeld and Bonde, Niels. 1991. 'Dateringen af Trelleborg—en kommentar', *Aarbøger for nordisk Oldkyndighed og Historie*, 231–33.
Christensen, Kjeld and Krogh, Knud J. 1987. 'Jelling-højene dateret', *Nationalmuseets Arbejdsmark*, 223–31.
Ellmers, Ditlev. 1980. 'Fränkisches Königszeremoniell auch in Walhall', *Beiträge zur Schleswiger Stadtgeschichte* 25, 115–26.
Fell, Christine. 1975. 'Old English *beor*', *Leeds Studies in English*. New Series VIII, 76–95.
From Viking to Crusader. Scandinavia and Europe 800–1200. 1992. Ed. Else Roesdahl and David M. Wilson. [Scandinavian ed.: *Viking og Hvidekrist. Norden og Europa 800–1200.* 1992. Ed. Else Roesdahl.]
Gräslund, Anne-Sofie. 1991. 'Var Mammen-mannen kristen?'. In *Mammen. Grav, kunst og samfund i vikingetid*. Ed. Mette Iversen, 205–10.
Gräslund, Anne-Sofie. 1992. 'Kultkontinuitet—myt eller verklighet? Om arkeologins möjligheter att belysa problemet'. In *Kontinuitet i kult och tro*. Ed. Bertil Nilsson, 129–50.
Hägg, Inga. 1983. 'Birkas orientaliska praktplagg', *Fornvännen* 78, 204–23.
Hvass, Steen. 1984. 'Wikingerzeitliche Siedlungen in Vorbasse', *Offa* 41, 97–112.
Iversen, Mette (ed.). 1991. *Mammen. Grav, kunst og samfund i vikingetid*.
Jensen, Stig. 1992. *Ribes vikinger*. [Also English ed. 1992]

Jeppesen, Jens and Madsen, Hans Jørgen. 1991. 'Storgård og kirke i Lisbjerg'. In *Fra Stamme til Stat i Danmark* 2. *Høvdingesamfund og Kongemagt*. Ed. Peder Mortensen and Birgit Rasmussen, 269–75.

Krogh, Knud J. 1983. 'The Royal Viking-Age Monuments at Jelling', *Acta Archaeologica* 53 (1982), 183–216.

META. Medeltidsarkeologisk Tidskrift. 1992:1–2.

Meulengracht Sørensen, Preben. 1991. 'Håkon den Gode og guderne. Nogle bemærkninger om religion og centralmagt'. In *Fra Stamme til Stat i Danmark* 2, *Høvdingesamfund og Kongemagt*. Ed. Peder Mortensen and Birgit Rasmussen, 235–44.

Müller-Wille, Michael. 1985. 'Frühmittelalterliche Bestattungen in Wagen und Wagenkasten'. In *Archaeology and Environment* 4, *In honorem Evert Baudou*, 17–30.

Nielsen, Leif Chr. 1991. 'Hedenskab og kristendom. Religionsskiftet afspejlet i vikingetidens grave'. In *Fra Stamme til Stat i Danmark* 2. *Høvdingesamfund og Kongemagt*. Ed. Peder Mortensen and Birgit Rasmussen, 245–67.

Nilsson, Bertil (ed.). 1992. *Kontinuitet i kult och tro från vikingatid till medeltid*.

Näsman, Ulf. 1991.'Grav og økse. Mammen og den danske vikingetids våbengrave'. In *Mammen. Grav, kunst og samfund i vikingetid*. Ed. Mette Iversen, 163–80.

Olsen, Olaf. 1966. *Hørg, hov og kirke*.

Roesdahl, Else. 1982. *Viking Age Denmark*. [Danish ed.: *Danmarks vikingetid*. 1980.]

Roesdahl, Else. 1983. 'Fra vikingegrav til Valhal'. In *Beretning fra Andet tværfaglige Vikingesymposium*. Ed. T. Kisbye et al., 39–49.

Roesdahl, Else. 1991a. 'Nordisk førkristen religion. Om kilder og metoder'. In *Nordisk Hedendom*. Ed. Gro Steinsland et al., 293–301.

Roesdahl, Else. 1991b. *The Vikings*. [Paperback 1992; Danish ed.: *Vikingernes verden*. 1987.]

Roesdahl, Else. 1992. 'Princely Burial in Scandinavia at the Time of the Conversion'. In *Voyage to the Other World. The Legacy of Sutton Hoo*. Ed. C. Kendall and P. Wells, 155–70.

Sawyer, Birgit, Sawyer, Peter and Wood, Ian (ed.). 1987. *The Christianization of Scandinavia*.

Stamsø Munch, Gerd. 1991. 'Hus og hall. En høvdinggård på Lofoten'. In *Nordisk Hedendom*. Ed. Gro Steinsland et al., 321–33.

Steinsland, Gro (ed.). 1986. *Words and Objects. Towards a Dialogue Between Archaeology and History of Religion*.

Steinsland, Gro. 1990a. 'Antropologiske og eskatologiske ideer i førkristen nordisk religion', *Collegium Medievale* 3, 59–72.

Steinsland, Gro. 1990b. 'De nordiske guldblekk med parmotiv og norrøn fyrsteideologi', *Collegium Medievale* 3, 73–94.

Steinsland, Gro. 1990c. 'The change of religion in the Nordic countries—a confrontation between two living religions', *Collegium Medievale* 3, 123–35.

Steinsland, Gro. 1991a. 'Religionsskiftet i Norden og Vǫluspá 65'. In *Nordisk Hedendom*. Ed. Gro Steinsland et al., 335–48.

Steinsland, Gro. 1991b. *Det hellige bryllup og norrøn kongeideologi*.

Steinsland, Gro, Drobin, Ulf, Pentikäinen, Juha and Meulengracht Sørensen, Preben (ed.). 1991. *Nordisk Hedendom. Et symposium*.

Tesch, Sten (ed.). 1990. *Makt och människor i kungens Sigtuna. Sigtunautgrävningen 1988–90*.

PETER FOOTE

HISTORICAL STUDIES: CONVERSION MOMENT AND CONVERSION PERIOD

THERE is, I regret to say, an element of fraud in this short paper, which is supposed to discuss the contribution of historical studies to the theme of the current session. I am not a historian; and it may well be that the questions I would ask of a historian are not those a historian would ask of himself. Indeed, I have a further suspicion that I may be talking not so much about the contribution of historians as about their lack of contribution. That doubtless results from my particular bias, for my curiosity is chiefly roused by that obscure interim period between the time of official conversion and the age of Church consolidation, especially at the Icelandic 'interface', to use a modish term. To my mind, what we need above all is a clearer understanding of the ambience in which genuine pagan poetry, for instance, and whatever went with it, could survive.

I have to be brief and will generalise cheerfully at the same time as I select wilfully. But this is a symposium, a party, in which hearty overstatements, likely to provoke rejoinder, should be the order of the day.

Mainstream historians generally agree, overtly or not, on distinguishing between a gradual process of conversion and a decisive conversion 'moment'. That occurred when a king or other public authority decreed that henceforth the population should depend on Christian rites alone for their peace and prosperity and for whatever else they looked for from divine aid. The 'moment' might be followed by a period of challenge and balance—it seems to have been long drawn out in eleventh-century Sweden—but the decisive step had been taken. Before the 'moment' there was obviously a period, longer or shorter, of growing familiarity with Christian imagery, notions and claims, and after it a period of gradual Christian consolidation. For practical purposes we can take the establishment of the metropolitan sees as marking the terminus of that transition period, in Denmark just after 1100, in Norway just after 1150, and in Sweden ten years or so later. It had taken about 150 years in each case, say five or six generations. The foundations of these national archbishoprics did not mean that the conversion process was at an end, but by then a sufficient ecclesiastical network for the cure of souls existed and could be extended. And in our secular world many historians, often inheritors of the anti-clerical attitudes of eighteenth-century rationalists and nineteenth-century liberals, tend to forget that cure of souls was what the new dispensation was fundamentally about.

By and large, mainstream historians have been more interested in the conversion 'moment', where we have at least some sources to dissect and discuss, than in the conversion process as a whole, where we must mostly work by inference and analogy; and they frequently prefer to analyse the sources and read the events in terms of power politics, kingship and commerce. Beliefs and cult practices, continuity and change, at the public level may receive some attention, but the extent and nature of the grasp that Christianity finally had on men's minds is largely neglected. A recent survey of early Norwegian history by Knut Helle, as we should expect a brilliant conspectus in many ways, pays heed, for example, to church organisation and to the alliance of hierarchy and monarchy in establishing the concept and imagery of kingship in Norway. But I find nothing in it on the adjustment of external attitudes, personal and communal, that followed the conversion 'moment', and the subsequent assimilation of Christian ideas—in ethical outlook, perspectives of the past and the future (matters on which Christian thinking has always been keen to let you know where you stand), and the part these played in changing social arrangements—marriage and slavery come to mind—and perhaps even in the 'emergence of the individual'. Neither the impact of Christianity on the idiom of language and the idiom of thought, nor its impact on the rhythm of life—for with Christian observance the day, the week and the year were all different from before—appear to be counted among *grunntrekk* of Norwegian medieval history. Which seems to me a pity, and different from fifty and more years ago when Sigrid Undset and Fredrik Paasche were not afraid of engaging with such matters, though not perhaps as critically as one could wish. In his time Arne Odd Johnsen tried something similar, but rather less effectively, for his large claims are often supported by untrustworthy detail. But whatever their defects, these authors and their topics should not be consigned to limbo—and that is an idiom with a good Christian history.

I naturally endorse such a broad and systematic programme of research desiderata as Birkeli (1982) has sketched for our field of study, but I would be content to ask historians for answers to much more limited questions. What can you tell us of the mingling of past and present, of pagan and Christian, in men's minds in the late tenth and through the eleventh century? What sort of syncretism existed? Where can it be reliably detected? In tackling such problems, those of us who have read a bit will naturally think first of looking to the poets and to the later entanglements of saga narrative in which much of their verse is preserved. We might do more to examine the circumstances of scalds and their wider circles— were there scaldic schools, as Dag Strömbäck once wondered? How do we account for the preservation of the stuff that appears to be authentically antique? Most people's ideas about such matters, including my own, I hasten to add, seem to remain quite inchoate. I shall come back to sagas.

Neither scaldic poetry nor sagas of any kind are much referred to by historians nowadays. In *The Christianization of Scandinavia*, for instance, papers published in 1987, edited by the Sawyers and Ian Wood, there is the odd reference to tenth-century poetry and cursory reference to Ari, Gunnlaugr (but not Oddr), *Hungrvaka*, and one or two other texts. *Heimskringla* is cited a little more frequently, but it is hard to see what sort of criticism has gone into it all. A reader would certainly like to know when Snorri is at one with his predecessors and when he differs from them; and what sort of authority the modern historian imputes to Snorri when he is alone in his information and interpretation, and why. Some mainstream historians, allegedly expert in sifting sources, show singularly little interest in the findings of literary historians.

Sources—what sources? Alongside the early verse, there is another class of texts whose status has long been politely acknowledged, but which have still not yet been fully exploited. I mean the corpus of so-called Christian laws from Norway and Iceland. In many cases their articles demonstrably belong to a comparatively early stage in the consolidation of the Christian dispensation, and certainly before Gratian and the elaboration of the study of canon law that the *Decretum* brought about. It has been encouraging to see Swedish scholars in the field of Church history making a new attack on restricted topics, where they bring in all kinds of evidence but have a fresh examination of the early laws at the heart of their study. They ask new questions of them, essentially in the light of comparison with the practices and legislation of the universal Church. What is decidedly local is thus isolated; and inherited forms and ways of thought in the native society are in turn illuminated. I may mention two comparatively recent studies by way of illustration. One is Smedberg's *Nordens första kyrkor* (1973); and, to my mind of still greater interest, Nilsson's book, *De sepulturis* (1989), on graveyards and burial practices, not nearly as gloomy an undertaking as it may sound. Perhaps because Swedish theologians have not yet received the good news of interdisciplinary effort, both these scholars appear to be better at Latin than they are at Norse: they occasionally mistranslate bits of vernacular law and are too often distressingly careless in quoting Norwegian–Icelandic forms. Sometimes their assumptions about pre-Christian religion and cult appear naive, as if we knew rather more about those matters than we actually do. Books like these cannot of course present a whole picture, but they take us close to some activities and attitudes which may reasonably be counted characteristic of the mingling of past and present, old and new, in an early phase of the period of Christian consolidation. Our cloud of unknowing is dense enough, but studies like these bring the occasional glimmer which may at least help to guide our fumbling speculation.

I have mentioned scaldic verse and early laws, but the problem of other texts, narrative texts, sagas—that is still with us. Mainstream historians mostly ignore them, and it is hard to blame them. They offer accounts that cannot be tested or substantiated; as 'sources' they are often centuries away from conditions they purport to describe. Professional students of the past are unable to read them as fragments of history made palatable and convincing by artistic shaping, and find it hard to grasp the notion that the authors who moulded them were very unlikely to have been starting cold, but were themselves recipients of what had already been shaped, whether as repeated, and perhaps conflicting, report or as chiselled anecdote.

Ninety-two years ago Björn Magnússon Ólsen published a remarkable 120-page monograph, *Um kristnitökuna árið 1000*, gratefully building on the work of Konrad Maurer, to whom he dedicated his study. In his account of the conversion 'moment' in Iceland and its background, he drew all strands together and interwove personal history, place-names, political and constitutional affairs, foreign relations, religious thinking—he did not leave out *Vǫluspá* and the tale of Þiðrandi whom the *dísir* slew—and produced a plausible whole, most beautifully integrated. But those strands were drawn from all the texts available to him, and to us, that touched the subject: *Landnámabók*, *Íslendingabók*, the *Kristni saga* that is found in *Hauksbók*, the *Kristniþáttr* in *Njáls saga*, the conversion section in the 'biggest' *Óláfs saga Tryggvasonar*, with its attendant *þættir* about Þorvaldr inn víðfǫrli and Stefnir Þorgilsson. Björn drew on these with selective and not insensitive fingers, but spent no time on the chronology of the texts or their tendencies and relationships—he maybe took that sort of knowledge, to be found in Maurer, and the validity of the record as a whole for granted. His approach is summed up in a sentence in which he says that he has followed *Íslendingabók* as far as it goes and from other sagas he has taken what seems to him to be nearest the truth—'það er oss þikir næst sanni'.

When Jón Jóhannesson published the first volume of his *Íslendinga saga* in 1956, he wrote more briefly and more cautiously, but in essence he appears to have accepted Björn Magnússon Ólsen's account from 1900 as a fundamentally sound analysis of all the factors to be considered in explaining, as far as may be possible, the events and the wider context of the adoption of Christianity as the national religion at the *Alþingi* of the year 1000. Icelandic historians, and others too, have since been much more taciturn on the subject and altogether more circumspect. Like Dag Strömbäck, they stick to Ari's early twelfth-century *Íslendingabók* and some scaldic verse, and leave aside the more detailed and colourful narratives of the thirteenth-century texts so skilfully synthesised by Björn Magnússon Ólsen.

Kristni saga, to speak briefly of just one of these neglected thirteenth-century texts, is admittedly difficult for us to get to grips with, but there may be ways of finding some historical pabulum in it. There are one or two things we know, or think we know, about this description of the Icelanders' adoption of Christianity, things of a kind to give us food for thought, though not for a moment do I suppose that we shall all draw the same nourishment from them. One thing is that the composition of *Kristni saga* is associated with Sturla Þórðarson, a man who would have been a professional historian or biographer in our day, writing for money and fame—and doubtless as accurately as possible in the circumstances. If we look at Sturla's other known works, we see that he did indeed behave like a historian and made all the use he could of available material, oral report, which was clearly extensive, written narratives, of which he knew many, and occasional letters and documents from archival sources. We can make the reasonable assumption that when he put *Kristni saga* together, or oversaw its composition, he thought he was retailing credible information about the past. I stress 'credible'—as Albani argued some years ago, he meant it as history—how could he tell whether his information, wherever it came from, was absolutely true to the facts? In other words, it seems to me much more natural to believe that Sturla in his situation was doing what Björn Magnússon Ólsen, in his situation at the turn of the century, was doing than to believe that his activity bore any close resemblance to what Halldór Kiljan Laxness was doing at any time in his situation, even when he was writing *Íslands klukkan* or *Gerpla*. If historians want to say something sensible about Rimbert or Adam of Bremen, they start by defining as closely as possible the man and his situation and assessing his personal and institutional bias. Might we not work harder on the same lines in the case of Sturla Þórðarson? And if Sturla can be shown not to have had any obvious institutional bias—and why should he have had?—I would count that an advantage. That he had evident preconceptions is another matter, and in a proper study of the subject it would obviously be needful to discuss how far and in what ways we may be justified in counting Sturla a representative voice—something which for the moment I merely take for granted.

But if we try to approach an author and a text in the way implied by these remarks, we are obliged to treat 'truth' as a relative matter. Sturla had miscellaneous information from the past and he sorted it to best advantage; we have small reason to assume he invented it. In the circumstances, I would be inclined to argue that, while a text revealing a thirteenth-century view of the past may, and probably can, tell us something about the writer's own time, it must also tell us something about that past itself. What *Kristni saga* purveys after all is a set of recollections formed, and maybe in some cases fixed and formalised, in the intervening period between event and written statement. It must represent, at least in a sort of semiotic way, some filtering of the sense which generations of Icelanders had made of the past whenever the subject of the conversion came up, whether in speech or writing, say between the year 1001 and Sturla's prime some 250 years later. Folklorists and ethnologists can also appreciate 'truth', the import of a record, on similarly appropriate lines. Several of them could be quoted, but I cite only Nils-Arvid Bringéus, of course out of context: '... verkligheten har olika dimensioner. För etnologen är det ofta ej en tillräcklig uppgift att utforska yttre skeenden och förhållanden. Det kan vara väl så viktigt att klarlägga människors uppfatning av verkligheten ...' (Bringéus, 86).

Another thing to ponder is the inclusion of scaldic stanzas in *Kristni saga* and the fact that these are generally acknowledged to be authentic and well preserved. How did they maintain themselves over so long a period? Most people would say because they were accompanied by anecdote, and that seems to me a reasonable enough explanation. We might try to draw up clearer rules for deciding when and if an anecdote authenticates a verse and when and if a verse authenticates an anecdote. But that is a fraught issue and, as experience has shown, it can lead to subtle special pleading and diametrically opposed conclusions. I am happy to do no more than mention it.

Kristni saga also has a good many little stories, some of them famous, that have no scaldic verse attached to them. They are interesting, even entertaining, but adventitious rather than integral in the narrative. By way of conclusion, I shall take the liberty of reminding you of one or two of the best known of these items—they bear repeating—along with a minimum of comment. They all come in the account of the decisive meeting of the *Alþingi* when Christianity was accepted.

Just after the opposing parties had declared themselves 'out of law' with each other, we are told:

> Then a man came at a gallop and said there was an eruption in Ölfus and the lava would run over Þóroddr goði's homestead. Then the pagans spoke up and said, 'No wonder the gods get angry at such talk.' Then Snorri goði said, 'What made the gods angry when the lava we are standing on now was on fire?'

Later, after Þorgeirr the Lawspeaker's decision:

> All the Northerners and the Southerners were baptized in Reykjalaug in Laugardalr when they rode from the assembly, because they would not go into cold water . . . Most of the men from the West were baptized in Reykjalaug in Syðri-Reykjadalr.

And further:

> When Rúnólfr [goði Úlfsson] was baptized, Hjalti [Skeggjason] said, 'Gömlum kennum vér nú goðanum at geifla á saltinu', [—or crudely paraphrased, with some lilt and too much alliteration] 'Now we teach the leader late in life to lick the salt.'

Naturally, I pluck out these three familiar bits for extrinsic as well as intrinsic reasons. There are considerations which make it plausible to think that they are stories that go back a long way. Jón Jónsson has recently been able to date an eruption in Nyrðri-Eldborg, followed smartly by another in Syðri-Eldborg (both lie between Lambafell and Blákollur), to about the time of the conversion, and the lava from them ran in the direction of Þóroddr's land at Hjalli, some 12 km. away. Snorri goði's sardonic response, with an Augustinian ring, is in itself timeless but, whether he actually made it at the *Alþingi* or not, it seems more likely that an association of the relativist attitude he is credited with and the fact of the eruption stems from a time when the lava, threatening the home of a well-known *goði* but one who otherwise plays no part in the narrative action of *Kristni saga*, was still a living memory. The identification of the places of baptism of most of the assembly participants is presumably a true recollection, and equally the explanation of their choice—'because they would not go into cold water'. Of course, it could be taken as an inference from the tradition which mentioned these warm-spring localities, but why anyone should wish to draw it long after the event is hard to see. What after all does the explanation convey? That in mid-summer a whole batch of the most notable men in Iceland shuddered at the prospect of a dip in the cold water of Öxará or Þingvallavatn? Or that those same men were of a haughty independent spirit, who made their own decisions, not much moved either way by the change of dispensation they had just accepted? Hjalti's utterance, verse-like in word-order, rhythm and alliteration, not out of keeping with the kviðlingr at Lögberg attributed to him by Teitr and Ari, stamps itself on the memory of anyone who hears it. Naturally, it could have been made up in the course of subsequent telling, but again more likely early than late.

Anecdotes like these encode attitudes. They are gestures which we observe at first hand only in a thirteenth-century literary context, but there is a fair amount of circumstance to suggest that they were not novel gestures. Should they not rather be seen as typical of the period of transition and transmission that followed the conversion 'moment' in Iceland? We shall differ on what we read out of them. For my part I find them significant of varying degrees of religious neutrality, tolerance, indifference, among leading groups in Icelandic society; which is, of course, entirely at one with Teitr Ísleifsson's account, in Ari's report, of the compromises which led to the acceptance of Christianity and which marked the following generation of legally regulated pagan–Christian coexistence in the country. If influential men of cool, unfanatical mind were not in an absolute majority at the time of the conversion, there were certainly enough of them to do better than hold the balance between the frændaskömm legislators on the one side and the convinced militant Christians on the other. But in that case we can hardly avoid the conclusion—far from new, needless to say—that they represented intellectually uncommitted attitudes, ranging perhaps from well-developed cynicism to active free-thinking, that were equally pervasive in late-pagan Iceland as well. And then the obscurity of the atmosphere in which pre-Christian poetry and mythology survived the conversion may seem perceptibly lightened.

NOTE

I should like to record my sincere thanks to Dr Sveinbjörn Björnsson of the University of Iceland for drawing my attention to Jón Jónsson's papers and sending me copies of them.

BIBLIOGRAPHY

Albani, Claudio. 1968. 'Ricerche attorno alla Kristnisaga', *Istituto Lombardo*... *Rendiconti. Classe di Lettere*... 102, 91-142.

Birkeli, Fridtjov. 1982. *Hva vet vi om kristningen av Norge?*

Bringéus, Nils-Arvid. 1975. 'Källkritiska problem inom etnologisk forskning', *Saga och sed* 1973-74, 85-131.

Helle, Knut. 1991. 'Tiden fram til 1536'. In Rolf Danielsson *et al.*, *Grunntrekk i norsk historie fra vikingtid til våre dager*, 13-106.

Íslendingabók. In Jakob Benediktsson (ed.), *Íslendingabók. Landnámabók* (1968), 3-28.

Jón Jóhannesson. 1956. *Íslendinga saga* I.

Jón Jónsson. 1977. 'Reykjafellsgígir og Skarðsmýrarhraun á Hellisheiði', *Náttúrufræðingurinn* 47, 17-26.

Jón Jónsson. 1979. 'Kristnitökuhraunið', *Náttúrufræðingurinn* 49, 46-50.

Jón Jónsson. 1983. 'Eldgos á sögulegum tíma á Reykjanesskaga', *Náttúrufræðingurinn* 52, 127-38.

Kristni saga. In Finnur Jónsson and Eiríkur Jónsson (eds.), *Hauksbók* (1892-96), 126-49.

Nilsson, Bertil. 1989. *De sepulturis. Gravrätten i Corpus iuris canonici och i medeltida nordisk lagstiftning.*

Ólsen, Björn Magnússon. 1900. *Um kristnitökuna árið 1000 og tildrög hennar.*

Sawyer, Birgit, Sawyer, Peter and Wood, Ian (eds.). 1987. *The Christianization of Scandinavia.*

Smedberg, Gunnar. 1973. *Nordens första kyrkor. En kyrkorättslig studie.*

Strömbäck, Dag. 1975. *The Conversion of Iceland. A Survey.*

R. I. PAGE

SCANDINAVIAN SOCIETY, 800–1100: THE CONTRIBUTION OF RUNIC STUDIES

JUST over a hundred years ago, when the Viking Society was but a gleam in the eyes of a group of genial Orcadian expatriates, there was published one of the most delectable books about Vikings, *The Viking Age: the early history, manners, and customs of the ancestors of the English-speaking nations: illustrated from the antiquities discovered in mounds, cairns, and bogs as well as from the ancient Sagas and Eddas.* By Paul B. du Chaillu, author of 'Explorations in Equatorial Africa', 'Land of the Midnight Sun', etc. London, 1889.

After a title like this a book seems hardly necessary. Yet there is one, two volumes of it, over a thousand pages altogether. It treats of the period from the Stone Age onwards, with discussion of material antiquities, religion and burial rites, superstitions, land and inheritance, social classes, legal assembly, law, social practices, war, ships and travel, buildings, dress, occupations and sports, moral principles and a host of other topics. Among this is a chapter on runes, some forty pages long, mentioning thirty or so northern runic monuments. In only two or three cases does du Chaillu bother to give a transliteration and translation of the text and so make its material content available to the reader. Indeed, the larger part of this chapter is devoted to literary accounts of runes, taken from the post-Viking period.

Such neglect of the runic evidence for the Vikings is typical of work published in the English language during most of the past hundred years. Runes have been noted, even described as a script, usually in rather perfunctory terms. But the fact that the Vikings speak directly to us, without the intermediary of the later Middle Ages, only in their runic inscriptions has seldom been found relevant to a serious study of the Viking Age.

If we take some of the major books on the Vikings written in English in the present century, we see this ignorance of, or perhaps I should say ignoring of, the evidence of runic texts clearly displayed. In reviewing the appropriate items I am uncomfortably aware that I shall be commenting on the work of honoured members of the Viking Society, indeed also of Honorary Life Members, Past Presidents, present Presidents and perhaps even future Presidents of our society.

T. D. Kendrick was not a professional historian, though his *A history of the Vikings,* published in 1930, is a beautifully controlled exposition of one part of the evidence. But it deals with the runes in a couple of pages and thereafter mentions a few specific monuments only casually and in passing.[1] As an art historian Kendrick could hardly ignore the great Jelling stone, and he commented briefly on a few Swedish rune-stones that record eastern journeys, but that is all.

Gabriel Turville-Petre was a literary historian. But his *The heroic age of Scandinavia* from 1951 failed to find anything heroic in the rune-stones, even in those that specifically invoke the heroic code in describing exciting exploits; those that break into verse whose language all but the most imperceptive must recognize as 'heroic'. Not that I suggest that Professor Turville-Petre was imperceptive; but I think he did not accept as heroic literature what was not recorded in the form that he thought proper for heroic literature, that is in manuscript. He also displays another attitude that seems common among those who look without sympathy at the runic field: 'it must be conceded that the inscriptions teach us little factual history,' he complains.[2] From the example he then gives it seems he thinks that (like biography) 'history is about chaps', and unless you have a chap's name which you can link to other sources, your inscription has no historical content.

Peter Sawyer, as befits a historian with an enthusiasm for primary evidence, devoted about three pages of the 250 or so in his *The age of the Vikings* to the runic record, and a good deal of that is complaint that we cannot often identify the people mentioned in the runic inscriptions. Noting the Hedeby stones that refer to the siege of that town, he says sadly, 'there are, however, very few "historical" stones of this kind',[3] history presumably gaining its validity by being confirmed by proper, non-runic, sources. The implication is that runic material is secondary evidence that is only important if it deals with people who also appear in real, manuscript, records. Thus Sawyer in his first edition of 1962. By the time of the second edition of 1971 he was no wiser.

Something of a contrast is Gwyn Jones's *A history of the Vikings* from 1968. Jones is not professionally an historian, though all his work shows a lively interest in historical record. He stresses in a single paragraph the range and variety of information that the runic texts, particularly the rune-stones, give on the Vikings.[4] Often he is concerned with runic confirmation of events and people known from historical sources, but he also notes the Swedish Ingvar stones, the records of various journeys east found on eleventh-century Swedish stones, inscriptions concerning Swedes who took part in raids on England, the Piraeus lion inscription and the memorials to Scandinavians who died at Hólmgarðr. Thus when writing about Vikings he very properly dwells on their ventures overseas; but this results in a comparatively slender reference to the Vikings in their home-lands, even though there are some rune-stones that make it clear that property in Scandinavia was the fruit of profits made on voyages abroad. In part they answer the question posed by the title of one of Sir David Wilson's memorable lectures, 'What did the Vikings do with their loot?'

The Viking achievement by Peter Foote and David Wilson, from 1970, shows no such inhibitions of principle in that it is largely concerned with medieval Scandinavians at home (are these Vikings?). Even though there are long sections of the book devoted to the nature of Norse society, the runic evidence is largely ignored. When it is included it is sometimes in trivial form: 'For the first time we begin to learn a little about the artists who carved the stones, for they begin to sign their work.'[5] An artist has no existence until you know his name. When you have a name he exists, even if you know nothing more of him than his name.

Luckily things have improved in recent years. As late as 1971 Peter Sawyer was still able to write that the rune-stones 'do something to compensate for the inadequacy of the more conventional written sources. It is, however, rarely possible to identify the individuals who are mentioned . . .'[6] Twenty years later, in contributing to his *Festschrift,* Mrs Sawyer saw the runic evidence in a more creative and positive light: 'considering the problems involved in using all this late evidence for conditions during the Viking Age it is remarkable that more attention has not been paid to the contemporary evidence of the runic inscriptions. These inscriptions . . . provide, for the first time, written evidence produced in the North that casts some light on contemporary circumstances.'[7] The difference in emphasis here is marked. Even the rune-stones that Professor Sawyer accepts as 'historical' derive their historicity from the fact that they refer to people, events, places that are known from formal (even if suspect) written sources. Mrs Sawyer properly regards rune-stones as historical documents in their own right.

The strange thing about the conventional attitude of historical writers to the use of runic sources in the last three decades is that the material was readily available to them, even to those who were not prepared to encounter it in a foreign language. In 1962, the year that saw the publication of the first edition of *The age of the Vikings,* appeared the English translation of Sven B. F. Jansson's *The runes of Sweden.* The book's title was misleading since it omitted most of the earliest inscriptions, which of course were in some ways the most interesting linguistically; indeed even the publishers seem to have thought so since they included a selection of further facts on runes on the dust-jacket. The revised and expanded version of the book had the more accurate title, *Runes in Sweden.*[8] Nevertheless, Jansson's 1962 book should have come as a revelation to an unlearned society, and encouraged its members to think more precisely about the significance of their evidence. For the first time there was available in modern English some account of the range, variety and style of these important documents. There was revealed the distinction between verse and prose memorials, between records of (to use Jansson's own sub-titles) 'the Viking expeditions' to a great number of destinations to the East and West, 'northern battles' within Scandinavia, a 'peaceful homeland', 'farms and farmers', 'good works' (that is, works of social charity), 'the conversion' to Christianity, legal meeting-places, the qualities that made up 'the good man', and so on. Professor Jansson's book is only an appetizer, but it should have been an aperitif that tempted the historian to taste further.

Of course, Professor Jansson had a mass of existing research to build upon, the individual volumes of *Sveriges runinskrifter* as well as his own personal contribution to this field which he made so much his own. Probably *The runes of Sweden* suffered from its readability, for it is axiomatic that a good read cannot also be a good piece of scholarship. Inevitably the book lacked a strongly explicated philological content since that was not the writer's intention. Those who could not repair this deficiency by going to the more austere pages of *Sveriges runinskrifter* were soon to find relief in a work compiled by perhaps the most distinguished of living Viking historians, Lucien Musset, who brought Fernand Mossé's material to the light of day in *Introduction à la runologie* in 1965. Here the *anthologie runique* gave the reader a more detailed, geographically distributed, picture of, among others, the Viking inscriptions.[9] Thus the historical content of the runic texts has been made available to non-specialists through recent decades.

But this underestimates the conservatism of scholars. If you kill a cow or sheep, flay it, clean, stretch, scrape and process the skin, get yourself a load of wood galls (perhaps imported from the Middle East), pound them in a pestle and mix the juice with a reagent to precipitate a dark deposit, catch a goose, pluck out a quill, sharpen it to a point, cut up the treated skin into arbitrary pieces, rule them with a stylus and fold them, and then use the quill, dipped in the darkened liquid, to paint arbitrary characters on the surface of the skin, you produce a historical document. If you incise a piece of wood with a knife or engrave a piece of stone with a punch, you don't.

Despite that, there has recently been a strong movement to make the runic material more accessible. Erik Moltke's monumental *Runes and their origin. Denmark and elsewhere*, published in 1985, is an example.[10] Though it is formally a book on the Danish inscriptions, it uses them to explicate social history. One of its chapters is challengingly entitled 'Runes reflect society', and examines the social and professional ranks mentioned in the inscriptions, with sections on servants, slaves, illiterates and women. For the immediately pre-Viking period (or what is now, by an ingenious redating, the proto-Viking period) Moltke treats of differently named social groups, the *goði* and the *þulr*, linked to religion and perhaps the law. There are chapters on the monuments whereby kings made their greatness manifest, on those that tell of heathendom and Christianity, on those inscribed objects that suggest literacy or the reverse. Altogether Moltke's book provides a feast of fine confused reading for the Viking historian to make use of.

It is well that in recent years we have found numbers of younger scholars prepared to make full use of this type of material. To give an example. Judith Jesch's *Women in the Viking Age*, published in 1991 devotes a chapter to 'Women's lives in runic texts'.[11] It is true that much of it is concerned with the quality of the men commemorated rather than of the women who commemorated them. Apparently the women gain their status by this relationship. But Jesch also makes deductions about women's importance within the family, their high rate of mortality in infancy and childhood, the impact of Christianity, their patronage of the arts. And specifically and most significant, their rights to inherit. This is natural in view of the immensely important inscription on the rock at Hillersjö, Uppland, Sweden and its related pieces, with their detailed account of a complex inheritance pattern that ends up with mother-in-law taking all. The main inscription begins with a stern admonition to the passer-by, *raþu*, 'Read (this)'; the information had to be made patent to everyone who was literate. When you consider that the section on women's right to inherit in *The Viking achievement* makes no reference to this essential document (but instead relies on the support of 'Danish historians towards 1200'—the word 'towards' is elegantly ambiguous—or on 'late medieval and subsequent records'—perhaps a little imprecise?)[12] you have to wonder why the prejudice against the runic evidence survived for so long. Jansson's comment on the Hillersjö text is worth noting. 'The Viking Age rules of inheritance that were applied in this case agree with the statutes of the Uppland Law, codified in 1296.'[13] The later legal texts only confirm what the Viking Age was already practising.

Questions of land ownership and inheritance of wealth are central in any study of the runic evidence for Viking society. I recall stating this as, I thought, a self-evident and generally accepted proposition in a lecture given some twenty years ago before a university in the south of England. A senior member of the audience (who later wrote a two-volume work on the Vikings) took me up on this; he seemed to think it fanciful. I suspect it is now generally accepted without demur. A number of scholars have worked to make it so, and if I pick out one it is without prejudice to the contribution of others. In recent years Birgit Sawyer has published a number of influential papers on the topic, and though one may not always agree with all her conclusions, one must pay tribute to her commitment.[14]

And of course, one need not be thinking of women's studies when adducing the rune-stones as land-holding and inheritance records. Jansson's monograph on the Malsta and Sunnå, Hälsingland, stones, from 1985, interprets the text of the first of these:

> Frømundr put up this stone (?these stones) in memory of Fægylfi Bræsi's son. And Bræsi was Lini's son. And Lini was Unn's son. And Unn was Ofæigr's son. And Ofæigr Þorir's son.
> Groa was Fægylfi's mother And then ... Guðrun.
> Frømundr Fægylfi's son cut these runes ...
> Gylfi took over this land and then land north in Vika in three townships, and then Lønangr and then Fæðrasio.

The genealogy is precise and detailed, the extensive property which presumably gave Gylfi his nickname Money-Gylfi is defined. Frømundr here attests his right to the property in direct male line. 'Thus,' says Jansson, 'the Malsta stone is not only a memorial in the usual sense. It is also a certificate of inheritance ('Den är även ett arvsdokument').'[15]

Most recently Marie Stoklund has suggested that in linking rune-stones to inheritance we are defining their use too narrowly. Though individual later inscriptions may serve this function, not all do. Their references to family relationships, social position, place and circumstances of death, and their laudatory epitaphs connect them with the *eptirmæli,* which I take it here means 'the good report after one's death'.[16] It is indeed salutory to have someone warning us against taking a simplistic view of a social practice that could serve more than one purpose.

Land-tenure is not the only subject which recent scholars have illuminated from the runic inscriptions of the Viking Age. There is also information on social ranks or classes, on duties or rights of individual groups within the Viking peoples. Such information is often not recorded anywhere else, but the runic examples require interpretation, and this can lead to dispute. As a case in point I quote the discussion of a number of terms—are they common words or technical ones?—found on rune-stones to describe a person's position within his social group.

How are we to define terms like *drengr, þegn, búmaðr, landmaðr, heimþegi* on these memorial stones? The trouble is that the meaning can be derived only from the contexts in which the word occurs. Some years ago, in lecturing on Vikings before a distinguished metropolitan university college, I ventured to translate the word *félagi* on a particular rune-stone as 'comrade-in-arms'. During questions afterwards the head of the department asked what was the evidence for such a translation. I answered that it was contextual. 'Ah, I thought there wasn't any real evidence,' he retorted, as though it was not self-evident that in most cases only context can be a safe guide to meaning in a dead language. Now I do not think he was really as daft as this anecdote suggests—I think he was trying to score up a public debating point without concern for scholarly values. But his question does enshrine a problem, and from this problem arise the controversies about the meanings of class describers in early Norse runic texts. In what way does the context help?—and context here includes the total context, not simply the linguistic one. Moltke has documented some of the dispute over the Danish use of terms like *drengr, þegn.*[17] Whether a *þegn* was a free peasant or a royal servant. Moltke's assertion that 'private individuals do not seem to have had "thegns", so it must have been the ruler's prerogative to appoint "thegns". . .' is hardly a precise one (or at least a precisely demonstrated one). And his follow-up, 'We may assume that "thegns" and certain "drengs" were associated in some way with the king's military organisation' is fine as long as you accept it is only Moltke's assumption and receives no demonstration in his book. On the other hand the total context— that these terms occur on rune-stones, which were presumably expensive luxuries—shows that the social groups involved were wealthy or at least well-off.

Jan Paul Strid has examined the Swedish use of the word *þægn* and found it regionally variable.[18] It is apparently frequent in Västergötland, there are two cases in Småland, one (together with some uncertain examples) in Södermanland; none in Uppland—these apart from the use of the element as a personal name. To clarify its significance Strid has to adduce the use of *þægn* as a place-name element, and on this basis suggests 'that at least one of the senses of Runic Swedish *þægn* was 'man (warrior) of high rank in the service of a king or chieftain', but he is pretty cagey about using this definition generally. The word *drængr* Strid sees as a more general word, one that could have a variety of meanings dependent upon context, 'to denote a member of an army unit, a fighting ship or a merchant fraternity', becoming 'associated with all the manly virtues that were so much esteemed in the Viking Age: courage, boldness, loyalty, and so forth.' This word's relationship to wealth or social rank he holds less secure, though inevitably the material contexts of the inscriptions, often on stones of some splendour, will imply riches. Whether one can go farther than Strid here I do not know. It would certainly be rash to ignore geographical distinctions, to assume that what applies to parts of Sweden may be taken for Denmark and Norway too.

There is, for instance, a problematic pair of examples from south Jutland. One of the Hedeby stones, no. 3, is set up by a king Sveinn in memory of his **himþiga** who, having travelled in the west, now met death at Hedeby.[19] Runic students inevitably connect this with Hedeby stone no. 1 which records that a **himþigi** of Sveinn (the same Sveinn presumably) erected it in memory of his **filaga** Eiríkr who met his death when **trekiaʀ** (*drengiar*) beseiged Hedeby: he was a ship's captain and a very good *drengr*. This is a case where I might suggest the translation 'comrade-in-arms' for *félagi*. Whether the word *drengr* is used in two different senses on Hedeby 1 I do not know. That Eiríkr was a *drengr harða góðr* might mean just 'a jolly good chap' as Moltke suggests with strong reservations,[20] but the context on these two stones requires a more serious interpretation. Why did King Sveinn set up a memorial stone to his *hempægi* at Hedeby? Why did someone who called himself Sveinn's *hempægi* set up one to his 'fellow' Eiríkr? Here we may get back to the concept of the rune-stones as legal documents. If the two dead men were formally in the king's service, he might be liable to pay compensation for their deaths. We remember the incident in *Egils saga* when Egill's brother Þórólfr had been killed in the service of Athelstan of England. Egill was very peevish until the king paid over lavish compensation: *tók Egill þaðan af at gleðask*, 'from then on Egill perked up.'[21]

In the same way Hedeby 3 may be a king's recorded admission of his duty to compensate for a *hempægi* killed under his command. Hedeby 1 may be a man's record of compensation paid to his 'fellow' (does this then have the primary and more technical meaning 'business partner'?) with the acknowledgment that it was his duty to repay a share of this to the dead man's family. Both these would be proper aspects of the *eptirmæli*. In these interpretations *drengr* might seem to have a more formal interpretation, 'officer called up in the king's service'. It is impossible to be sure without more examples.

One of the cheering, and sometimes terrifying, aspects of runic studies is that there is always the possibility of new finds that could lighten our darkness. To give an illustration. Between the publication of the first edition of Moltke's *Runerne i Danmark og deres oprindelse* and the second edition in English translation nine years later the Danish corpus had increased by over 90 inscriptions. Or to compare great things with little, consider the Manx runic material. When I recorded this in 1983 it had 29 Viking Age inscriptions.[22] In December 1991 Sir David Wilson took up residence on the island. He had been there barely a week when I received from him the record of another fragmentary inscription found, he assured me, 'under the Communion Table at Kirk Braddan Church.' While I was gloating over this new accession, the colleagues to whom I reported it speculated what Sir David was doing under the communion table at Kirk Braddan church. Some weeks afterwards I had the chance of examining the new rune-stone, and found its inscription was part of a maker's formula. At the same time the Manx Museum authorities made available to me a fragment found some years earlier but hitherto unreported. It is a tiny piece, part of the upper surface and one side of a slate slab. The top has the lower part of an elegant warrior with a sword at his belt, cut in low relief. The side shows the tops or bases of up to five staves, with a punctuation point. Not enough remains for any single letter to be identified, so this is one of the handful of Manx stones that provides only a point on a distribution map. But two new points added to about thirty is not a negligible number.

The most astonishing increase in runic finds—not necessarily Viking Age—in recent decades is the effect of urban archaeology. This began when some wise man burned down half of Bryggen, Bergen, in 1955. Archaeologists moved into the devastated site and uncovered huge numbers of pieces of wood and bone inscribed with runic characters. Norwegian runologists have been playing with them ever since.[23] The effect has been twofold. The simple one was to increase the number of known Norwegian runic inscriptions dramatically—by over a half. The more complex one was to reveal a common use of runes, for commercial, social, practical, epistolary and scurrilous purposes, that had hitherto only been hinted at. Later research on other Scandinavian urban sites, Trondheim, Ribe and Lödöse, for example, confirmed something of the Bergen observations: that runes were often used in the early post-Viking period in a variety of ways neither memorial nor formal. The effect of this was to make some runologists speculate on whether the same range of use could be postulated for the Viking Age. Did Vikings use the script for everyday purposes, for sending messages, recording business transactions, making rude comments on their neighbours, and so on? Could some of the later medieval written accounts of *rúnakefli* have a basis in fact?

The scholar who went farthest in this direction was our late and much missed colleague Aslak Liestøl who put forward in 1971 the hypotheses that (a) newly-found runic inscriptions on portable objects, and in particular on sticks of wood whose sole purpose was to hold the inscription, suggest that the Viking Age also may have used runes in this way, though as yet there were few examples known, (b) letter-writing on runic sticks such as those found in Bergen may have been a Viking practice, (c) short-twig runes, being simple in form and easy to cut, would have been a perfect script for this, and so (d) many Vikings were probably literate in this sense.[24]

> Runes were not solely or even chiefly a monumental form of writing—that I must be allowed to maintain. Their use in memorial inscriptions and the like is secondary—first and foremost they were employed in practical, everyday life. Indeed this should be self-evident. I find it difficult to conceive of someone learning to write simply in order to carve tomb-stones, but even if there were such people, their work would be in vain—unless others were prepared to learn to read, simply in order to decipher those same tomb-stone inscriptions!

Of course, this argument is less forceful than it appears at first glance. Rune-stones are not necessarily, and are sometimes clearly not, tomb-stones. If their texts are not simple memorials but also legal or formal documents, cut on stone because of the greater permanence of that material and because a stone could be exposed in a public place where its claims would be visible to all, people could well be persuaded to read and inscribe them. To return to Liestøl's own words:

> I think we are bound to conclude that the majority of Viking Age Scandinavians—at least those of any standing, and those intent on making their way in life—were able to read and write. Their system of writing was in constant use, and the inscriptions extant today are merely the pitiful remains of the wealth of documents written by them.

Finally a prophecy that is still unfulfilled:

> True, only a few texts have come down to us—but quite an unusually fortunate combination of circumstances is required if such inscriptions are to be preserved. For one thing, we must presume that most of them were intentionally destroyed in their own day, being reduced to waste, broken, burned, chopped or cut up ... If a rune stick escaped such a fate, it would still have to be lodged in a hermetically sealed place within a fairly short time of its making if it was to have any chance of surviving for a thousand years and more. It is our job to find the rune letters which have been preserved in this way, we must dig them up, we must draw attention to them and see to it that they are taken care of. When the odds against preservation are so great, it is remarkable that any have come to light at all ... We believe more runic inscriptions on wooden sticks are yet to be found in the unexcavated parts of Viking Age and early medieval towns, and we have no doubt but that the leaders of excavations now and in the future will do all they can to bring them to light.

Of the importance of Viking Age runic correspondence—were any to be found—there could be no doubt. One of the most revealing of the Bergen letters is a late twelfth-century one calling up a ship for the king's service.[25] Could we have something like this for the tenth century we might learn much about the king's right to summon support for the defence of the realm. The melancholy fact is that little has so far appeared. Consider the cases of two Viking towns where a great deal of archaeological investigation has been completed in recent years, York and Dublin. York is surprisingly deficient in Norse runes. This may be a chance survival effect even though the ground here preserves organic materials—I cannot think it the result of indifferent excavation techniques. Dublin, however, has runes.

There are twelve inscribed pieces altogether, with runes cut on wood, on rib and other bones of animals, on a red deer's antler. Some are worked and served other purposes than the holding of texts; a handle, a wooden plane, a wooden textile-beater. Others are unworked and their only interest is that they bear runes. Though we claim twelve pieces, there are at least two of them where, though their characters have the same general effect as runes, they are not runes; only 'rune-like symbols'. They could be a cryptic script on a runic base but I do not think so—they are not carefully enough cut to sustain that hypothesis, and they do contain, mixed with arbitrary characters, occasional genuinely runic forms. They may be people's attempts to appear literate though they were not; which would tell us something of the status of literacy in the society. There is a comparison here with the silver pseudo-penannular brooch found at Hunterston, near Largs, Ayrshire, which has a comprehensible inscription on one section, **malbriþa a stilk**, 'Melbrigda owns (this) brooch', followed in the next by a matching group of lines which Magnus Olsen describes as 'carelessly carved signs resembling runes.'[26] The brooch was owned by someone with a Celtic name, and it may be relevant that Dublin also is in Celtic territory—Celts were notoriously addicted to cryptic formulae.

Other of the Dublin runic inscriptions have occasional odd letter-forms that make them hard to interpret, others again have letter sequences that look to be without meaning. Only occasionally do we get meaningful and unambiguous groups, as the personal name **kirlak** ($=$ *Geirlákr*) on the textile-beater and the group **hurn:hiartaʀ**, 'hart's horn' on the deer's antler, though in each of these cases there is a less clear continuation of the text. But there is nothing in all these finds that suggests that runes had a practical and commercial application, and they give no support to Liestøl's thesis. Liestøl's warning of the problems of survival that wood, bone and similar materials face is a proper one, and we should also take into account the fact that, here as generally in runic studies, we have a small and not necessarily representative sample of what was once cut. Yet for all that the Dublin finds prove that wood and bone survive for many centuries in Dublin earth, and the absence of 'commercial' inscriptions in what should be a commercial city is striking.

In working on these inscriptions Michael Barnes has asked the very apposite question of whether there is any Celtic influence on their language, a question not yet answered and indeed not yet precisely posed. It will be remembered that when I wrote on the Manx runic crosses some years ago I referred to the possibility that their language might represent that of a racially mixed society, and that this was in some degree supported by the mix of Celtic and Norse names in the commemorative inscriptions as well as the occasional intrusion of a Celticism into the written Norse.[27] Dr Jesch took the point up in her *Women in the Viking Age,* and in the absence of other contemporary records of the Norse Manx settlement, it suggests something of the mixed nature of Manx society in the tenth century.[28] Other runic inscriptions in Ireland—though they are few—suggest a similar cultural intermix, though whether of creoles or pigeons I do not know. A swordmount from Greenmount, Co. Louth, has the ownership inscription **tomnal selshofoþ a soerþ [þ]eta**, 'Dufnall sealshead owns this sword', with both an Irish personal name and an Irish spelling of it.[29] The cross at Killaloe, Co. Clare, has the runic text **Þurkrim risti+ | [k]rusþina**, 'Thorgrim raised this cross.'[30] Celtic influence may perhaps be seen in the lack of inflexional -R in the masculine personal name nominative, as in contemporary Manx texts. It is certainly in the accompanying ogham inscription which is alleged to have the remains of an Irish prayer, 'a blessing on Thorgrim'. Again there may here be information on a mixed-language community not noted in the formal records.

At this point I note the subtitle of this series of papers: *current problems.* So I sum up a few of my points in problem form.

(1) The difficulty of convincing historians that runic inscriptions may also be historical documents. To some extent this is the fault of runologists, because they fail to make their material easily available to non-runologists, preferring to write for one another in the rather forbidding format that specialists adopt to convince their colleagues of their scholarship. We must experiment in making inscriptions and their contexts readily accessible; but we must also make our methodology comprehensible to others, so that they can understand the reasons for our readings and interpretations, and be able to judge how much is fact, how much interpretation. Moreover, runologists of different disciplines must communicate more freely as indeed they have begun to do in recent years. For instance, to an English runologist it is astonishing how long it has taken some Scandinavian experts to become aware of the influence Roman scripts have sometimes had on runic texts.

(2) The statistical background. We must keep in mind the probability that what survives is only a small and very likely random sample of what was produced. How do we know if it is representative? Representative of what? Social class, wealth, literacy, nation, date? At first glance, major stones ought to survive more easily than minor objects on wood or bone, or perhaps than objects of precious

metal. How far this is true I do not know, but some study of the history of runic studies might help here. The Manx experience shows that in the eighteenth and nineteenth centuries rune-stones were being freely broken up for use in new building;[31] indeed, there is some indication this may have happened as recently as the second half of the twentieth century. And this is in an island where building stone is not hard to come by. The Bergen finds, on the other hand, show how modern excavation of a single site can revolutionize runic knowledge of a particular district or a particular period. Taking a smaller case: before the Dublin excavations Ireland had only three certainly known runic inscriptions, those of Killaloe, Greenmount and Beginish. Now it has in the region of fifteen. The increase may not be significant statistically, but it is striking to the non-statistician.

We must also ask whether runes were always more common in some areas than others. Why has Sweden so many more rune-stones than Norway or Denmark? Why is the distribution within Sweden so patchy? Why are there large areas of Denmark without known Viking Age runes? Can we say simplistically, as Sawyer could in 1962, 'the distribution of rune stones in Sweden, by and large of the eleventh century, gives a reasonably reliable indication of the areas then settled and the correspondence between the distributions of rune stones and of hoards of treasure is very close...'?[32] Do rune-stones occur as a matter of course in the more densely populated areas, or does the nature of the population, its social class, awareness of history, its religious or political affiliations, have some effect? Do rune-stones have a comparable regional distribution to treasure hoards because both indicate people of wealth within the area, or are there other reasons? How can we explain, on any of these hypotheses, the relatively large number of rune-stones of the Viking Age on Man, and their rarity in the Danelaw?

(3) Related to (2). When historians are short of information from a particular region or time they tend to combine a variety of sources to get a fuller picture. Is it appropriate to do this with runic data? Should we use Swedish illumination to penetrate the deeper darkness of Norway and Denmark? How far do local variations—of education, social custom, religion—affect the content, meaning and status of rune-stones?

(4) Should we attempt to define hierarchies of script, introduce a more 'palaeographical' element into runology? Is it possible, as Aslak Liestøl attempted, to identify a 'cursive' variant of runic script which might work within different bounds from a more formal one? What sort of training did different runemasters have? Do different types of script derive from different social or commercial groups; or different regional groups as implied by the rather old-fashioned terms 'Danish runes' and 'Swedo-Norwegian runes'? Swedish scholars have, of course, worked on individual traditions within their rich rune-stone corpus, but the principle needs wider examination. Was the maker of a rune-stone usually also the

carver of its runes? Or did you send for a specialist for specialist work? And—this applies to some Viking areas—to what extent was a rune-master literate in other scripts such as roman or ogham?

(5) Why is there so much uncertainty in our interpretations of runic texts and can we do anything about it? What an archaeologist, faced with an inscription, asks his epigraphist is the simple question, 'What does it say?' And all archaeologists I have worked with tend to get exasperated when I reply, as I often do, that I could put forward some suggestions, but I cannot guarantee a meaning. In the case of rune-stones we often have a general pattern of text into which an individual inscription can be fitted; and this gives a preliminary interpretation though there may be pockets of uncertainty as well as linguistic peculiarities. This makes the rune-stones more open to use than the inscriptions on other objects, and should give any summary of runic usage an improper bias. When we get to inscriptions on miscellaneous portable objects we are so often unable to define the sort of texts they are and this makes interpretation perilous. A modern sceptic should ponder how much he might make out of some present-day demotic inscriptions if he were to find them completely out of intellectual context: 'For best before see cap', 'This door is alarmed', 'Heavy plant crossing', 'Disabled toilet', 'No right turn mandatory', 'Away coaches and fans', 'Unisex hair' and so on. Armed with a minimal word-list and a minimal grammar (which is all we have for runic Norse) would he be sure he could identify parts of speech, word separation, extended meanings of words? So with the runologist: he can make suggestions, but seldom is it possible to do more. And this means that most interpretations must be put in the subjunctive. When three field-workers, Michael Barnes, Jan Ragnar Hagland and I, came to contemplate our individual contributions on the Dublin inscriptions, we found we were on occasion able to put forward alternative interpretations of the other's text. But had these any validity other than to show that the text was ambiguous to a modern reader unable to share the original context? Much runic time has been spent exchanging, for interpretations that could not be proved, alternatives of no greater probability. We cannot spend our lives suspending judgment. But what else can we suspend unless it is disbelief?

(6) It was that wise Swedish scholar, Lena Petersen, who defined for us the greatest runic problem of all, how to get enough money to support runic research. In a sense this derives from some of the issues I have presented above, the need for runology to achieve recognition and credibility, to be shown as central rather than marginal to historical and linguistic study. That can be done if we make our material and its methodology more readily available to our fellow-workers than perhaps we have done hitherto.

NOTES

[1] Kendrick 1930, 100–01, 137, 163.
[2] Turville-Petre 1951, 23.
[3] Sawyer 1962, 43.
[4] Jones 1968, 266–67. He also gives an appendix, two pages long, on runes as a script, 419–20.
[5] Foote and Wilson 1970, 313.
[6] Sawyer 1971, 43.
[7] Sawyer 1991, 215.
[8] Jansson 1962 and 1987.
[9] Musset 1965, 380–444. For those scholars who dared venture into German there was a good selection of material in Ruprecht 1958.
[10] Moltke 1985, a revised version in English translation of Moltke 1976.
[11] Jesch 1991, 42–74.
[12] Foote and Wilson 1970, 109.
[13] Jansson 1987, 98.
[14] Sawyer 1988, 1989 and 1991. Birgit Sawyer has a number of other articles on related topics in Swedish, for which see the running bibliographies in *Nytt om runer*.
[15] Jansson 1985, 34.
[16] Stoklund 1991, 296.
[17] Moltke 1985, 287. Dr Jesch discusses these words in her paper in this volume. There is still more work to be done on them: cf., for example, the implications of *drenc* used in a precise sense in a Latin context in the *Chronicon Laudunensis*, noted in Fell 1974, 182.
[18] Strid 1987.
[19] Moltke 1985, 196–97.
[20] Moltke 1985, 290.
[21] Nordal 1933, 145.
[22] Page 1983, 134.
[23] The first volume of *Norges innskrifter med de yngre runer* to deal with inscriptions from Bryggen is Liestøl 1980 together with Johnsen 1990. There have, of course, been numbers of discussions of Bryggen runes earlier than this, notably Liestøl 1964 and Dyvik, Seim and Grandell 1988.
[24] Liestøl 1971, particularly pp. 75–78.
[25] Liestøl 1964, 54–56.
[26] Olsen 1954, 169–71
[27] Page 1980, 196–97; 1983, 135, 142–43.
[28] Jesch 1991, 72–74.
[29] Olsen 1954, 180.
[30] Olsen 1954, 180–81.
[31] Page 1980, 185–86.
[32] Sawyer 1962, 103.

BIBLIOGRAPHY

Dyvik, Helge, Seim, Karin Fjellhammer and Grandell, Axel. 1988. *The Bryggen papers. Supplementary Series* 2.

Fell, Christine. 1974. 'The Icelandic saga of Edward the Confessor: its version of the Anglo-Saxon emigration to Byzantium', *Anglo-Saxon England* 3, 179—96.

Foote, Peter and Wilson, David M. 1970. *The Viking achievement: the society and culture of early medieval Scandinavia.*
Jansson, Sven B. F. 1962. *The runes of Sweden.* (Trans. P. G. Foote.)
Jansson, Sven B. F. 1985. *Två runstenar i Hälsingland: Malsta och Sunnå.* Filologiskt arkiv 33.
Jansson, Sven B. F. 1987. *Runes in Sweden.* (Trans. P. G. Foote.)
Jesch, Judith. 1991. *Women in the Viking Age.*
Johnsen, Ingrid Sanness. 1990. *Bryggen i Bergen* I (= *Norges innskrifter med de yngre runer,* vol. 6, 2, ed. James E. Knirk).
Jones, Gwyn. 1968. *A history of the Vikings.*
Kendrick, T. D. 1930. *A history of the Vikings.*
Liestøl, Aslak. 1964. *Runer frå Bryggen.* [A reprint of Liestøl's article in *Viking* 27, 1964, 5–53, with an added postscript reporting the letter of Sigurðr Lávarðr.]
Liestøl, Aslak. 1971. 'The literate Vikings'. In Peter Foote and Dag Strömbäck (ed.), *Proceedings of the Sixth Viking Congress. Uppsala 1969,* 69–78.
Liestøl, Aslak. 1980. *Bryggen i Bergen* (= *Norges innskrifter med de yngre runer,* vol. 6, 1).
Moltke, Erik. 1976. *Runerne i Danmark og deres oprindelse.*
Moltke, Erik. 1985. *Runes and their origin. Denmark and elsewhere.* (Trans. P. G. Foote.)
Musset, Lucien. 1965. *Introduction à la runologie.*
Nordal, Sigurður (ed.). 1933. *Egils saga Skalla-Grimssonar.* Íslenzk fornrit 2.
Olsen, Magnus. 1954. 'Runic inscriptions in Great Britain, Ireland and the Isle of Man'. In Haakon Shetelig (ed.), *Viking antiquities in Great Britain and Ireland* 6, 151–233.
Page, R. I. 1980. 'Some thoughts on Manx runes', *Saga-Book* 20:3, 179–99.
Page, R. I. 1983. 'The Manx rune-stones'. In Christine Fell *et al.* (ed.), *The Viking Age in the Isle of Man. Select papers from The Ninth Viking Congress, Isle of Man, 4–14 July 1981,* 133–46.
Ruprecht, Arndt. 1958. *Die ausgehende Wikingerzeit im Lichte der Runeninschriften.*
Sawyer, Birgit. 1988. *Property and inheritance in Viking Scandinavia.*
Sawyer, Birgit. 1989. 'Women as landholders and alienators of property in early medieval Scandinavia'. In Karen Glente and Lise Winther-Jensen (ed.), *Female power in the Middle Ages. Proceedings from the second St Gertrud symposium, Copenhagen 1986,* 156–71.
Sawyer, Birgit. 1991. 'Women as bridge-builders: the role of women in Viking-Age Scandinavia'. In Ian Wood and Niels Lund (ed.), *People and places in northern Europe 500–1600. Essays in honour of Peter Hayes Sawyer.*
Sawyer, P. H. 1962 and 1971. *The age of the Vikings.* 1st and 2nd editions.
Stoklund, Marie. 1991. 'Runesten, kronologi og samfundsrekonstruktion. Nogle kritiske overvejelser med utgangspunkt i runestenene i Mammenområdet'. In Mette Iversen, Ulf Näsman and Jens Vellev (ed.), *Grav, kunst og samfund i vikingetid.*
Strid, Jan Paul. 1987. 'Runic Swedish thegns and drengs'. In *Runor och runinskrifter. Föredrag vid Riksantikvarieämbetets och Vitterhetsakademiens Symposium 8–11 september 1985,* 301–16.
Turville-Petre, G. 1951. *The heroic age of Scandinavia.*

JUDITH JESCH

SKALDIC VERSE AND VIKING SEMANTICS

SKALDIC verse is an important but underused source for the historical study of the Viking Age in Scandinavia and elsewhere. In this paper I will outline some principles for the study of skaldic vocabulary and show how such a study illuminates the social history of early Scandinavia.

Skaldic verse: the nature of the evidence

Most skaldic poetry is preserved in Icelandic manuscripts of the thirteenth century or later. In the prose contexts in which the verses are preserved, they are often linked to a specific historical moment and usually attributed to an identifiable historical individual, and scholarly consensus would therefore assign to most skaldic verses a date of composition before their first extant recording. On the basis of these medieval attributions, we appear to have a substantial body of verse that is roughly dateable to the period before 1100. Naturally, not all medieval attributions can be correct, and we need to distinguish verse that has been correctly attributed and is therefore dateable from spurious verse which remains of uncertain date. The principles for making this distinction have yet to be subjected to a full and rigorous scrutiny, but most scholars would probably go along with Foote's 'pragmatic distinction' (1984, 74) between verse in the Kings' Sagas and the poetic treatises that is 'on the whole more likely than not to be correctly ascribed', and the verse in *Íslendingasögur* and related texts which should be left out of the historical 'canon' in the absence of any clear indications as to its date and circumstances of composition.

This historical 'canon' of both praise poems and *lausavísur* from the Kings' Sagas and the treatises, although substantial and dateable, has its limitations. The subjects that interested the skalds are few and predictable: war, gold and sailing predominate, with topics like love and more mundane matters largely restricted to the 'non-canonical', possibly spurious, corpus. The scholar searching for enlightenment about Scandinavian society before 1100 will find that only certain aspects of that society are illuminated, directly or indirectly, by skaldic verse.

As well as being circumscribed in subject-matter, skaldic poetry is an art-form that does not give much away, with its brilliant formalism drawing attention from the message to the medium. That message is generally cliché-ridden, repetitive and often deceitful, and even where skaldic verse attempts narrativity, its main tactic is to link a series of set-pieces. But it is possible to make a virtue of this skaldic failing. The elaborate static quality of skaldic verse is both cause and effect of a largely nominal style, a discourse that is rich in nouns and adjectives.

SKALDIC VERSE AND VIKING SEMANTICS

The vocabulary of skaldic verse, with its many synonyms and near-synonyms for human beings and their social relationships, deserves particular attention.

Principles of the semantic study of skaldic verse

Some general principles need to be agreed before the vocabulary of skaldic verse can receive this attention. The principles I suggest here arise out of my work on the Old Norse nouns *þegn* and *drengr*,[1] often untranslatable and hovering between being general terms of approbation and technical terms of rank. These terms have been discussed in a series of earlier studies (Aakjær 1927–28; Kuhn 1944; Lindow 1976; Strid 1987), but none of these is restricted to the skaldic usages; they are all etymological, comparatist and, often, decontextualised in approach.

There is much to be gained from a recontextualisation of semantic studies and from a more precise application of the comparative method. As for etymology, I tend to agree with Fell (1987, 295) that it 'may obfuscate discussion of meaning and translation'. Thus, any study of skaldic semantics should pay particular attention to the following:

(1) *Defining the corpus*. For a historical investigation it is essential to limit the material to verse that can be localised in a particular historical and chronological context. Using the Foote principle, this means restricting the analysis to verses that are preserved in Kings' Sagas and Snorri's *Edda*.

It is useful to further delimit the corpus by date. Once we have applied Foote's principle, we find a preponderance of verse dated to the eleventh century, greatly helped of course by such prolific poets as Sigvatr, Arnórr and Þjóðólfr. It is wise to concentrate on this material which is relatively abundant and relatively near the time of writing. However, I would argue for stretching the eleventh century somewhat, and making the limits c.980–1105.

(2) *Editorial problems*. Using skaldic verse as the basis for such a study because it originated in the Viking Age presupposes a text-critical approach in which the aim is to reconstruct the original form of the verse as far as is possible, independent of its prose context. Since Finnur Jónsson, few strides have been made in the direction of providing such an edition. However, the absence of a reliable text-critical edition of the corpus (see Fidjestøl 1985) should not present an insuperable obstacle. The textual difficulties of skaldic verse are not evenly spread and, as Foote pointed out (1978, 59), 'a very large number of scaldic stanzas are extraordinarily well-preserved'. My own impression is that textual problems do not greatly affect our understanding of the type of vocabulary items under consideration here.

(3) *Special problems of skaldic diction*. The concept of 'skaldic vocabulary' is not an uncomplicated one. In skaldic verse we have to contend with at least three levels of vocabulary. Thus, many words have a straightforward denotative mean-

ing, while others have a denotation that is limited to their use in poetry, or acquire a new denotation when entering into the metaphorical collocations we call kennings. While kennings present their own special problems, the first two categories are also not always easy to distinguish. For instance, when faced with the word *ekkja* in a skaldic verse, we need to decide whether it literally denotes a 'widow', or whether it has the more generalised poetic sense of 'woman'.

Terms for social status and rank are particularly vulnerable to this kind of imprecision. The skalds needed many synonyms for and variations on terms for men of high rank and warrior status, and the exigencies of skaldic metre would not have allowed them to be too fastidious about their choice of word. Thus, for any noun in the skaldic corpus, we have to allow for the following possibilities:

— that it has a meaning which is not specific to poetry, and which may or may not be precise;

— that it has a meaning restricted to poetry which is nevertheless coloured by its non-poetic meaning, and which may or may not be precise;

— that it has a meaning restricted to poetry which is not coloured by any meanings it may have elsewhere, and which may or may not be precise.

Recognising the theoretical possibility that a term has a straightforward, non-poetic meaning is of course not the same thing as being able to determine that meaning, since most of our prose instances of the word will be from a later period. However, despite the problems, the only way to determine the meanings available to any one term in the poetic corpus is to examine the full range of occurrences.

(4) *Defining the semantic unit.* As well as the simple terms like *þegn* and *drengr*, account needs to be taken of adverbial derivatives such as *fulldrengila* or compounds such as *búþegn*. It may be that the component *-þegn* or *-dreng-* is not semantically identical to the simplex but, again, this can only be discovered when the whole range has been investigated.

(5) *The semantic contexts.* The meaning of a word is not intrinsic but determined by its relationship to other words in the linguistic system.

(a) *Collocations.* In skaldic verse, with its fairly free word order and often multiple possibilities of combining lexical units, it is sometimes difficult to determine precisely which collocations the terms being investigated enter into. Recasting the stanza in prose misrepresents the way skaldic poetry works, and it may be necessary to take the *helmingr* in which the term appears as the collocational unit.

(b) *Contrasts.* The meaning of a word is also delimited by the ways in which it contrasts with related words in the same semantic field. Thus, terms like *þegn* and *drengr* need to be considered in relation to functionally parallel terms such as *húskarl*, *rekkr*, *hirðmaðr*. The wider semantic field also needs to be considered, including words that are functionally different but conceptually related, such as *drótt*, *lið*, *verðung* representing the social unit in which the *þegn* or *drengr* operates, or *dróttinn*, *þengill*, etc., for the leader whom he serves.

(6) *The literary contexts*. We must also consider the wider literary context in establishing the meaning of a word.

(a) *The poem*. On occasion a word may have an idiosyncratic meaning that is characteristic of one poem or poet. Thus, I believe that Sigvatr uses the word *drengr* in such an anomalous way in his *Austrfararvísur*, as I will demonstrate below.

(b) *Intertextuality*. As a small, professional class, most poets probably knew each other's work well, and either borrowed from it or made use of formulaic expressions. A number of the examples of *þegn* and *drengr* occur in lines that are identical or nearly identical in two or more poems by different poets and this phenomenon may affect our understanding of their meaning.

(c) *The saga*. The text-critical approach, in which we aim to work with a text that is the closest possible to the original Viking Age composition, would seem to preclude any serious consideration of the prose context in which the verse is found. However, it is a fact that skaldic verse is mediated to us through thirteenth-century Icelandic prose texts and it is better to acknowledge this influence and make allowances for it if necessary, rather than to pretend we are able to read the verse unmediated.

(7) *Comparative angles*. Even a contextual semantic study needs to take account of occurrences of the word in non-skaldic texts. This comparative material can be of many kinds, but two seem especially relevant to the current investigation:

(a) *Runic inscriptions*. The eleventh-century date of much skaldic verse coincides neatly with the date of the numerous late Viking Age runic inscriptions from mainland Scandinavia. East Norse forms of the terms *þegn* and *drengr* occur in Swedish and Danish memorial inscriptions.

(b) *Old English texts*. Þegn is a perfectly good Old English word, widely used in both literary and historical sources, *dreng* is a loan-word that appears in *The Battle of Maldon* and sporadically after 1066. Again, the period c.980–1105 neatly covers the bulk of the relevant English material.

Skaldic meanings of drengr and þegn

With these principles in mind, I propose to discuss the meanings of *drengr* and *þegn* as they emerge in skaldic verse of the late tenth to the early twelfth century. The range of questions raised by these two terms can be seen from the following selection of conclusions scholars have reached about their meanings:

For Svend Aakjær (1927–28, 28–29), 'the Nordic thegns and drengs were once . . . royal servants, members of the king's attendant nobility and of his hird or bodyguard.' But, 'as time went on . . . they came to connote the possession

... of certain moral qualities, especially nobility, generosity, chivalrousness and courage.'

Hans Kuhn concluded (1944, 111–14) that neither *þegn* nor *drengr* was originally used as a term of rank in Norway and Iceland, but that there is evidence that *drengr* developed such a meaning in Denmark and that this spread to Norway, as shown by some skaldic examples.

John Lindow wrote (1976, 106) that 'if *drengr* and *þegn* ever were technical terms in contemporary West Norse, this usage left no trace in the language of the skalds.' From the runic evidence, he deduced (pp. 111–12) that *drengr* and *þegn* belong to the sphere of 'the large, free middle class of farmers who made up the backbone of old Scandinavian society' but that they 'did not make up part of Nordic *comitatus* terminology.'

Jan Paul Strid concluded (1987, 313) that 'there is no substantial difference between the runic *drængiaʀ* of Svealand and the *drengir* of the Old Icelandic literature' and he followed Peter Foote in suggesting that 'they are similar to English *gentleman* in their variety of connotations.'

The importance of determining the meanings of *drengr* and *þegn* is shown by the kinds of conclusions historians and archaeologists wish to draw from their uses.[2] Thus, Peter Sawyer (1989, 34) believed on the basis of Danish and west Swedish runic inscriptions that 'Drengs who fought for Cnut and survived may well have continued, as thegns, to acknowledge him as their royal lord after returning home where some may have acted as his local agents.'

A close analysis of the dateable skaldic evidence presents a quite different picture in which *drengr* and *þegn* are neither technical terms of rank nor general terms of approbation. Instead they belong to a semantic sphere that demonstrates the workings of the society that produced and consumed skaldic verse. Of particular interest are the relationships between a king or military leader and his immediate companions, his wider group of supporters, both military and political, and his subjects at large. These relationships occur in the spheres of both war and more peaceful political activity. It is clear that these relationships are in flux in the eleventh century and the terminology reflects this.

Drengr

A primary meaning of *drengr* appears to be that of the member of the *comitatus*, as we know him from many generations of explication of Old English and Old Norse heroic literature, in which the follower fights by the side of his lord in battle and is in turn richly rewarded. This element of reciprocity is important, and almost overshadows the hierarchical nature of the relationship. This idea of the first among equals is expressed quite clearly in three stanzas of Halldórr ókristni's *Eiríksflokkr*, describing the battle at Svǫlð (*Skjd.* A I 203–04; B I 194; *Hkr.* I 360, 365, 367).[3] In st. 4a, we see the *drengir* performing their duties:

> Gerðisk snarpra sverða,
> slitu drengir frið lengi,
> þars gollin spjǫr gullu,
> gangr of Orm enn langa.

There was movement of keen swords around Ormr enn langi, *drengir* broke the peace for a long time, where gilded spears called out.

In st. 6a their leader jarl Eiríkr calls on his *drengir*:

> Hét á heiptar nýta
> hugreifr, með Óleifi
> aptr stǫkk þjóð of þoptur,
> þengill sína drengi.

The cheerful ruler called on his *drengir*, useful in battle, the troop sprang back across the rowing-benches with Ólafr.

And in st. 7b Eiríkr, the *dýrr drengja stjóri*, does his bit in the battle:

> Gnýr varð á sjá sverða.
> Sleit ǫrn gera beitu.
> Dýrr vá drengja stjóri.
> Drótt kom mǫrg á flótta.

There was crash of swords on the sea. The eagle tore the wolf's food. The excellent leader of *drengir* fought. Many warriors fled.

The rhyme with *þengill* in st. 6a is common for *drengr* and occurs in Steinn Herdísarson's *Óláfsdrápa*, where the equation between military support and the leader's generosity is made explicit in st. 16 (*Skjd*. A I 413; B I 382):

> Dyggr lætr þungar þiggja
> þengill af sér drengi,
> vás launar svá vísi
> verðung, Hóars gerðar.

The valiant ruler lets his *drengir* receive heavy Óðinn's gear [armour], thus the leader repays his retinue for their trouble.

Finally, it should be noted that the term *drengr* could be used to refer to the enemy, as when Vígfúss Víga-Glúmsson mentions the Danish *drengir* at the battle of Hjǫrungavágr (*Skjd*. A I 120; B I 115; *Fsk*. 134).

It could be argued that it is not the word *drengr* itself that implies membership of the *comitatus*, but the contexts in which it occurs; that *drengr* simply means 'man', or possibly 'warrior', and takes on the more specific connotation because everyone knew that was what the relationship between a lord and his 'man' entailed. There is some support for this view in stanzas where the term *drengr* is explicitly paralleled by another term in the same semantic field, as in st. 2 of Hallfreðr vandræðaskáld's *Erfidrápa*, where the *rekkar* are in the same relationship to their leader as the *drengir* (*Skjd*. A I 159; B I 150; *Hkr*. I 356; *Fsk*. 152–53).

Where I believe it is possible to trace the particular connotations of *drengr* is, paradoxically, when the term begins to lose this specific meaning and takes on other connotations. It is the specific meaning of *drengr* (close follower of a military leader) and not a more general meaning (man, warrior) that enables new meanings of the word to develop in the eleventh century. From Sigvatr onwards, we can trace the twofold development of *drengr*, with emphasis on one hand on the semantic component of 'intimacy', on the other of 'followership'.

Sigvatr rings the changes on the element *-dreng-* in his *Austrfararvísur* (*Skjd.* A I 233–40; B I 220–25). He is called *armi drengr* by a heathen woman he meets in Sweden (st. 5; *Hkr.* II 137; Turville-Petre 1976, 82), and when his horse stumbles it is referred to as *fákr drengs* (st. 11; *Hkr.* II 93–94; Turville-Petre 1976, 80; Frank 1978, 72–74). Despite the fact that it is a difficult and uncomfortable mission (*drjúggenginn vas drengjum*), the poet (*drengr*) still feels able to praise his *þengill* (st. 14; *Hkr.* II 139–40). Indeed, he triumphs over adversity and emphasises that he has managed the journey *fulldrengila* (st. 15; *Hkr.* II 140; Turville-Petre 1976, 83), and he achieves an agreement for equal treatment of Rǫgnvaldr's *húskarlar* with Óláfr's *drengir* (st. 18; *Hkr.* II 142; *Fsk.* 180). Throughout the poem, Sigvatr contrasts his happiness on the king's ship with his troubles on land, and uses *drengr* when the discomforts are being emphasised. The implication is that the king's followers are more than willing to endure trouble and difficulty for his sake, but also that they are intimate enough with him to make open and complaining reference to this. Sigvatr's usage is individual, even idiosyncratic, but builds on the semantic components of the basic term. His verse is very much the poetry of camaraderie, of the in-group. Speaking, as Sigvatr does, from within that in-group, it is logical for *drengr* to develop the first-person meaning. This meaning is common in non-canonical skaldic verse, where the poet refers to himself in the third person as *drengr*. The semantic component 'intimacy' that seems important to the meaning of *drengr* can lead to the use of the term in other contexts than that of the relationship between the war-lord and his followers. Thus *drengr* is commonly used in poetry about women and love.

In a *lausavísa* preserved in *Orkneyinga saga*, Arnórr Þórðarson expresses his unwillingness to get involved in a battle between the two Orkney jarls Þorfinnr and Rǫgnvaldr, referring to himself as *drengr* (*Skjd.* A I 354; B I 326–27; *Orkn.* 66–67). But besides demonstrating the common first-person meaning of this term, this verse also reminds us (*gótt's fylgja vel dróttni*) of the important collocation with the term *dróttinn*. In Arnórr's poetry we sense a new relationship between a *drengr* and his *dróttinn* that is no longer the easy camaraderie of the *comitatus*. In his *Magnúsdrápa*, for instance, the king is *drengja harri* in the centre of the fighting (st. 14; *Skjd.* A I 342; B I 314), or *drengja dróttinn* when he wins both Denmark and Norway (st. 7a; *Skjd.* A I 340; B I 312–13):

> Náði siklingr síðan
> snjallr ok Danmǫrk allri,
> mǫttr óx drengja dróttins,
> dýrr Nóregi at stýra.

The courageous, excellent prince then achieved rule over Norway and all Denmark, the power of the lord of *drengir* increased.

This stanza is a good example of the type of praise poetry that centres entirely on the king, heaping up nouns and epithets referring to him—the *drengir* have only a shadowy substance, providing at most an unspecific background to the achievements of their king. This style reaches its culmination in the *Eiríksdrápa* of Markús Skeggjason which always seems to me to have a flavour of pastiche about it. In st. 7, describing Eiríkr's generosity, the emphasis is entirely on the king and the gifts he is distributing, while the *drengir* are the mere passive recipients of his bounty (*Skjd.* A I 445–46; B I 415; *Knýtl.* 214–15):

> Drengir þǫgu auð at yngva.
> Ǫrr fylkir gaf sverð ok knǫrru.
> Eiríkr veitti opt ok stórum
> armleggjar rǫf dýrðar seggjum.
> Hringum eyddi hodda slǫngvir
> hildar ramr, en stillir framði
> fyrða kyn, svát flestir urðu,
> Fróða stóls, af hǫnum góðir.

The *drengir* received wealth from the king. The generous captain gave swords and ships. Eiríkr granted often and lavishly arm's amber [gold] to men of excellence.
The battle-brave distributor of treasure destroyed rings, and the occupant of Fróði's throne honoured men so that most became enriched by him.

With the growing power and ambitions of kings, then, the *drengir*, far from being their most trusted followers and intimates, have become mere cannonfodder (Steinn, *Óláfsdrápa*, st. 4; *Skjd.* A I 410; B I 379; *Hkr.* III 180–81; *Fsk.* 279) or rowing-power (Þjóðólfr, *lausavísa* 19; *Skjd.* A I 381; B I 351; *Hkr.* III 142). And anyone who is not totally loyal to his *dróttinn* is accused of the crime of *drengspell* (Þjóðólfr, *Sexstefja*, st. 11; *Skjd.* A I 371; B I 341; *Fsk.* 264). Sigvatr, who reserved the right to criticise his kings, would not have approved.

Þegn

Also reserving their right to criticise the king are the *þegnar* of skaldic poetry. In the corpus under investigation, the term *þegn* first appears in stanza 19 of Óttarr svarti's *Hǫfuðlausn* (*Skjd.* A I 295–96; B I 272; *Hkr.* II 172–73; *Fsk.* 181; *Orkn.* 41):

> Gegn, eru þér at þegnum,
> þjóðskjǫldunga góðra
> haldið hæft á veldi,
> Hjaltlendingar kenndir.

Engi varð á jǫrðu
ógnbráðr, áðr þér nóðum,
austr, sás eyjum vestan,
ynglingr, und sik þryngvi.

You rule skilfully and worthily the dominions of good folk-kings, the Shetlanders are acknowledged to be your *þegnar*.
There was no vehement king in the east [Norway], before we got you, who forced the islands in the west under him.

Here, the word *þegn* appears to mean 'subject'. In the prose introduction to this verse in ch. 31 of *Fagrskinna*, this relationship is interpreted as one of tax-payment: *Óláfr konungr lagði undir sik fyrst Nóregskonunga ok tók skatta um Orkneyjar ok Hjaltland ok Færeyjar*. But in the verse itself, the relationship between the king and the Shetlanders, while clearly one of subordination, is not a legalistic fiscal one but is expressed in basic terms of subjugation. The poet addresses the king and praises him for having a firm hold on his kingdom, and for being the first Norwegian king to have subjugated the islands in the west.

This connotation of resistance that must be crushed is present in almost all the occurrences of *þegn* in eleventh-century skaldic verse. Sigvatr, as usual, uses the connotations for his own purposes: in *Bersǫglisvísur*, he is on the side of the *þegnar* who are in a state of opposition to the rule of Magnús the Good. But they are in opposition because of the king's heavy-handed behaviour in keeping them in line. *Hverr eggjar þik hǫggva . . . bú þegna?* he asks (st. 11; *Skjd*. A I 254; B I 237; *Hkr*. III 29; *Fsk*. 213–14), and he reports their amazement that *mínn dróttinn leggr sína eign á óðal þegna* (st. 14; *Skjd*. A I 255; B I 238; *Hkr*. III 30). In his verses on the Battle of Stiklestad, the idea of opposition is also present: the *þegnar* opposed to the king gained an advantage because they were twice as many (*Erfidrápa*, st. 9; *Skjd*. A I 259; B I 241; *Hkr*. II 377), and in a *lausavísa* warning King Óláfr of treachery, it will be every *þegn* for himself (*lausavísa* 20; *Skjd*. A I 271; B I 251; *Hkr*. II 304).

Sigvatr could usually see both sides of a question, but other poets adopted a more single-mindedly royalist tone, and the *þegnar* are there seen entirely from the king's point of view, as unruly subordinates to be curbed. Thus, echoing a line from Sigvatr, Arnórr Þórðarson praises Magnús for that which Sigvatr criticised him for: *Eignask namt þú óðal þegna* (*Hrynhenda*, st. 8; *Skjd*. A I 334; B I 307–08). The *þegnar* become as much a part of the king's possessions as the land, so that Magnús and Haraldr harðráði can share them out between them (Þjóðólfr, *Sexstefja*, st. 9; *Skjd*. A I 371; B I 341; *Hkr*. III 97–98). Stanzas 19–23 of *Sexstefja* illustrate how Haraldr subjugates the different parts of Norway, and this section of the poem is summed up in st. 24 with the statement that *Haraldr refsir þegnum reyndan ofsa* (*Skjd*. A I 375; B I 344–45; *Hkr*. III 199).

Haraldr was not the only king admired for dealing with his subjects with a hard hand. Even the mild Óláfr kyrri was praised by Steinn Herdísarson for forcing (*kúga*) the *þegnar til friðmála* (*Óláfsdrápa*, st. 13; *Skjd.* A I 412; B I 382; *Hkr.* III 203; *Fsk.* 299). As usual, the eleventh-century attitude is summed up by Markús Skeggjason. Stanza 8a of his *Eiríksdrápa* enumerates four classes of miscreants that the king has dealt with (*Skjd.* A I 446; B I 415; *Knýtl.* 216):

> Vǫrgum eyddi Vinða fergir.
> Víking hepti konungr fíkjum.
> Þjófa hendr lét þengill stýfa.
> Þegnum kunni hann ósið hegna.

The conqueror of the Wends destroyed outlaws. The king decisively stopped piracy. The ruler had thieves' hands chopped off. He curbed the rebellion of the *þegnar*.

Placing *þegnar* in the company of outlaws, pirates and thieves is hardly flattering!

Thus, in skaldic verse about 11th-century Scandinavia, the term *þegn* was clearly used in the context of growing royal power, which felt the need to assert itself strongly against its own subjects.

Comparisons

The occurrence of the word *dreng* in a pre-1066 English source,[4] *The Battle of Maldon*, l. 149 (Scragg 1981, 61), is undoubtedly a loan-word and corresponds fairly closely to the meaning outlined above. In borrowing the word *dreng*, the English poet used it very much as it would have been used in an equivalent skaldic verse about the battle, if only we had one.

Two lines later in the poem, we find the word *þegen*, referring to the hero, Byrhtnoth, as *Æþelredes þegen*. The word occurs three more times in the poem, always clearly referring to men of rank, in the context of emphasising their loyalty to, and willingness to die for, their lord. These two semantic components of high rank and loyalty to a superior are basic to the secular uses of the word *þeg(e)n* in Old English. This is not the place to embark on a semantic analysis of the Old English word, which is extremely common, except to say that the Old English term is generally quite specific and there seems to be little or no overlap with the skaldic usage as I have sketched it above. The English influence on the meaning of the word, if any, must come later (Hofmann 1955, 77).

Post-1066 uses of the word *dreng* (including the Lancashire Domesday) have a very different meaning from that of *The Battle of Maldon* and seem, like *þegn*, to refer to a specific rank (Harmer 1952, 532). It is likely that this usage was introduced in the time of, or as a result of, the reign of Cnut, and that it came from Denmark. Thus a more proper comparison would be with its use in East Norse runic inscriptions rather than West Norse skaldic verse, and this is a topic that needs further investigation.

At the same time, runic inscriptions raise a different set of questions compared with skaldic verse. With runic inscriptions we have the original text and dating is more secure, if not very precise. Perhaps more significant is the fact that we are dealing with an entirely different type of text, in a different register, composed for different reasons and for a different audience, in East rather than West Norse. Yet there are also areas of overlap. Both skaldic verse and runic inscriptions could be said to have the general function of 'praise', and some runic inscriptions have poetic pretensions.

Despite this overlap, it seems clear that both terms, *þegn/þiagn* and *drængR*, are used very differently in runic inscriptions from the way they are in skaldic verse.[5] In general, it can be said that the runic usages of these two words are not as clearly differentiated as the skaldic ones. In the runic inscriptions, the two terms are used in very similar ways, usually referring to the dead, very often in collocation with an adjective, usually *góðr*, *goþr* etc. There is nothing in the inscriptions to indicate whether these were terms of rank or not. The only discernible differences between the two terms are generational and regional: the *drængiaR* are more likely to be commemorated as sons or brothers (or in Denmark as partners), the *þegnaR* as fathers and husbands; in eastern Sweden, *Þiagn* is known only as a proper name. There is also, in the Swedish inscriptions, a fairly strong correlation between use of the term *drængR* and what might be called 'viking' activity, expeditions or death abroad, particularly if we include the few inscriptions containing the adverb *drængila*.

The only safe conclusion is that the skaldic poems and the runic inscriptions are using an entirely different vocabulary, despite the apparent identity of the two terms under investigation. Whether this is because the words meant something different in East Norse and West Norse, or whether it is because either the skalds or the rune-carvers (or both) were using a specialised vocabulary, remains to be seen.

NOTES

[1] I am grateful to David Parsons who, financed by the Scandinavian Studies Fund of the University of Cambridge, has created a machine-readable version of a large proportion of *Skjd.* B and has thereby made the task of finding individual words considerably easier.

[2] Recently, Marie Stoklund (1992, 295–96) has wisely warned against drawing too wide-ranging conclusions from the variable and not always securely dated runic material.

[3] For all skaldic stanzas and half-stanzas cited, I give references both to *Skjd.* and to one or more *Íslenzk fornrit* editions, if relevant. I tend to follow the latter, if cited, in matters of both normalisation and punctuation (though not slavishly). The translations are my own and aim at consistency and accuracy rather than elegance.

[4] In fact, the term (spelt *ðreng*) is also used in Gospatric's writ which, although surviving in a 13th-century transcript, almost certainly represents an original from the late Anglo-Saxon period (Harmer 1952, 421).

[5] The occurrences of these words in Danish and Swedish runic inscriptions can be deduced from the concordances in Andersen and Holmboe 1983, and Peterson 1989. For discussion, in addition to the studies already cited, see Jacobsen and Moltke 1942, cols 643, 730–31.

BIBLIOGRAPHY AND ABBREVIATIONS

Aakjær, Svend. 1927–28. 'Old Danish thegns and drengs', *Acta philologica Scandinavica* 2, 1–30.
Andersen, Ingeborg, and Holmboe, Henrik. 1983. *Kondordans over de danske runeindskrifter—Transskription.*
Fell, Christine. 1987. 'Old English *wicing*: a question of semantics', *Proceedings of the British Academy* 72, 295–316.
Fidjestøl, Bjarne. 1985. 'On a new edition of scaldic poetry'. In *The Sixth International Saga Conference, 28.7.–2.8. 1985. Workshop papers*, 319–35.
Foote, Peter. 1978. 'Wrecks and rhymes'. In Thorsten Andersson and Karl Inge Sandred (eds.). *The Vikings. Proceedings of a symposium of the Faculty of Arts of Uppsala University, June 6–9, 1977*, 57–66.
Foote, Peter. 1984. 'Things in early Norse verse'. In Bjarne Fidjestøl et al. (eds.). *Festskrift til Ludvig Holm-Olsen på hans 70-årsdag den 9. juni 1984*, 74–83.
Frank, Roberta. 1978. *Old Norse court poetry: the dróttkvætt stanza.*
Fsk. = Bjarni Einarsson (ed.). 1984. *Ágrip af Nóregskonunga sǫgum. Fagrskinna—Nóregs konunga tal.*
Harmer, F. E. 1952. *Anglo-Saxon writs.*
Hkr. = Bjarni Aðalbjarnarson (ed.). 1941–51. Snorri Sturluson. *Heimskringla.*
Hofmann, Dietrich. 1955. *Nordisch-englische Lehnbeziehungen der Wikingerzeit.*
Jacobsen, Lis, and Moltke, Erik. 1942. *Danmarks runeindskrifter. Text.*
Knýtl. = Bjarni Guðnason (ed.). 1982. *Danakonunga sǫgur.*
Kuhn, Hans. 1944. 'Altnordisch *rekkr* und Verwandte', *Arkiv för nordisk filologi* 58, 105–21.
Lindow, John. 1976. *Comitatus, individual and honor. Studies in North Germanic institutional vocabulary.*
Orkn. = Finnbogi Guðmundsson (ed.). 1965. *Orkneyinga saga.*
Peterson, Lena. 1989. *Svenskt runordsregister.*
Sawyer, Peter. 1989. *The making of Sweden.*
Scragg, D. G. (ed.). 1981. *The Battle of Maldon.*
Skjd. = Finnur Jónsson (ed.). 1912–15. *Den norsk-islandske skjaldedigtning.*
Stoklund, Marie. 1992. 'Runesten, kronologi og samfundsrekonstruktion'. In *Mammen. Grav, kunst og samfund i vikingetid*, 285–97.
Strid, Jan Paul. 1987. 'Runic Swedish thegns and drengs'. In *Runor och runinskrifter. Föredrag vid Riksantikvarieämbetets och Vitterhetsakademiens Symposium 8–11 september 1985*, 301–16.
Turville-Petre, E. O. G. 1976. *Scaldic poetry.*

PREBEN MEULENGRACHT SØRENSEN

HISTORICAL REALITY AND LITERARY FORM

IN ITS broad sense, the term 'philology' implies not only the studies that are necessary to produce an edition of a text—work on manuscripts and language, along with emendation and comment—but also consideration of its form and significance; in fact what is more usually thought of as literary study. Saga studies have traditionally belonged both to the domain of philology in this broad sense and to the domain of history—and in that order. Most modern contributions reveal the same divide, at least if we count historical anthropology as a legitimate branch of historical scholarship. The two approaches are closely related but the boundary-line between them is clearly drawn. Philological and literary study seeks the reality *in* the text. Historical and ethnological study seeks some kind of reality *behind* the text.

The subject I have been asked to speak on is the contribution of saga studies to our understanding of Scandinavian society in the early Middle Ages, seen as a current problem. I find I am best able to do this by looking at the present-day situation in saga research and then casting a glance to the future. But inevitably I shall start with a quick look at the past.

In the course of this century no small confusion has arisen in the study of Norse–Icelandic literature: a collapse of the consensus that once existed about its origin and significance. When the Viking Society was founded, and for some time after that, it was possible to read sagas, even Sagas of Icelanders, as truthful historical accounts; and Eddaic poems, myths and legends were still accepted by most scholars as valid sources of information about the pre-Christian North. This general attitude was an outcome of the Romantic movement, whose nineteenth-century sons found no difficulty in reading sagas as history, poetry, mind and spirit, all at the same time. In his history of Old Norse literature, published in 1865, N. M. Petersen could say: 'The word has two revelations: poetry and history.' He goes on: 'The idea goes forth and creates the particular; particulars form an assemblage, and therein the human mind perceives the idea. It is the task of history to achieve this perception.' On these lines, and with a reference to Alexander von Humboldt, he explained the creation of sagas: 'The narrator discovers the idea inherent in an age ... An idea reveals itself in the narrative. It becomes critical history presented with historical art. The saga turns into history' (Petersen 1966, 182; my translations).

The seeds of schism in our own century were already sown in the Romantic dichotomy between history and poetry (imaginative creative writing, as we would probably call it). When Carsten Hauch, Petersen's colleague at the University of

Copenhagen, lectured on Sagas of Icelanders in 1848 and 1849, he spoke of the differences between the realm of poetry and the realm of history—but only to see saga literature as a higher unification of the two (Hauch 1855, 467). A generation later the synthesis was being dissolved. Positivism and her straightlaced daughters, source-criticism and the 'book-prose' theory, made an either/or distinction between poetry and history; and now it could no longer be a question of perceiving the coherent idea of a past age through the particulars of saga literature. On the contrary, it was the particulars themselves that attracted all the attention. Historians tried to sort sagas, which they referred to as 'sources', into historical and unhistorical groups. Philologists and literary historians did the same and went even farther down that road. They regarded sagas as written compositions, the work of authors with individual personalities; and their most obsessive search was for the sources those authors used, for their preoccupations and prejudices, sometimes even for their names and addresses.

Sagas of Icelanders were dissected with particular zeal. Scholars tried to distinguish between written sources and oral tradition, between historical fact and authorial fiction, between native inheritance and foreign influence, between pagan and Christian, between honest description of the past and contemporary roman à clef. But it rarely happened that a saga was considered as what it primarily is: letters on a page, a text, which irrespective of its origin presents itself as a coherent whole to anyone who hears or reads it. The scholars who based their approach to a saga on the axiom that it was the work of a creative author seldom or never went the whole way, which would have entailed a purely literary interpretation of the text they studied. And few scholars attempted to explain why, if the sagas are fictions, the texts themselves persist in claiming they are works of history; or why, if they were thus regarded as history, they should be presented in aesthetic form, in literary mode.

The uncertainty that has lingered over the status of sagas as texts, Sagas of Icelanders in particular, has meant that there has been no firm hermeneutic base to build on. When the historians dismissed sagas as usable sources, they left a void which literary scholars have not succeeded in filling. It is true that much time and effort have gone into analysis of sagas from fresh points of view, and many valuable additions have been made to our knowledge, but we have not reached any new consensus on how sagas are to be read and understood. Most studies of a literary kind have been concerned with something outside the text rather than with the text itself. That is not my idea of literary scholarship, and I hope it is not yours either.

Sagas were deprived of their status as records of historical reality. Debate about what they meant and what value-system or systems they represented nevertheless continued. A central point round which discussion revolved concerned the ethics of the Sagas of Icelanders. The traditional idea had been that they portrayed an authentic heathen code, but when the notion of their immaculate oral conception in the pre-literate past was abandoned, that idea had to be abandoned too. But as the sagas now came to be seen as products of the Christian Middle Ages, so their ethical ideas came to be seen as Christian as well. The argument was, and is, that since sagas were written by Christians for the benefit of a Christian public, then they must be interpreted on the basis of received Christian values.

A good many studies have sought to demonstrate Christian modes of thought and theological perspectives behind the sagas' apparently pre-Christian façade. There is plenty of academic discord in this field too. Acknowledgment that Christian literary culture affected sagas as written texts has served a useful purpose, but in the last resort the approach has only stretched sagas out on a new Procrustean bed. Older scholars saw Sagas of Icelanders as lineal kin of heroic poetry, and equated 'honour' with the Germanic heroic outlook. Younger scholars believe the same sagas are ruled by ideas that were shaped and fostered by the moral theory of medieval churchmen. Both attitudes start with value-systems that are external to the sagas, and neither approach does more than throw fitful light on the themes and principles offered by the texts themselves.

Some attempts at a strictly literary interpretation of individual sagas have been made, but few have been successful. But if we miss the mark in approaching sagas with the literary methods at our disposal, the fundamental reason for the failure is obvious. The fact is that these very methods put us off our aim from the start. The sagas present themselves as factual historical narratives and it by no means immediately follows that instruments developed for the critical dissection of fiction of one kind and another are suitable tools for the analysis of a saga-text. Or to put it another way: saga-language imitates the language of everyday life, which has direct reference to reality, and it does not contain the rhetorical and figurative significances, the symbolic play with ordinary speech, which our practice of literary criticism is primarily designed to observe and evaluate.

Saga style, particularly in the Sagas of Icelanders but in Kings' Sagas and Contemporary Sagas as well, is an imitation of spoken narrative, of a tale told; and the style itself is indicative of the truth of what is reported. The form is the form of tradition, and the stock phrases in sagas, 'It is told', 'Now to be told is', convey the primary setting, where the narrator is face to face with his audience, guaranteeing with his personality the truthfulness of his account. If we want to understand what a saga means, we must take it seriously for what it claims to be in all its language and form: a truthful report of past events. A historian may find this difficult, because he is committed to a narrow modern definition of truth; but it is not hard for students of literature or ethnology: they can operate with other notions of truth, not bound by the concept paramount in their own culture.

There has recently been a reorientation in attitudes towards sagas and Norse–Icelandic literature as a whole. As at the turn of the century, the impulse has mainly come from historical studies, but characteristically enough not so much from the mainstream discipline as from kindred branches, legal history, cultural history, history of religion, and from social anthropologists who are now reoccupying the territory deserted by the historians. The interminable discussion about truth and fiction, the inherited and the novel, has worn itself out. The relegation of Norse–Icelandic texts from the realm of history to the realm of invention, which has now in effect lasted for nearly a century, cast a pall, but it has not stifled a perceived need to confront saga literature afresh and profit from the rich material it can contribute to our knowledge of ancient Northern culture. I shall in all brevity attempt to illustrate the new attitude by reference to recent work by four scholars who, we can say, have lifted corners of that pall and let fresh light in. None of them is concerned primarily with sagas as texts, but all have consequences for saga study and all have a bearing on aspects of early Scandinavian society.

Social anthropology has played a key part in the current change of attitude, not so much by the direct contributions of the discipline as by the inspiration it has given to scholars in the fields of history and literature. The most important and substantial of the direct contributions have been made by Kirsten Hastrup in her Oxford dissertation, *Culture and history in Medieval Iceland* (1985), and in a number of papers collected in *Island of anthropology. Studies in past and present Iceland* (1990). The first of these is an attempt at historical ethnography, taking a by-pass, as it were, round the historians' blockade of the Norse–Icelandic source-material, though certainly at such a level of abstraction and with such a generalising use of texts, chiefly laws and Ari's *Íslendingabók,* that her study will not meet the historian's demand for an account of the past as close to reality as possible. But the value of her book lies as much in her concepts and method as in any concrete results. What is new is the social anthropologist's overall view, which once again makes it possible to synthesise on the basis of those relics of Norse civilisation we still possess. For Kirsten Hastrup this kind of cultural totality is discovered as a conceptual system which can be described by means of ethnographic models. It is no less important that in subsequent studies she comprehends that system as formed in narrative—she maintains that the past cannot be understood without 'some kind of narrative structure'. So the problem of the relationship between the tale and the truth simply dissolves. The text *is* history, and in that sense it is true. She concludes: 'The sagas were representations of a timeless history that was kept alive in the collective memory by being repeatedly "said"' (Hastrup 1990, 142, 153).

It is not difficult to find less convincing stuff in other recent ethnographic studies of sagas. Some social anthropologists seem to move into this field in a spirit like that of their predecessors plunging into darkest Africa; but, apart from a sometimes deficient acquaintance with primary sources and ignorance of the long history of scholarship in the Norse field, social anthropologists run the general risk, noted by Vilhelm Grønbech in 1909, of reducing all problems to one low level, 'a crude cross-section of different people far removed from each other in culture', to a common denominator which is imposed on 'Negroes and Indians and Greeks without distinction' (Grønbech 1955, II 347; my translations). Something of the kind has happened in recent saga studies. Society as portrayed in sagas is compared with 'primitive, stateless societies' anywhere in the world, and it is claimed that the outcome tells us something about the Icelandic past, though in fact it throws no more light on it as a historical reality than it does on the sagas themselves.[1]

The social anthropological approach gives better results when it is combined with the methods of the historian and literary scholar, or at least it should. William Ian Miller is to some extent representative of this kind of combined operation, a legal historian who uses Sagas of Icelanders as a source for the description of social institutions. He has reproached Kirsten Hastrup, not wholly without justification, for an uncritical use of sources, and in particular for not making use of saga-literature. In a number of papers (e.g. Miller 1983 and 1986) and in his book, *Bloodtaking and peacemaking* (1990), he himself employs Sagas of Icelanders and *Sturlunga saga*, along with *Grágás*, as his primary sources of Icelandic social history in the last century of the Free State. His own source-criticism is limited to defending in general terms the use of literature as material the historian cannot neglect and emphasising that 'the saga sources are admirably suited to certain social and legal historical enquiries concerning the time in which they were written' (Miller 1990, 45). He maintains that 'the sagas describe a real world external to themselves' and that it is possible to 'recover' this world 'in those areas where the saga description is thick enough and makes sense in the light of relevant comparative data' (Miller 1990, 76). Here we are back to unhesitating confidence in the value of sagas as sources but, be it noted, not as sources of information about people and events. The focus is now on social patterns and cultural institutions.

As with Kirsten Hastrup, Miller's strength lies in his desire to make a coherent whole of the images of society conveyed in sagas. His weakness is that he takes the descriptions of the past in Sagas of Icelanders to be sources of knowledge about the contemporary world of the writers of those sagas, and neglects to consider the problems which arise as a result. He does not make much of the fact that sagas are narratives given literary form, that they are reality but with a construction put upon it. He on the other hand accepts them without qualification: for him they are trustworthy accounts of an immediate reality on which a social history can be based. His results show that his method is effective. Sagas and laws together give a homogeneous all-round picture, but it remains an open question whether this picture is of historical reality or only of the reality of the text—and if it is historical, is it then tenth-century history or thirteenth-century history? Miller cannot tell us the answer, for he does not put it to the test. He rarely analyses any text as a literary creation.

Miller's method is as much that of the social anthropologist as of the legal historian, and only very few 'straight' historians have dared to start using sagas as sources again. One of them is Sverre Bagge, brought up in the Scandinavian school of source-criticism. Bagge strikes off on a different path from that followed by older members of the profession—Erik Lönnroth, for example, who has counted both the sagas and Saxo 'absolutely useless' as sources for the history of pre-Christian Scandinavia (Lönnroth 1977, 7–8). In a paper given in 1984 Bagge maintained that the general picture of social conditions, kinship and customs which we can draw from sagas does not depend on the truthfulness, as such, of the account of any event, and he consequently finds it justifiable to use them as sources for particular enquiries (Bagge 1986, 148). His words have been quoted several times since, not because they express something never said before, more because it comes as a relief to hear a historian say them. More recently Bagge has devoted several smaller studies (e.g. Bagge 1991b–c, 1992) and a whole book, *Society and politics in Snorri Sturluson's Heimskringla* (1991a), to an analysis of Kings' Sagas as historical evidence. He claims that, insofar as they show no consistent preference for any party in a conflict, *Sverris saga* and *Heimskringla* must be held to represent 'objective' historiography. Their ideology is common to all the characters depicted and also in agreement with the values of the audience their authors addressed. Therefore, he says, the sagas can be used to understand fundamental aspects of the society in question, its culture and mentality. On the other hand, like the traditional historians, he also considers the 'literary character' of sagas to be an impediment when it comes to seeking factual historical information in them (Bagge 1992, 67–70).

Miller and Bagge are on common ground in using texts like *Íslendingasögur* and *Heimskringla* as sources relevant to the contemporary world of their authors. This is based on no more than an assumption, or in Miller's words: 'It is simply safest to assume that the society of the family sagas is the society that the author knew by experience, idealised somewhat to advance his narrative agenda' (Miller 1990, 50). But his 'safest' offers no security at all. The Sagas of Icelanders claim to be telling their audience about the Viking Age, and if they are treated as sources for some later period, questions arise to which no answers are as yet forthcoming.

One or two literary studies, closely related to those of the historians I have just mentioned, have perhaps brought us in closer touch with the Viking world; but the best current example of the way in which the early literature can be used to contribute to a fresh understanding of Scandinavian society in the period from AD 800 to 1100 is a work by a historian of religion. It is Gro Steinsland's Oslo dissertation, *Det hellige bryllup og norrøn kongeideologi* (1991), a book with a very specific aim. It is based on a study of the poems, *Skírnismál, Ynglingatal, Háleygjatal* and *Hyndluljóð*. Her thesis is that a myth of sacred marriage between a god and a giant-woman explained the origin of the royal dynasties of the North and provided the model for the special status accorded to rulers. She too claims to be saying something about a historical reality behind the texts; but the reality in this case is a myth with cult function, a myth which finds expression in the four poems she deals with. Literary interpretation and description of the past thus become one and the same thing. Her analysis of the texts reveals a pattern of thought and belief which proves to have had wide currency in the pre-Christian Nordic world. The pattern accommodates a conception of polarised groups or forces which, when united, lead to a new creation or a new beginning. This is a fundamental factor, perhaps the fundamental factor, in Norse mythology, but it also becomes the model for the perception of the past found in Kings' Sagas and Sagas of Icelanders.

The studies I have mentioned all deal with conceptual structures. Kirsten Hastrup looks for general models which can describe both the Norse world-picture and the historical development of Icelandic society in the Commonwealth Period. From sagas and laws Miller seeks to demonstrate concrete social relations and the patterns into which they fall. Sverre Bagge considers that reliable information about institutions and mentality can be read out of Kings' Sagas. Gro Steinsland focuses on a mythical concept which was active in an ideology and which both explained history and influenced its course. A number of other studies in the last few years, including some of a more strictly literary or historical kind, have been similarly concerned with structures in Nordic culture, society, politics or religion. Their authors are not interested in people and events, either in the saga-writers' own time or in the past they describe. They do not relate a text to any external system of norms but interpret it purely on its own terms. At the same time, some of these scholars appear relaxed, not to say nonchalant, in the face of questions traditionally asked—about dating, transmission, authorial individualism, intention, genre, and so on. Where interest lies in behavioural paradigms and social institutions, the source-value of sagas is taken for granted.

The works I have referred to are important for the literary study of sagas because they reveal set patterns of thought and attitude in the early medieval Norse mentality. On the other hand, it is equally clear that if the social anthropologist and the historian in any relevant branch is to achieve valid results, he or she needs what the text-disciplines can provide. The prime reason is simple: the source-material in question is written as literature or, to use the term of the Romantics, as poetry.

In his *Etymologiæ* (I. xli. 1), Isidore says that history is a form of narrative. That remained the prime medieval concept. Are we not then obliged to study medieval historiography first and foremost as narrative? So, if I am asked in what way saga research can contribute to our knowledge of Scandinavian society in the Viking Age, then against the background I have sketched I can only answer that renewed interest in the reality behind sagas must entail new recognition of the reality of the text: that is, a need for philological and literary study. We must both reconsider the content of sagas and attempt to comprehend their whole mode of expression, their style, rhetoric, motives. Older historians believed sagas were windows through which they could view reality. Rejecting that, the strict source-critics said there was nothing at all to view except the saga itself. Now we must grasp the fact that the text in itself is the truth, is the history.

I should like to propose three tasks. First, deeper study of the 'meaning' in saga literature. At the beginning of this century Alexander Bugge and Lauritz Weibull dismissed the Kings' Sagas' account of the chain of events that led to the death of Óláfr Tryggvason because they detected a similarity between Sigríðr in stórráða's plot against Óláfr and Brynhildr's treatment of Sigurðr in heroic legend (Bugge 1910, 21–28; Weibull 1911, 125–26; further discussed in Meulengracht Sørensen 1993, 19–21). They did not explain why such a sequence in history should follow a pattern from legend; but we can now see, for example, that in sagas kinship and marriage provide explanatory models of a basic kind. The poetic model made the history true by making it comprehensible to the medieval public.

I may stick with this example for a little longer in further illustration of the relationship between literary form and historical reality. Both Queen Sigríðr in the Kings' Sagas and Brynhildr in heroic legend are manifestations of the stock character who has been called 'the female inciter': a woman who eggs on her husband or son to take revenge. She is a type familiar in sagas of every kind and has been paid a good deal of attention in recent studies. Some writers think she reflects the actual role of women in the Viking Age, others that the woman's goading is purely a literary motive. Judith Jesch, who as far as I know has uttered the latest word on the subject, is in the latter camp. She counts 'the female inciters of the sagas' as 'literary clichés' (Jesch 1991, 190). But what does it mean to say that something is a literary cliché? Are we not rather bound to assume that this very widespread motive had significance among the ideas which the original audience of a saga had about women and their role in relation to honour and vengeance, and that it was that significance which could, for example, make Sigríðr in stórráða's machinations true as history?

A second pressing need is for studies of the style and rhetoric of sagas, and by rhetoric I mean not merely the influence of classical doctrine and example on Icelandic prose but equally the specific character and specific development of saga style. In what ways does saga rhetoric differ from European rhetoric in general? Study of developments in style from the twelfth to the fourteenth century and of the conventions that governed the individual saga genres will be able to teach us something about what saga-writers thought they were doing, how they related to reality, and what their original public made of their work.

That leads to my third desideratum: studies of the reception of sagas. The old preoccupation with oral sagas and then the succeeding concentration on individual authors and their background both let the limelight fall on hypothetical originals and left the transmission of our extant texts in the shade. We need a shift which will put the spotlight on audiences and readers of sagas and on the work of recension and revision which in the course of the Middle Ages actually shaped the texts we have. Instead of dogma about original or archetype, we must recognise the text as a process, a moulding by different ages and different outlooks. Such consideration has found a more natural place in comment on Kings' Sagas than on Sagas of Icelanders; but the study of Kings' Sagas as literature is in a feebler state even than comparable study of Sagas of Icelanders—and both still in infancy. What is needed then is a better understanding of sagas as forms of literary communication addressed to a public; and studies of the kind I have proposed will help us to see more clearly what use we can make of sagas as sources of information about the historical world they portray. Research in reception history will also contribute to a new conception of literary history, where instead of starting from an author and his non-existent autograph we shall start from the extant manuscript record. Last but not least, reception studies will make their mark on the work of editing, when principal interest is switched from a hypothetical original to the preserved text.

I shall end by referring to a development of the last few decades which seems to me to present the biggest problem of all in our current practice of Northern Research. This is the splitting of scholarship into separate disciplines which, like petty self-sufficient kingdoms, impose heavy tolls on any exchange of ideas and methods. Recognising the fact that texts in all their meanings express historical reality—and those meanings are all we have—we are basically back to the Romantics' perception of poetry and history, of text and reality, as one and the same. I shall be optimistic and reckon that there is a fair prospect that we shall be able to benefit from saga literature both as literary art and as a valid introduction to the early Nordic past. To realise that prospect will require collaboration in scholarly effort and a fusion of the experience gained in branches too long divided: philology, literary study, history and anthropology. And we need the sympathetic insight and the sovereign view—and the courage—which will allow us to attempt syntheses in the manner of earlier philologists, such as W. P. Ker, Vilhelm Grønbech, Sigurður Nordal—only our syntheses will be built on all the new knowledge and understanding that have come into being since their day. It is a work which might nicely fill most of the next hundred years.

NOTE

[1] The phrase quoted is from E. Paul Durrenberger (1992, 46). His article is an example of the failure to heed Grønbech's warning. He concludes, 'The sagas are neither art nor history, but articulation of what Lévi-Strauss (1973) calls a "totemic operator" . . .' This looks like a misunderstanding both of sagas and of Lévi-Strauss; cf. what Lévi-Strauss (1962, 307–08) has to say on the conflict between history and totemistic classification.

BIBLIOGRAPHY

Bagge, Sverre. 1986. 'Borgerkrig og statsutvikling i Norge i middelalderen', [Norwegian] *Historisk Tidskrift*, 145–97.
Bagge, Sverre. 1991a. *Society and politics in Snorri Sturluson's* Heimskringla.
Bagge, Sverre. 1991b. 'Ideology and propaganda in *Sverris saga*', *The audience of the sagas*. Preprints of the Eighth International Saga Conference . . . Gothenburg University, 32–42.
Bagge, Sverre. 1991c. 'Propaganda, ideology and political power in Old Norse and European historiography: a comparative view', *L'Historiographie médiévale en Europe* (ed. Jean-Philippe Genet), 199–208.
Bagge, Sverre. 1992. 'From sagas to society: the case of *Heimskringla*', *From sagas to society. Comparative approaches to early Iceland* (ed. Gísli Pálsson), 61–75.
Bugge, Alexander. 1910. 'Sandhed og Digt om Olav Tryggvason', *Aarbøger for nordisk Oldkyndighed og Historie*, 2nd series 25, 21–28.
Durrenberger, E. Paul. 1992. 'Law and literature in medieval Iceland', *Ethnos* 57, 31–47.
Grønbech, Vilhelm. 1955. *Vor folkeæt i oldtiden*. 2nd ed. (First published 1909–12.)
Hastrup, Kirsten. 1985. *Culture and history in medieval Iceland. An anthropological analysis of structure and change.*
Hastrup, Kirsten. 1990. *Island of anthropology. Studies in past and present Iceland.*
Hauch, Carsten. 1855. *Afhandlinger og æsthetiske Betragtninger.*
Isidore. 1911. *Isidori . . . etymologiarum . . . libri XX* (ed. W. M. Lindsay).
Jesch, Judith. 1991. *Women in the Viking Age.*
Lévi-Strauss, Claude. 1962. *La Pensée sauvage.*
Lévi-Strauss, Claude. 1973. *The savage mind.*
Lönnroth, Erik. 1977. *The Scandinavians: selected historical essays.*
Meulengracht Sørensen, Preben. 1993. *Fortælling og ære. Studier i islændingesagaerne.*
Miller, William Ian. 1983. 'Justifying Skarphéðinn: of pretext in the Icelandic bloodfeud', *Scandinavian studies* 55, 316–44.
Miller, William Ian. 1986. 'Gift, sale, payment, raid: case studies in the negotiation and classification of exchange in medieval Iceland', *Speculum* 61, 18–50.
Miller, William Ian. 1990. *Bloodtaking and peacemaking. Feud, law and society in saga Iceland.*
Petersen, N. M. 1966. *Bidrag til den oldnordiske litteraturs historie.* (First published in *Aarbøger for nordisk Oldkyndighed og Historie* 1861, issued 1865.)
Steinsland, Gro. 1991. *Det hellige bryllup og norrøn kongeideologi. En analyse av Hierogamimyten i Skírnismál, Ynglingatal, Háleygjatal og Hyndluljóð.*
Weibull, Lauritz. 1911. *Kritiska undersökningar i Nordens historia omkring år 1000.*

BJØRN MYHRE

THE BEGINNING OF THE VIKING AGE—SOME CURRENT ARCHAEOLOGICAL PROBLEMS

Introduction

THIS year we are celebrating the centenary of the Viking Society. Next year it will be 1200 years since Alcuin wrote his letters to King Æthelred of Northumbria in 793. His description of a sudden attack by heathen barbarians, ignorant of the Christian belief and culture, is still, I feel, influential in our image of the Vikings.

In this paper I shall look for a different picture. I shall briefly present some tentative ideas I am working on about the economic and political organization of southern Norwegian societies at the beginning of the Viking Period, about the earliest contact between Norway and the British Isles and about the problem of when and why the Viking Period actually started. Some of these ideas have an empirical basis, while others are only working models that are to be refined or, if necessary, rejected.[1]

The Borre research project

The ideas presented in this paper have grown out of my participation in the reseach project at Borre in Vestfold. We have studied the history of the well-known cemetery with its nine very large barrows. We have tried to locate possible settlement sites, to study the contemporary agricultural landscape and to set the political centre of Borre into a regional and north European context (Myhre 1992).

One of the large barrows was plundered and levelled in 1852, with the destruction of the famous Borre ship-burial from about AD 900. Only a few objects and ship's nails are still preserved, but this must have been a princely burial of a quality similar to the Oseberg and Gokstad graves (Brøgger 1916). Only minor archaeological investigations have been carried out at Borre since 1852.

Our investigations so far have discovered that the oldest of the nine large barrows at the site is from the late 6th or the early 7th century, and that the cemetery was used for at least 300 years. A contemporary settlement site with buildings has been located, but has so far only been excavated in trial trenches. From about AD 600, cultivation and settlement in the area was intensified; at the same time—according to our hypothesis—as Borre developed into a political centre for this part of eastern Norway.

In earlier work, I have argued that chiefdoms or petty kingdoms may have existed along the coast of southern and western Norway during the 5th and 6th centuries AD (Myhre 1987). Their centres were strategically placed in good agricultural areas with a dense population, along the fjords or at the mouths of large river valleys. Various goods could have been transported to such centres from different ecological zones of the neighbouring territory, and it would also have been possible to exercise some control over the important communication and trading route along the coast from these strongholds. Chieftains could use valuables and commodities collected through a redistributive economic system to further their own prestige and authority through gift-exchange, feasts and controlled trade (Odner 1972 and 1974; Christophersen 1989, 121). Craftsmen and artists may have worked at these centres (Ramqvist 1991a and b).

The archaeological finds from southern and western Norway are of a similar kind as those from Denmark, Anglo-Saxon England and northern Germany. This does not mean that political organization was necessarily of a similar kind in all regions around the North Sea during the Migration Period, but I think it is fruitful to use other early Germanic kingdoms or political entities as working models for analysing the organization of polities in southern Norway.

This model has been adjusted to eastern Norway of the 6th to 8th centuries, the date of the Borre cemetery and of similar sites with large barrows or rich finds. Such sites are found along the main river valleys and Oslo fjord at places where valuables and commodities from the mountains and the forests could be collected: goods like iron, soapstone, furs, antler, hones and so on. Borre has an especially strategic location by a narrow part of the fjord from which it was possible to control the route from the hinterland to the North Sea area. At Borre itself we have found pieces of two claw beakers that may have been manufactured in southern England (Evison 1982a; Näsman 1986, 68–71). Numerous Insular objects and some sherds of claw beakers have been found at the nearby trading site of Kaupang, albeit mostly from the 9th century (Blindheim 1976). Most of the glass sherds at Kaupang are probably of Frankish origin (Hougen 1969).

The first barrows at Borre were built at an important stage in economic and political development in northern Europe. On both sides of the English Channel the first emporia or market sites had been established by the early 7th century; shortly after 700 at Ribe in Jutland (Bencard and Bender Jørgensen 1990a, 130–48; 1990b; Jensen 1991a, 79; 1991b). Ulf Näsman has argued that luxury articles and prestige goods like glass and jewellery were distributed between these centres, as part of controlled trade as well as gift-exchange between political leaders (Näsman 1986; see also Hedeager 1992). Richard Hodges has suggested a stepwise development of exchange and trade around the southern coasts of the North Sea. For the late 7th and early 8th centuries he finds indications that not only prestigious goods were exchanged but also commodities produced by craftsmen in the emporia, as well as natural resources from the districts (1989, 162–64; see also Steuer 1987; Näsman 1990, 105; Jensen 1990, 132).

I would place Borre and the district of Vestfold during the late 7th and the 8th centuries in a large-scale system of communication and exchange such as this. I propose the hypothesis that the petty kings in Vestfold participated in a social and economic network of alliances and warfare between royal courts in Scandinavia and along the southern shores of the North Sea. In addition to commodities, there was probably also an exchange of ideas, ideologies and knowledge.

Archaeology and the Viking Period

Ideas and models emerging from the Borre project, together with recent reseach in Denmark into economic and political developments during the 7th and 8th centuries, have led me further to reconsider the prevailing hypotheses about political organization in western Norway during this period. The chronology of the 7th and 8th centuries has to be reconsidered, as well as the date and the character of early contacts between western Norway and the British Isles.

The study of this period has to take account of relevant written sources. We are, however, faced with a general problem in that interpretations of written texts, even if they are fragmentary or questionable, tend to have too much influence on archaeological research. I feel that, generally speaking, the archaeology of the Viking Period is overdependent on interpretations made by historians, especially when it comes to problems concerning religion, social and political organization and the first contacts between Scandinavia and Britain. Archaeologists have mainly concerned themselves with problems of chronology, art, technology, settlements, graves and so on.

During the last three decades, Scandinavian archaeology has made progress in three main fields of relevance to the study of the early Middle Ages. I would note first the very large body of data which has been brought to light from settlements, graves and trading sites, not least the many finds indicating large-scale exploitation of inland and mountain resources for iron, furs, antler, soapstone, hones and so on.

Secondly, I would emphasize the cooperation of archaeologists and natural scientists with respect to vegetation history, osteology, physical anthropology and dating methods like radiocarbon chronology and dendrochronology. New datings of sites and a new picture of the development of the human environment have forced archaeology to reassess its hypotheses.

Last but not least, I would note the theoretical debate within archaeology of recent decades. Since the 1960s, archaeology has come out of the systems theory of primarily functionalistic thinking to apply structuralist and post-processual theories that also emphasize the symbolic and ideological aspects of material culture (Hodder 1991; Myhre 1991). This new approach has brought the so-called New Archaeology of the 1970s back into closer cooperation with other human disciplines.

Generally speaking, I feel that the archaeologist is now better equipped to meet with historians and other scholars in the study of the Viking Period. In Denmark in particular we have recently seen how the cooperation of different disciplines can produce impressive new results and understandings of this important transitional phase between prehistory and historical times (Mortensen and Rasmussen 1988 and 1991). There, it is particularly the archaeologists who have discovered important data which show that social and political organization was more developed during the 7th and 8th centuries than was previously thought. The evidence for strong political authorities in southern Scandinavia in the 8th century is another foundation-stone in a real understanding of when and why the Viking Age began.

The problem of chronology

Recent archaeological investigations and absolute dating methods like radiocarbon chronology and dendrochronology have led many archaeologists to question the current absolute and relative chronologies of the late pre-Viking[2] and Viking Periods (Näsman 1989, 160). We are faced with the general problem of phasing together results based on archaeological methods like typology, stylistic analysis and stratigraphy with the absolute chronology obtained by methods based in the natural sciences. We also, of course, have the problem of correlating dated historical events with archaeological material and phases.

It has been shown that the traditional Viking-Period styles, like the Oseberg, Borre, Jelling and Mammen styles, do not form a simple chronological sequence. Instead they seem to overlap (Näsman 1989, 172). The definition of different styles has also been discussed (Fuglesang 1982; 1987; 1991).

For my work, the transition between the Vendel styles III/E and the Oseberg style is of special interest. Linked with this problem is the question of the start of the Viking Period, archaeologically speaking, in terms of both relative and absolute chronology.

Recent work on the Merovingian Period on the Continent seems to support Hermann Ament's phasing of it into an Early and a Late Period, each with subperiods I, II and III. Absolute datings are based on the evidence of coins, dendrochronology, historical events and radiocarbon dates. The Early Merovingian Period starts with the establishment of the Merovingian dynasty by Childeric and ends when the first mayors of the palace come to power and the Carolingian Period begins. Ament suggests two possible final dates: 719 when Charles Martel nominally came to power, or 751, when Pepin III was crowned. From an archaeological point of view, he prefers the date of AD 719, which is closer to the end of the period of the 'Reihengräbersitte' (1977).

Studies by Birgit Arrhenius, Ulla Lund Hansen and Karen Høilund Nielsen on Scandinavian material, compared with Ament's chronological system as well as recent dendrochronological dates of important Merovingian graves on the Continent, indicate that the Vendel styles III/B–E should be dated earlier than previously thought (Arrhenius 1983; Lund Hansen 1988; Høilund Nielsen 1987; 1991). The transition between the Migration and the Vendel Period may be placed as early as shortly before AD 550, and style III/E probably occurs as early as phase JM ('jüngere Merowingerzeit') III: that is between AD 680 and 720. The date of style F is a crucial problem in this discussion. It must have appeared at least before 768–88, when the Tassilo-chalice was probably made (Haseloff 1951, 1).

Ulla Lund Hansen poses the question in this way: 'The problem now is with what kind of material are we to fill up the second half of the 8th century? Is it to be material identical with what we previously called Early Viking Period, or with parts of that material?' (1988, 33; my translation).

Karen Høilund Nielsen has recently studied Vendel-style elements by means of correspondence analysis, leading to a new division of the Vendel Period into well-defined phases: first into phases 1A–D and 2A–C (1987; based mainly on Bornholm material); later into phases VII:A–D (1991, 130–46; based on Danish and Swedish material). It is important to note that traditionally Early Viking Period objects occur as early as her phase 2B–C or VII:D, i.e. the so-called Berdal oval brooches (Petersen's types 11–24) and objects decorated with gripping beasts, style III/E, style F and the Broa style. Archaeologically speaking, such styles and objects should then be earlier than AD 800, perhaps even predating the last quarter of the 8th century (Høilund Nielsen 1987, 69).

In his study of the oval brooches from Birka in Sweden, Ingmar Jansson came to a similar conclusion. He found that the Broa style (Early Oseberg style), gripping beasts and style III/E-elements occur together during the late 8th century. In his opinion the beginning of the 'archaeological Viking Period' is closely connected to the beginning of the Birka period. He places the transition rather vaguely in the last quarter of the century (1985, 176–95).

The recent excavations in Ribe, Jutland, have proved to be extremely important in this respect. Moulds of early Berdal brooches have been found in stratified layers together with *sceattas* of the Wodan/Monster and Porcupine types, probably made some time between 720 and 755 (Bendixen 1984). The dating of some of these layers is confirmed by dendrochronology (Christensen 1990). There are problems in that the *sceattas* may have remained in circulation until the late 8th century, and there is a possibility of the layers having been disturbed (Bencard and Bender Jørgensen 1990a, 130–48).

Mogens Bencard's conclusion (1990) that these early Berdal brooches were made during the middle part of the 8th century is, however, disputed (see Frandsen and Jensen 1988 and 1990). I find it persuasive that Bencard's dates based on the material from Ribe fit very well with the conclusions drawn by Høilund Nielsen,

Ulla Lund Hansen and Ingemar Jansson, even if these authors are much influenced by interpretations of the Ribe finds.

Discussion of the Ribe finds continues, but all in all it seems that the circumstantial evidence for dating the Broa style, the earliest occurrence of the gripping beast motif and the early Berdal brooches (P 11–22) to the middle or late part of the 8th century is convincing (see Fuglesang 1987, 12). The Oseberg style and the developed oval brooches P 25 and 27, should, accordingly, be placed at the end of the 8th century, with early oval brooches (P 37) appearing shortly after AD 800 (Jansson 1985).

I have re-examined a series of Norwegian graves that have traditionally been placed in the early 9th century in the light of this conclusion (see Figs 1–9 and note 3). The absolute chronology of the early Viking Period in Norway has been based on the so-called 'Shetelig axiom' that the period started after the Lindisfarne raid of 793, and that, accordingly, most Insular objects of an ecclesiastical character came to Norway after that incident, even if they were made in the British Isles during the 7th or 8th centuries (Shetelig 1927; 1933, 166; Bakka 1963; 1973, 11; 1982, 33; Geber 1991; Jansson 1985, 177). Many of these Insular objects were reused as dress-ornaments in Norway. They have been described as having been savagely torn from their original context and reused by barbarians who were ignorant of their sacral character (Henry 1967; Wamers 1985, 40, 64, 85–86).

The late Egil Bakka saw the connection between objects with ornaments in style III/D–F and Insular artefacts very clearly, and the chronological problem that the combination of this fact with the Lindisfarne axiom posed. His solution to the problem was to date style III/E–F to as late as about 800; to the beginning of the Viking Period according to his chronological system (1973; 1982, 32, 53).

It is a fact that many of the Insular objects in Norwegian graves must originally have been made during the 8th or even the 7th centuries. This fact has been explained away by postulating old material that was still in use in churches and monasteries in the British Isles around and after 793. The new chronology indicates, however, that graves with Insular objects could be dated to the middle and late parts, maybe even the early parts, of the 8th century.[3] This shift brings the date of the Insular objects and the local Norwegian artefacts into line, and in my opinion it brings order to the Norwegian chronology. It also shows that Shetelig's axiom was incorrect.

The Insular imports include not only ecclesiastical objects but also glassware, brooches, pins, buckles, a hanging bowl, beads and scales with weights. It does not appear to me that most of the ecclesiastical objects were carelessly ripped from their original context; rather that they have often been cut up neatly and made into fine ornaments. A suprisingly large number of objects have not been modified (Fuglesang 1989, 259; see also Blindheim 1978, 173; Wamers 1985, 41; Geber 1991).

The objects belonging to the 8th century do not differ in type from those that can be dated after 800, so that the objects in themselves do not indicate any different kind of contact or exchange on either side of the Lindisfarne plundering. In Ireland there seems to be no doubt that churches and monasteries were already being plundered during the 7th and 8th centuries by the Irish themselves (Lucas 1967; Morris 1979, 180). Charlotte Blindheim has suggested that ecclesiastical objects could have been traded and exchanged like other Insular commodities, and that some of them could even have been used as gifts or bribes in connection with conversion or missionary activity abroad (1978, 173–76). If it is correct that such Insular objects came to Norway already during the early 8th century, her hypothesis becomes even more interesting, and should be the subject of renewed discussion.

It is of special interest that we find so many Insular objects in graves along the coast of western Norway, all the way up to Vesterålen in northern Norway. One possibility is that they were distributed via Denmark and the Continent in the same way as the artefacts of Continental make. It is, however, striking that very few Insular objects have been found in southern Scandinavia outside Hedeby (Wamers 1985, 45–49, Karte 2–4). A more likely proposition is that even 7th- and 8th-century objects came to western Norway along the direct route via Scotland and the Northern Isles.

Contact between Norway and the British Isles before 793

In many publications John Hines has argued for a direct line of communication between England and Norway across the North Sea in the Migration Period (1984; 1992; forthcoming). He has also presented arguments for the continuation of a direct connection during the Vendel Period down to the Viking Period. He alludes to Insular objects found in Norwegian graves, and to written sources like Bede's *Historia* and the poems *Widsith* and *Beowulf* which include comments that may indicate a general knowledge of Norway amongst English writers.

Most important, in my opinion, is the passage quoted from Alcuin's letter to King Æthelred of Northumbria after the plundering of Lindisfarne. Usually only one of Alcuin's sentences is quoted: '... never before has such a terror appeared in Britain as we have just suffered from a pagan people, nor was it thought possible that a navigium of this kind could be made'. In a later passage in the same letter, however, Alcuin writes about these pagan people: 'Consider the dress, the hairstyle, and the luxurious habits of the princes and people. Look at the hairstyle, how you have wished to imitate the pagans in your beards and hair. Does not the terror now threaten of those whose hairstyle you wished to have?' (Hines 1984, 293–94). I agree with John Hines that it seems that Alcuin and the people of Northumbria must have known these pagans relatively well before the Lindisfarne raid.

Much of the discussion about early contact across the North Sea has run into problems connected with the technology of shipbuilding. Most scholars have argued that regular crossings were not possible before more advanced ships, with a sail, had been constructed, and therefore the dating of the first known real Viking ship, the Oseberg ship from about 800, has become a *terminus post quem*. Ole Crumlin-Pedersen has recently indicated that sailing-ships may have been used in Scandinavia as early as the 7th century (1990, 111), and, like Martin Carver (1990), I find it difficult to accept that large ships like the ones from Sutton Hoo or Kvalsund could not have been used on the open sea, even if they were rowed.

What changed with the Lindisfarne incident, according to John Hines, was that the Scandinavians no longer 'acted only as traders but also as raiders'. His argument is that Lindisfarne and later attacks cannot be explained simply on the basis of a new shipbuilding technology but rather as the result of a 'cultural change in Scandinavia, a change in the attitudes and ambitions of the Scandinavians relative to the North Sea area' (1984, 300–01). It is my intention to search for indications of such a change in attitude.

When John Hines wrote his thesis, the new chronology of the 8th century was not well developed, and the number of artefacts or graves that supported his view was small. New studies by Vera Evison (1982a and b) and Ulf Näsman (1986) of Vendel Period glass enlarged the number of Insular finds in Scandinavia. But these and other early Insular objects found in Norway could easily have been traded along the southern shores of the North Sea, as for instance Bakka (1971), Vierck (1970; 1978), Näsman (1986) and Müller-Wille (1985) argued.

If it is correct that as many Insular objects as I have suggested ended up in western and northern Norwegian graves during the 8th century, it is a substantial point in favour of Hines's hypothesis.[3] It is also appropriate to mention here Mogens Ørsnes's arguments for Insular influence on Scandinavian styles III/C–D, and his hypothesis that Scandinavia lay within the Anglo-Irish missionary area during the 8th century. Style III/D in particular, he suggested, was influenced by direct communication between Scandinavia and northern England (1966, 227; 1970, 108).

The best evidence for such contacts would be to find graves or settlements of a Norse character in the Northern Isles. During the 1930s, Haakon Shetelig and A. W. Brøgger suggested that some of the Norse finds in Orkney, Shetland and the Hebrides indicated a Norwegian settlement as early as the 8th century. Brøgger was the most categorical, concluding that 'colonization commenced long before the year 800' (1930, 282), while Shetelig disregarded some of Brøgger's datings and made a more modest declaration: 'Archaeologically the conclusion appears unavoidable that at least some stray colonists were established there from the time about 750 AD, but the one isolated find scarcely affords satisfactory evidence to settle the first Viking invasion in the Hebrides' (1954, 102; see also Shetelig 1933, 84). Such a conclusion was in line with his general opinion of contact between the British Isles and western Norway.

In her book *Scandinavian Scotland*, Barbara Crawford has cautiously suggested that the early raids 'on the English coast indicate a possible establishment of pirate bases in the Scottish Isles by the late eighth century. This is not to say, however, that these early raids were a by-product of settlement in the north' (1987, 40). Peter Sawyer, on the other hand, once suggested that the Norse had settled peacefully on the islands some time before raiding started (1971, 206). Arguments for an early phase of integration or coexistence between Picts and Norse have recently been advanced among other possible hypotheses (Ritchie 1974; Morris 1991). Some British archaeologists have, however, questioned the evidence even for early 9th-century Norse settlement on the British Isles (Graham-Campbell 1980; forthcoming), while others keep this possibility open, pointing out how inadequate our knowledge is (Wilson 1976, 95; Ritchie 1977, 189; Morris 1985, 221 and 241; 1989, 287). All scholars agree, however, that further investigations are needed before it is possible to reach firmer conclusions.

One way of attacking the problem is to study the earliest grave-finds in the light of the new chronology of the 8th century. I would draw particular attention to the following finds:

Oronsay, Hebrides	Berdal brooch. Similar to P 14.	Brøgger 1930, 216.
Kilmainham, Dublin	Berdal brooch. Similar to P 11.	Bøe 1940, 40.
Barra, Hebrides	Oval brooch. P 27.	Brøgger 1930, 233.
Sanday, Orkneys	Oval brooch. P 25.	Brøgger 1930, 172.
Arran, Hebrides	Single-edged sword.	Brøgger 1930, 205.

These brooches may belong to phase VII:D (earlier 2B–C) of Høilund Nielsen's Vendel Period, in the 8th century. The Kilmainham Berdal brooch is of a type of which moulds have been found in 8th-century layers at Ribe (Fig. 11; Brinch Madsen 1984, 67). According to Norwegian chronology, single-edged swords like the one from Arran should be dated before 800 (Helgen 1982, 67). Grave-finds like these, however, are always difficult to date accurately (Wilson 1976, 100). There is always the possibility that early objects remained in use for more than one generation, and some of them could have been heirlooms deposited in later graves as, for example, a pair of Berdal brooches found in a grave at Clibberswick, Unst, Shetland together with a mid-Viking-Period trefoil brooch (Graham-Campbell forthcoming, 8; Brøgger 1930, 157). But the argument becomes special pleading when all early objects are explained away in this manner.

I wish also to draw attention to a number of finds in which developed oval brooches of early Petersen type 37 appear. It is now time to reconsider the possibility that some of these finds too may be dated to about AD 800, or at least to the beginning of the 9th century (Petersen 1928, 33–44):

Unst, Shetland	(with a bronze bowl)	Brøgger 1930, 159.
Lewis, Hebrides	(with Insular objects)	Brøgger 1930, 236.
N. Ronaldsay, Orkneys	(with a pennanular brooch)	Brøgger 1930, 165.
Westness, Orkneys	(with an 8th-century Celtic pin)	Kaland 1973, 95.
Islandbridge, Ireland		Bøe 1940, 39.
Ballyholme, Ireland		Bøe 1940, 75.

It should also be mentioned that the graves from Kilmainham, Dublin, produced a number of single-edged swords of Petersen's types C and H that should be dated to the beginning of the Viking Period (Petersen 1919, 66, 89; Bøe 1940, 12–25; Coffey and Armstrong 1910). But as the weapon-chronology at the moment is not well adjusted to the new chronology of styles and brooches, it is not possible to put an accurate absolute date to these. Some of these graves may, however, be much earlier than 841, when, according to the written sources, Dublin was established by the Vikings (see also Shetelig 1933, 86).

These few finds are not definite evidence of an early Norse settlement in the Northern Isles. The new chronology of the 8th century is still uncertain, and it is not known whether it can be applied to the whole of the northern area. I do, however, consider it very significant that there are Norwegian graves that put early oval brooches, style III/D–E, and Insular objects in the same context; graves that now should be from the middle part of the 8th century.[3] Contact with Britain, and even with Ireland, may therefore have been established by that time.

This conclusion is supported by recent analysis of combs from the late Iron Age and the early Norse Period from Orkney. Combs of both traditonally Pictish and Norse types found on settlement sites in stratified layers have been shown to be made of reindeer antler, most probably from Norway. The earliest so-called Pictish combs of reindeer antler may be of the 7th century onwards (Smith forthcoming). Antler may represent trade, or at least some form of continuous contact, between Norway and Shetland/Orkney since that time (Weber forthcoming).

There are also other indications of early colonization in the Western Isles during the 7th and 8th centuries. I have in mind above all the many early radiocarbon dates from settlement sites in Iceland. At Herjólfsdalur on the Vestmannaeyjar, Margrét Hermanns-Auðardóttir has excavated a farm site with several buildings, some of which in a western Norwegian context could as easily be dated to the pre-Viking as to the Viking Period. At least three radiocarbon dates from good contexts may be pre-800 AD (1989, 46–53). The excavations in Reykjavík by Else Nordahl have also produced several early radiocarbon dates (1988, 113). At the moment a vigorous debate is going on over the use of radiocarbon dating in Iceland, and we are still waiting for more decisive proof of such early settlement on the island (Margrét Hermanns-Auðardóttir 1991 with comments by Sigrid Kaland, Barbara Crawford, Ditlev Mahler and Christopher Morris; see also Vilhjálmur Örn Vilhjálmsson 1990 and Guðrún Sveinbjarnardóttir 1990).

On the Faroes too, radiocarbon-dated pollen analysis indicates pre-Viking husbandry, perhaps as early as the 7th century. Johannes Johansen interprets these finds as a reflection of an early Celtic or Scandinavian settlement (1985). His early-dated pollen diagram has not, however, been supported by archaeological finds, and further investigations need to be made (Arge 1986, 14–16; Krogh 1986). These conclusions are to a great extent in conflict with the preserved written sources. I feel that it is time to sit down and examine both the written texts and the archeological material with a mind both open and critical, while remembering that both types of source are biased.

Many hypotheses have been produced to explain the first Viking raids on the coasts of the British Isles and the Continent. Amongst these we find arguments of overpopulation at home, a search for new land to settle, advances in ship technology, and a more or less casual discovery of an easy way to get rich.

Peter Sawyer has recently presented a hypothesis that I find most stimulating, and which I would like to develop further: 'It was the western European demand for northern products and the parallel Scandinavian demand for western goods, that caused close contacts between the two areas, and encouraged Scandinavians to search for new supplies in the far north or east of the Baltic. This trade enhanced the power of some Scandinavian rulers, by increasing their wealth. Others who were less successful or even exiled could resort to piracy first in the Baltic and later in the west, an extension that was facilitated by the adoption of the sail' (1982, 7). I would also stress the evidence for trading and the development of strong political authority in Scandinavia during the centuries before 800, but while Sawyer credits all the Viking attacks to 'the unsuccessful and the exiled', I would suggest that many of the assaults were deliberately planned by Scandinavian leaders or petty kings as a response to growing political and ideological pressure from Frankish or Anglo-Saxon powers like Charlemagne and Offa. I would stress the possibility of there having been a long period of trade, exchange and more peaceful contact between powers on all sides of the North Sea before the raiding started.

The Viking attacks would therefore be a result of economic, ideological and political developments all around the North Sea, and they tell us just as much about the strength and complexity of the 8th-century polities in Denmark and southern Norway as about those in the British Isles and on the Continent.

Archaeological theory, ethnicity and ideology

During the 1960s and 1970s, archaeological theory was dominated by the positivist and functionalist New Archaeology. System theory in particular came to be the main explanatory tool, with an emphasis on economic, ecological, technological and demographic factors and on social systems.

In the 1980s, archaeological theory turned to structuralism and semiotics, critical theory and poststructuralism, led by Cambridge archaeologists like Ian Hodder and Christopher Tilley. It has now been generally accepted that the symbolic and ideological elements of material culture have to be taken just as seriously as functional aspects. Objects have form and substance, but also a meaning; they may be used for communication between people, and for the expression of values and feelings.

Material culture can be studied as a form of text. It has to be produced or written, as well as interpreted or read. Like text, material culture is produced to have a social effect, and cultural traditions may be manipulated in relation to social ends. Material culture is normally individually produced, but is so in a social context where not only may this context influence production; production itself may have the aim of changing the context. Material culture is thus used in social negotiations, and may accordingly be manipulated and used either to uphold or to change society (Hodder 1989; Tilley 1989).

One important consequence is that material culture cannot simply be interpreted as a mirror of society, or a window to look through into the past (Tilley 1989, 188). It is, as Ian Hodder has put it, a structured transformation of reality. As archaeologists, we face similar problems when trying to understand the meaning of material things to those historians or literary scholars face when interpreting written texts.

Symbolic and structuralist theory has inspired the study of prehistoric ethnic groups. Most archaeologists have followed Fredrik Barth's definition of an ethnic group as 'a collection of people who in their interaction confirm and maintain an identity vis-à-vis another collection of people with a different tradition'. Barth further states that 'the cultural contents of ethnic dichotomies would seem, analytically, to be of two orders: (i) overt signals or signs—the diacritical features that people look for and exhibit to show identity, often such features as dress, language, house-form or general style of life; and (ii) basic value orientations—the standards of morality and excellence by which performance is judged' (1969, 10–14).

It is important to note that ethnic identity is generated by interaction between groups, and that the symbolic emphasis of interacting groups will often be most active and contrastive during periods of stress and competition or when collaboration between groups is desirable (Hodder 1982, 185). The implication of such a definition is that in some periods ethnic differences may be difficult to observe in material culture, while during other periods such symbolic communication may be marked. Ethnic symbols may also be manipulated or actively used by individuals or groups of people for personal advantage, and it is possible to change ethnic identity. Consequently ethnicity is not a static phenomenon; rather it is part of a complex and changing system. Archaeologically, changing ethnic symbolic expression can be studied by focusing on special ethnic markers like house-form, dress, ornament, graves and so on, but such traits are not necessarily a straightforward mirror of reality. We have to take into consideration their specific social and historical context (Odner 1983 and 1985; Olsen 1985).

The theoretical basis of ethnic categorization should be reconsidered in the light of the discussion referred to above, with regard to archaeological material from the Northern Isles of the early Middle Ages. I believe that distinctions between Picts, Celts and Norse are sometimes made rather mechanically, perhaps only on the basis of a few ordinary, domestic objects found on settlement sites. A priori arguments are sometimes found: for instance that sites radiocarbon-dated earlier than AD 800 must be Pictish or Celtic (see Morris 1989, 279–95). Anne Ritchie, however, has argued that 'there was a greater degree of overlap between native and Norse culture in the Northern Isles in the 9th century AD than has hitherto been suspected. The colonists adopted native artefacts and other aspects of material culture such as grave-enclosures, and their farms display the same mixture of dispersed and nucleated settlement patterns and the same basic economy as those of the native population. All this points to considerable integration, which was undoubtedly aided by the basic similarities between the life-styles and cultural development of the two peoples' (1974, 34). She therefore advises us to be careful when giving ethnic labels to settlement sites.

The new chronology of the 7th to 9th centuries, recent excavations in Orkney referred to above and post-processual archaeological theory make it necessary for archaeologists to take another look at the ethnic interpretations of the material culture of the Northern Isles along the lines suggested by Anna Ritchie in 1974. In this paper I wish to propose the hypothesis that the ethnic symbolic expression of the natives and the Norse is difficult to recognize in the material culture of the 7th and 8th centuries. When we notice a change in the ethnic expression of the Norse during the 8th century, it is mainly in burial customs and the objects deposited in graves; a new development that has to be seen in the light of a change in the general economic, political and ideological situation in the North Sea area.

Moral values, ideologies and religious allegiances may also be symbolically expressed in material culture. Different opinions have been expressed on the character of the change of religion in the Nordic countries during the Viking Period. Hypotheses suggesting an evolutionary process, in which an old and weakening religion lost its grip and was gradually superseded by a superior religion, Christianity, have been challenged by scholars who argue that we should see the situation as one of conflict between two strong and vital religions (Steinsland 1990; Mundal 1990). Others argue for quite a long transitional period of coexistence between the two religions, at some times quite peaceful, at others with more antagonistic situations occurring, depending on the social and political situation in each region (Brink 1990, 17–67).

Most scholars agree that large-scale changes of religion were motivated by the upper strata of the society and are often closely connected with political power-struggles. In pre-Christian Scandinavia, religion was part of social organization, and was so closely connected with law, ideology, mythology and the political system that a change in religion could not appear without changing society itself (Steinsland 1990; see also Meulengracht Sørensen 1991). The religious issue might, however, also have been used by competing petty kings as an instrument with which to challenge the power of their neighbours. Christian and heathen symbols like ecclesiastical objects or heathen cult-objects could themselves have played a role in such conflicts.

Early missionary activity amongst heathen Scandinavians may be seen as an attack on the existing social and political system. Christianity, for instance, was not accepted in Norway before the unification of the country in the late Viking Period when the leading king could use religion as part of his strategy of power. Before that time we should expect hostility to missionary activity just as much as we would expect a violent response to a military threat. It is obvious that Carolingian expansionism and the eventual conquest of the Saxon and Frisian territories during the 8th century was correlated to missionary activities. The same strategy seems to have used by Charlemagne from 777 onwards, when the Danish kingdom was threatened.

The so-called Missionary style—the Tassilo chalice style—and the Carolingian style are symbolic expressions of the new ideology and main concepts of Christianity (Haseloff 1951, 64–75). We might expect the Danes and probably other Scandinavian peoples too to have feared Merovingian and Carolingian expansion and to have acted against the military and ideological pressure it involved. If so, some of the changes we can observe in the material culture of the Scandinavians during the 8th and early 9th centuries may be interpreted as expressions of a reaction to this outer pressure. The population of Scandinavia may have used building-forms, costume, ornament, special artefacts, burial practice, religious cults and sacrificial offerings and styles or style-elements to express their ethnic identity and to strengthen their religious and political orientation.

A hypothetical scenario of the North Sea area during the 8th century

Let me end by presenting an alternative view of the political and ideological situation in southern Norway during the 8th century and of the possibility of early contact and interaction between Norway and the British Isles. This is offered as a series of hypotheses that need further investigation but which might well stimulate discussion of the archaeology and history of the important century between 700 and 800 where the origins of the Viking Period must be sought.

A large-scale economic and political network developed around the southern shores of the North Sea about 700 (Wood 1983; Hodges 1989). Market-sites or emporia were established by political leaders and contact between royal dynasties can be assumed to have been more intensive than before. Both commodities and ideas were exchanged. A strong Danish kingdom with a centre in Jutland, maybe at Ribe, developed after 700, which gradually grew even to rival the Carolingian Empire (see also Näsman 1991). In my model, Borre and Vestfold were part of this network, mainly because of the area's control over important inland resources of eastern Norway, like fur, antler, iron, soapstone and hones. During the 8th century and throughout the Viking Period Danish kings tried to take control over Vestfold and Viken, with intermittent success (first documented in 813; Sawyer 1988, 57).

During the 8th century a strong west Norwegian polity developed also in south-western Norway, maybe with a centre at Avaldsnes in Rogaland. At this strategic location on the main sailing-route along the coast there are large barrows, with at least two rich ship burials, which may be dated to the end of the 8th century (Magnus and Myhre 1986, 411). Avaldsnes continued to be the political centre of the leading Norwegian kings for most of the Viking Period. At some stages they successfully competed with the petty kings of eastern Norway, and even with the Danish kingdom, for power over Vestfold and Viken.

The political élite in both eastern and western Norway were well informed about the kingdoms of the British Isles and the Continent during the 8th century. They lay within the range of Insular missionary activities (see Ørsnes 1966, 227; 1970, 108), and since the 7th century some form of contact and trade between chieftains or petty kings in western Norway, the Northern Isles, Scotland and Northumbria had been established. Some Norse farmers may have settled on the islands, perhaps even in the Faroes and Iceland. In the beginning of this period the relationships between Picts, Celts and Norse were relaxed and peaceful, and there was no need for the Norse population to demonstrate or express their ethnic identity through material culture. It is possible, for instance, that the first Scandinavian settlers and traders assimilated peacefully to the local population and their material culture.

During the 8th century the situation changed. Insular missionary activities on the Continent intensified, perhaps too among Norse settlers and in Scandinavia. Some time between 695 and 714 the missionary Willibrord travelled to the Danes, maybe to Ribe, to meet 'King Ongendus, a man more gruesome than a wild beast and harder than a stone,' as Alcuin wrote (Skovgaard-Petersen 1981, 21; Bencard and Bender Jørgensen 1990a, 147). South of the Danish border neighbouring kingdoms were acting in a threatening way, and the Danevirke was strengthened in 737. The Carolingians expanded northwards with sword and cross. A military and ideological conflict developed between Scandinavian kingdoms and the Christian powers of the Continent and the British Isles, although there were also periods of peaceful interaction and trade. Control over economic and strategic resources, and over trade, not only from the Baltic but also from the Norwegian mountains and northern Norway, may have been important for the Carolingian and Anglo-Saxon rulers.

Alcuin's letters about the Lindisfarne raid should be interpreted in such a political and religious context. He was one of Europe's most learned men at the turn of the century; he had studied in York, travelled widely in Europe, and had had meetings with Church leaders as well as kings. He was called to the court of Charlemagne in 781 to assist him in his educational and cultural reforms, and he stayed with Charlemagne until 796, when he acquired the abbacy of Tours. He was sent to visit the mighty King Offa of Mercia and was an important link between Anglo-Saxon and Continental scholarship (Duckett 1965; Godman 1982). Also at Charlemagne's court from 781 to 785 was the learned scholar Paul the Deacon, who was preparing the *Historia Langobardorum*. Both Paul and Alcuin knew the works of Jordanes, Bede, Gregory of Tours, Isidore of Seville and Fredegar, and other written sources on the histories of different Germanic tribes. Alcuin was therefore well informed of the current ideas concerning the Scandinavian homeland of many of these tribes (Goffart 1988, 3, 333, 382, 432).

When Alcuin wrote the Lindisfarne letters from the Frankish court in 793, Charlemagne was in conflict with the Danish king. In 800 Alcuin further described his countryman Willibrord's missionary visit to the Danish king Ogendus of about 700. He should, therefore, have known the Danish people quite well, and he must have been aware of the Scandinavian kingdoms and of Scandinavian involvement in the north of the British Isles. Alcuin's letters cannot be treated as separate from the political strategy of the Church or from that of Charlemagne and the Anglo-Saxon kings. Probably they all had a common interest in a presentation of the Scandinavians as frightening barbarians who ought to be Christianized as well as conquered.

I would suggest, then, that Alcuin's letters are not to be regarded as objective descriptions of the situation but rather as arguments in a political and ideological conflict.

I would further suggest that the archaeological material too should be analysed and interpreted in the light of this growing interaction and competition between political powers around the North Sea. Only during the stressed and competitive phase of the 8th century was a distinct ethnic identity symbolically expressed by the Norse on the islands, principally in burial practice, costume, jewellery and art-styles. As the Scandinavians gradually took political control in the North the situation reversed, and many of the local population adjusted their material culture to the Norse, symbolically becoming Norse.

I would also suggest that the Scandinavians were well aware of the ideological conflict, so that the chieftains and petty kings in particular must have felt Christianity as a threat to their power. One symbolic counteraction would be to destroy ecclesiastical objects by cutting them up and reshaping them into daily artefacts such as dress-ornaments. Another move could be to use Christian style-elements in their own styles or mythology. A third possibility was to use violence, to destroy centres of missionary activity like Lindisfarne and Iona, just as the Carolingians plundered heathen temples of the Saxons, Frisians and Slavs (Reuter 1985, 77).

According to this view, many of the Viking actions were deliberately planned by Scandinavian chieftains and petty kings. They were not ignorant barbarians; they knew very well the military and ideological pressure they were facing. Some of their responses can be read in their material culture. But of course there were also entrepreneurs and pirates who took advantage of the unstable situation and acted outside the chieftain's control. Historians and writers since Alcuin's days have made the mistake of portraying the Vikings in the image of pirates like this, forgetting that plundering, even of churches, was common in all countries around the North Sea during these centuries (Reuter 1985, 78; Lucas 1967). They have also underestimated the complexity and strength of authority and kingship in southern Scandinavian polities during the 8th century (see also Wormald 1982, 144). Organized plundering may have been an important source of income for the Scandinavian kings, just as it was for the Merovingian and early Carolingian kings (Reuter 1985).

My main hypothesis is that the archaeological material from the 8th and 9th centuries should be read and interpreted as a corpus of symbolic expressions of economic, ideological and political negotiation. We have tended to treat this material as functional and thus as an objective source that could be used to state quite directly what the Viking Period involved.

If the material culture of the Northern Isles developed and changed in the context of a gradual and continuous contact across the North Sea, the starting-point of the Viking Period could be fixed at any of several points along a timescale running from AD 700 to 800, depending on the criteria chosen.

One possibility is to follow the Continental periodization, with its Merovingian and Carolingian periods, and like Herman Ament date the change from the Merovingian to the Viking Period to either 720 or 750, that is primarily on the basis of political events documented by written sources. Another possibility would be to base the periods on archaeological material like dress, jewellery, weapons or styles. Like Karen Høilund Nielsen and Ingmar Jansson we could date the start of the Viking Period by developed oval brooches (about 775–800), or we could use the gripping-beast motif and the Broa phase as our criteria and draw the line about 750 (depending on what the earliest dates prove to be). Alternatively, if we give priority to economic and political developments around the North Sea, we could, like Richard Hodges, put special emphasis on the establishment of trading-sites such as his type B emporia, with their specialization in production and trade in utilitarian as well as prestigious objects, a development that he dates to about AD 700 (1989, 162). Such a date would be in line with recent suggestions by Klavs Randsborg (1990), Lotte Hedeager and Henrik Tvarnø (1991, 309) and Lise Bender Jørgensen and Palle Eriksen (forthcoming).

NOTES

[1] My sincere thanks to Lise Bender Jørgensen, Charlotte Blindheim, Stefan Brink, Martin Carver, Signe Horn Fuglesang, Karen Høilund Nielsen, Ulla Lund Hansen, Christian Keller, Egil Mikkelsen, Ulf Näsman and Birthe Weber who made valuable comments on various drafts of this manuscript. I am grateful to Øystein Geber who let me use his unpublished thesis on imported objects in Viking graves in west Norway (1991). Especially I want to thank John Hines for correcting my English and for commenting constructively on my text. All faults are my own.

[2] The pre-Viking Period (Montelius period VII) has been given different names in the Scandinavian countries, in Sweden 'Vendeltid', in Denmark 'Yngre Germansk Jernalder', in Norway 'Merovingertid'. In this article the name 'Vendel Period' is used to avoid confusion with the Continental 'Merovingian Period'.

[3] A list of Norwegian grave finds with Insular objects from about AD 800 or earlier has been compiled but would have taken up too much space if it had been included here. The finds are arranged in five groups:
1. Early/middle 8th century. Find contexts with small, thin-bodied and zoomorphic oval brooches, and objects decorated in style III/D–E.
2. Middle/late 8th century. Find contexts with Berdal brooches like P 11–22.
3. Late 8th century. Find contexts with oval brooches like P 25 and 27 (R. 650 and R. 648).
4. Early 9th century. Find contexts with oval brooches like early P 37 (R. 647).
5. Other Insular objects from the 7th and 8th centuries, in context.
6. Other Insular objects from the 7th and 8th centuries with no context.

BIBLIOGRAPHY AND ABBREVIATIONS

Almgren, Bertil. 1955. *Bronsnycklar och djurornamentik.*
Ament, Hermann. 1977. 'Zur archäologischen Periodisierung der Merowingerzeit', *Germania* 55, 133–40.
Arge, Simon. 1986. *Landnamet på Færøerne.*
Arrhenius, Birgit. 1983. 'The chronology of the Vendel graves'. In J. P. Lamm and H. Å. Nordström (eds). *Vendel Period Studies* 2, 39–70.
B. = Museum number of Historisk Museum, University of Bergen.
Bakka, Egil. 1963. 'Some English decorated metal objects found in Norwegian Viking graves. Contributions to the art history of the eighth century AD', *Universitetet i Bergen, Årbok,* 3–66.
Bakka, Egil. 1971. 'Scandinavian trade relations with the Continent and the British Isles in the pre-Viking times', *Antikvarisk arkiv* 40. Early Medieval Studies 3, 37–51.

Bakka, Egil. 1973. 'Eit gravfunn frå Fosse i Meland, Hordaland og det arkeologiske periodeskiljet mellom merovingartid og vikingtid', *Finska Fornminnesföreningens tidskrift* 75, 9–17.
Bakka, Egil. 1982. 'Ein Beschlagfragment mit Tierornamentik von der Karolingischen Pfalz in Paderborn. Westeuropäische und nordische Tier-ornamentik des 8. Jahrhunderts im überregionalen Stil III', *Studien zur Sachsenforschung* 4, 1–56.
Barth, Fredrik. 1969. Introduction to Fredrik Barth (ed.). *Ethnic groups and boundaries.*
Bencard, Mogens. 1990. 'The stratigraphy and dating of 8th-century Ribe', *Journal of Danish Archaeology* 7, 225–28.
Bencard, Mogens and Bender Jørgensen, Lise. 1990a. 'Excavation and stratigraphy'. In Mogens Bencard (ed.). *Ribe Excavations 1970–76* 4, 15–167.
Bencard, Mogens and Bender Jørgensen, Lise. 1990b. 'The foundation of Ribe', *Antiquity* 64, 576–83.
Bender Jørgensen, Lise and Eriksen, Palle. Forthcoming. *Trabjerg. En vikingetids bebyggelse i Nordvestjyllland.* To be printed in *Jysk Arkæologisk Selskabs Skrifter.*
Bendixen, Kirsten. 1984. 'Sceattas and other coin finds'. In Mogens Bencard (ed.). *Ribe Excavations 1970–76* 1, 63–101.
Blindheim, Charlotte. 1949. 'Et unikt vendelstilsarbeide fra Romsdal', *Viking* XIII, 55–75.
Blindheim, Charlotte. 1976. 'A collection of Celtic (?) bronze objects found at Kaupang (Skiringssal), Vestfold, Norway'. In Bo Almqvist and David Greene (eds). *Proceedings of the Seventh Viking Congress. Dublin 15–21 August 1973,* 9–27.
Blindheim, Charlotte. 1978. 'Trade problems in the Viking Age. Some reflections on Insular metalwork found in Norwegian graves of the Viking Age'. In Thorsten Andersson and Karl Inge Sandred (eds). *The Vikings. Proceedings of the Symposium of the Faculty of Arts of Uppsala University June 6–9, 1977,* 166–76.
Böhner, Kurt. 1958. *Die fränkischen Altertümer der Trierer Landes.* 1. Teil.
Brinch Madsen, H. 1984. 'Metal-casting. Techniques, production and workshop'. In Mogens Bencard (ed.). *Ribe Excavations 1970–76* 2, 15–189.
Brink, Stefan. 1990. *Sockenbilding och sockennamn. Studier i äldre territoriell indelning i Norden.*
Brøgger, A. W. 1916. *Borrefundet og Vestfoldkongernes graver.*
Brøgger, A. W. 1930. *Den norske bosetningen på Shetland-Orknøyene.*
Bøe, Johs. 1940. 'Norse Antiquities in Ireland'. In Haakon Shetelig (ed.). *Viking Antiquities in Great Britain and Ireland* III.
C. = Museum number of the museum of National Antiquities, University of Oslo.
Carver, Martin O. H. 1990. 'Pre-Viking traffic in the North Sea'. In Seán McGrail (ed.). *Maritime Celts, Frisians and Saxons.* Council for British Archaeology Research Report 71, 117–25.
Christensen, Kjeld. 1990. 'Wood-anatomical and dendrochronological studies'. In Mogens Bencard (ed.). *Ribe Excavations 1970–76* 4, 169–81.
Christophersen, Axel. 1989. 'Kjøpe, selge, bytte, gi. Vareutveksling og byoppkomst i Norge ca 800–1100: en modell'. In Anders Andrén (ed.). *Medeltidens fødelse,* 109–45.
Coffey, George and Armstrong, E. C. R. 1910. 'Scandinavian objects found at Islandbridge and Kilmainham', *Proceedings of the Royal Irish Academy* XXVIII, 107–22.
Crawford, Barbara E. 1987. *Scandinavian Scotland.*
Crumlin-Pedersen, Ole. 1990. 'Boats and ships of the Angles and Jutes'. In Seán McGrail (ed.). *Maritime Celts, Frisians and Saxons.* Council for British Archaeology Research Report 71, 98–116.
Duckett, Eleanor Shipley. 1965. *Alcuin, friend of Charlemagne.*

Evison, Vera I. 1982a. 'Anglo-Saxon glass claw-beakers', *Archaeologia* 107, 43–76.
Evison, Vera I. 1982b. 'Bichrome glass vessels of the 7th and 8th centuries', *Studien zur Sachsenforschung* 3, 7–21.
Frandsen, Lene B. and Jensen, Stig. 1988. 'Pre-Viking and Early Viking Age Ribe', *Journal of Danish Archaeology* 6, 175–89.
Frandsen, Lene B. and Jensen, Stig. 1990. 'The dating of Ribe's earliest culture layers', *Journal of Danish Archaeology* 7, 228–31.
Fuglesang, Signe Horn. 1982. 'Early Viking art'. In Hjalmar Torp and J. Rasmus Brandt (eds). *Acta ad archaeologiam et artium historiam pertinentia*. Series altera in 8° II, 125–73.
Fuglesang, Signe Horn. 1986. Review of Jansson 1985. *Fornvännen* 81, 234–37.
Fuglesang, Signe Horn. 1987. 'Vikings, Scandinavia'. In *The Dictionary of Archaeology*.
Fuglesang, Signe Horn. 1989. Review of Wamers 1985. *Fornvännen* 84, 258–62.
Fuglesang, Signe Horn. 1991. 'Animalistici, Stili. Paesi Nordici'. In Angiola Maria Romanini and Marina Righetti Tosti-Croce (eds). *Enciclopedia dell'arte medievale* II, 21–31.
Geber, Øystein S. [1991.] *Brede seil over Nordsjø går. Import til Vestlandet i vikingtid*. Mag. art. thesis, Historisk Museum. Universitetet i Bergen.
Goffart, Walter. 1988. *The narrators of barbarian history (AD 550–800). Jordanes, Gregory of Tours, Bede and Paul the Deacon*.
Godman, Peter (ed.). 1982. *Alcuin. The Bishops, Kings and Saints of York*.
Graham-Campbell, James A. 1980. *The Viking World*.
Graham-Campbell, James A. Forthcoming. 'The Irish Sea Vikings'. The Munro Lecture at the University of Edinburgh 19/10 1989.
Guðrún Sveinbjarnardóttir. 1990. Review of Margrét Hermanns-Auðardóttir 1989. *Saga-Book* XXIII:2, 84–87.
Haseloff, Günther. 1951. *Der Tassilokelch*.
Hedeager, Lotte. 1992. *Iron Age Societies: from tribe to state in Northern Europe, 500 BC–AD 700*.
Hedeager, Lotte and Tvarnø, Henrik. 1991. *Romerne og germanerne*. In Søren Mørch (ed.). *Det europæiske hus* 2.
Helgen, Geir. 1982. *Odd og egg. Merovingertidsfunn fra Hordaland, Sogn og Fjordane*.
Henry, Françoise. 1967. *Irish art during the Viking invasions 800–1020 A.D.*
Hines, John. 1984. *The Scandinavian Character of Anglian England in the pre-Viking Period*. BAR. British Series 124.
Hines, John. 1992. 'The Scandinavian Character of Anglian England: an update'. In M. O. H. Carver (ed). *The Age of Sutton Hoo*, 315–29.
Hines, John. Forthcoming. 'På tvers av Nordsjøen. Britiske perspektiver på Skandinaviens senere jernalder', *Universitetets Oldsaksamlings Årbok* 1991–92.
Hodder, Ian. 1982. *Symbols in Action*.
Hodder, Ian. 1989. 'Post-modernism, post-structuralism and post-processual archaeology'. In Ian Hodder (ed). *The meaning of things. Material culture and symbolic expression*, 64–78.
Hodder, Ian. 1991. *Archaeological theory in Europe. The last three decades*.
Hodges, Richard. 1989. 'Charlemagne's elephant and the beginnings of commodisation in Europe', *Acta Archaeologica* 59, 155–68.
Hougen, Ellen Karine. 1968. 'Glassbegre i Norge fra sjette til tiende århundre', *Viking* XXXII, 85–109.
Hougen, Ellen Karine. 1969. 'Glassmaterialet fra Kaupang', *Viking* XXXIII, 119–37.

Høilund Nielsen, Karen. 1987. 'Zur Chronologie der jüngeren germanischen Eisenzeit auf Bornholm', *Acta Archaeologica* 57, 47–86.
Høilund Nielsen, Karen. 1991. 'Centrum og periferi i 6.–8.årh. Territorielle studier af dyrstil og kvindesmykker i yngre germansk jernalder i Syd- og Østskandinavien'. In Mortensen and Rasmussen, 127–54.
Jansson, Ingmar. 1985. *Ovala spännbucklor. En studie av vikingatida standardsmycken med utgångspunkt från Björköfynden.*
Jensen, Stig. 1990. 'Handel med dagligvarer i vikingetiden', *Hikuin* 16, 119–38.
Jensen, Stig. 1991a. 'Dankirke-Ribe. Fra handelsgård til handelsplads'. In Mortensen and Rasmussen, 73–88.
Jensen, Stig. 1991b. *Ribes vikinger.*
Johansen, Johannes. 1985. 'Studies in the vegetational history of the Faroes and Shetland Islands', *Annales Societatis Scientiarum Færoensis* XI.
Kaland, Sigrid Hillern Hanssen. 1973. 'Westness-utgravningene på Rousay, Orknøyene', *Viking* XXXVII, 77–102.
Krogh, Knud. 1986. 'Um Føroya fyrstu buseting', *Mondul* 12, 1.
Lucas, A. T. 1967. 'The plundering and burning of churches in Ireland, 7th to 16th century', *North Munster Studies*, 172–229.
Lund Hansen, Ulla. 1988. 'Hovedproblemer i romersk og germansk jernalders kronologi i Skandinavia og på Kontinentet'. In Mortensen and Rasmussen, 21–35.
Magnus, Bente and Myhre, Bjørn. 1986. *Norges Historie* 1.
Margrét Hermanns-Auðardóttir. 1989. *Islands tidiga bosättning.*
Margrét Hermanns-Auðardóttir. 1991. 'The early settlement of Iceland', *Norwegian Archaeological Review* 24, no. 1, 1–33.
Meulengracht Sørensen, Preben. 1991. 'Håkon den Gode og guderne. Nogle bemærkninger om religion og centralmagt i det tiende århundrede'. In Mortensen and Rasmussen, 235–44.
Morris, Christopher D. 1979. 'The Vikings and Irish monasteries', *Durham University Journal* LXXI, no. 2, 175–85.
Morris, Christopher D. 1985. 'Viking Orkney: A survey'. In Colin Renfrew (ed.). *The prehistory of Orkney*, 210–42.
Morris, Christopher D. 1989. *The Birsay Bay Project* 1.
Morris, Christopher D. 1991. 'Native and Norse in Orkney and Shetland'. In C. Karkov and R. Farrell (eds). *Studies in Insular art and Archaeology.* American Early Medieval studies 1.
Mortensen, Peder and Rasmussen, Birgit M. (eds). 1988. *Fra stamme til stat* 1.
Mortensen, Peder and Rasmussen, Birgit M. (eds). 1991. *Fra stamme til stat* 2.
Müller-Wille, Michael. 1985. 'Westeuropäischer Import der Wikingerzeit in Nordeuropa'. In S. O. Lindquist (ed.). *Society and trade in the Baltic during the Viking Age*, 79–102.
Mundal, Else. 1990. 'Kristninga av Noreg og Island reflektert gjennom samtidig skaldedikting', *Collegium Medievale* 3, 145–62.
Myhre, Bjørn. 1987. 'Chieftains' graves and chiefdom territories', *Studien zur Sachsenforschung* 6, 169–87.
Myhre, Bjørn. 1991. 'Theory in Scandinavian archaeology since 1960: a view from Norway'. In Hodder, 161–86.
Myhre, Bjørn. 1992. 'The Royal Cemetery at Borre, Vestfold: A Norwegian Centre in a European Periphery'. In M. O. H. Carver (ed.). *The Age of Sutton Hoo*, 301–13.
Nordahl, Else. 1988. *Reykjavik from the archaeological point of view.*

Näsman, Ulf. 1986. 'Vendel Period glass from Eketorp II, Öland, Sweden', *Acta Archaeologica* 55, 55–116.
Näsman, Ulf. 1989. 'The Germanic Iron Age and Viking Age in Danish archaeology', *Journal of Danish Archaeology* 8, 159–87.
Näsman, Ulf. 1990. 'Om fjärrhandel i Sydskandinaviens yngre jernålder', *Hikuin* 16, 89–118.
Näsman, Ulf. 1991. 'Det syvende århundrede—et mørkt tidsrum i ny belysning'. In Mortensen and Rasmussen, 165–80.
Odner, Knut. 1972. 'Ethno-historic and ecological settings for economic and social models of an Iron Age society'. In David Clarke (ed.). *Models in Archaeology*, 623 ff.
Odner, Knut. 1974. 'Economic structures in Western Norway in the Early Iron Age', *Norwegian Archaeological Review* 7, no. 2, 104–12, 148–58.
Odner, Knut. 1983. *Finner og Terfinner. Etniske prosesser i det nordlige Fenno-Skandinavia*.
Odner, Knut. 1985. 'Saamis (Lapps), Finns and Scandinavians in history and prehistory. Ethnic origins and ethnic processes in Fenno-Scandinavia', *Norwegian Archaeological Review* 18, nos. 1–2, 1–12, 29–35.
Olsen, Bjørnar. 1985. 'Comments on Odner 1985', *Norwegian Archaeological Review* 18, nos. 1–2, 13–19.
P = Petersen 1928.
Petersen, Jan. 1919. *De norske vikingesverd*.
Petersen, Jan. 1928. *Vikingetidens smykker*.
Petersen, Jan. 1940. 'British Antiquities of the Viking Period found in Norway'. In Haakon Shetelig (ed.).*Viking Antiquities in Great Britain and Ireland* V.
R. = reference with no. to Rygh 1855.
Ramqvist, Per H. 1991a. 'Perspektiv på regional variation och samhälle i Nordens folkvandringstid'. In Ch. Fabech and J. Ringtvedt (eds). *Samfundsorganisasjon og sosial variasjon*, 305–17.
Ramqvist, Per H. 1991b. 'Über ökonomische und sozio-politische Beziehungen der Gesellschaften der nordischen Völkerwanderungszeit', *Frühmittelalterliche Studien* 25, 45–72.
Randsborg, Klavs. 1990. 'The periods of Danish antiquity', *Acta Archaeologica* 60 (1989), 187–92.
Reuter, T. 1985. 'Plunder and tribute in the Carolingian empire', *Transactions of the Royal Historical Society* 35, 75–94.
Ritchie, Anna. 1974. 'Pict and Norseman in Northern Scotland', *Scottish Archaeological Forum* 6, 23–36.
Ritchie, Anna. 1977. 'Excavation of Pictish and Viking-Age farmsteads at Buckqouy, Orkney', *Proceedings of the Society of Antiquaries of Scotland* 108, 174–227.
Rygh, Oluf. 1855. *Norske Oldsager*.
Sawyer, Peter. 1971. *The Age of the Vikings*.
Sawyer, Peter. 1982. 'The Causes of the Viking Age'. In R. T. Farrell (ed.). *The Vikings*, 1–7.
Sawyer, Peter. 1988. *Da Danmark blev Danmark. Fra ca. år 700 til ca. 1050*.
Shetelig, Haakon. 1927. 'Tidsbestemmelser i vikingetidens stilhistorie', *Finska Fornminnesföreningens tidskrift* XXXVI, 106–12.
Shetelig, Haakon. 1933. *Vikingeminner i Vest-Europa*.
Shetelig, Haakon. 1954. 'The Viking Graves'. In Haakon Shetelig (ed.).*Viking Antiquities in Great Britain and Ireland* VI, 65–111.
Sjøvold, Thorleif. 1974. *The Iron Age settlement of Arctic Norway* II. *Late Iron Age*.
Skaare, Kolbjørn. 1963. 'Angelsaksiske mynter', *Viking* XXVI, 113.

Skovgaard-Petersen, Inge. 1981. 'The written sources'. In Mogens Bencard (ed.). *Ribe Excavations 1970–76* I, 21–62.
Smith, B. B. (ed.). Forthcoming. *The excavations at Howe, Stromness, Orkney*. Society of Antiquaries of Scotland. Monographs.
Steinsland, Gro. 1990. 'The change of religion in the Nordic countries—a confrontation between two living religions', *Collegium Medievale* 3, 123–35.
Steuer, Heiko. 1987. 'Der Handel der Wikingerzeit zwischen Nord- und West-Europa auf grund archaeologischer Zeugnisse'. In K. Düwel *et al.* (eds). 1987. *Untersuchungen zu Handel und Verkehr der vor- und frühgeschichtlichen Zeit in Mittel- und Nordeuropa* IV, 113–197.
Tilley, Christopher. 1989. 'Interpreting material culture'. In Ian Hodder (ed.). *The meaning of things. Material culture and symbolic expression*, 185–94.
Vierck, Hayo. 1970. 'Zum Fernverkehr über See im 6. Jahrhundert'. In K. Hauck. *Goldbrakteaten aus Sievern*. Münsterische Mittelalterschriften 1, 355–95.
Vierck, Hayo. 1978. 'Ein angelsächsische Zierscheibe des 7. Jahrhunderts n. Chr. aus Haithabu'. In *Berichte über die Ausgrabungen in Haithabu* 12, 94–109.
Vilhjálmur Örn Vilhjálmsson. 1990. 'Dating problems in Icelandic archaeology', *Norwegian Archaeological Review* 23, nos. 1–2, 43–53.
Wamers, Egon. 1985. *Insularer Metallschmuck in wikingerzeitlichen Gräber Nordeuropas. Untersuchungen zur skandinavischen Westexpansion.*
Weber, Birthe. Forthcoming. 'Norwegian reindeer antler export to Orkney and Shetland? An analysis of combs from Pictish/early Norse sites', *Universitetets Oldsaksamlings Årbok* 1992–93.
Wilson, David M. 1976. 'Scandinavian settlement in the North and West of the British Isles—an archaeological viewpoint', *Transactions of the Royal Historical Society* 26, 95–113.
Wood, Ian. 1983. *The Merovingian North Sea*.
Wormald, C. Patrick. 1982. 'Viking Studies: Whence and Whither?' In R. T. Farrell (ed.). *The Vikings*, 128–56.
Ørsnes, Mogens. 1966. *Form og Stil. Sydskandinaviens yngre germanske jernalder.*
Ørsnes, Mogens. 1970. 'Südskandinavische Ornamentik in der jüngeren germanischen Eisenzeit', *Acta Archaeologica* XL, 1–121.

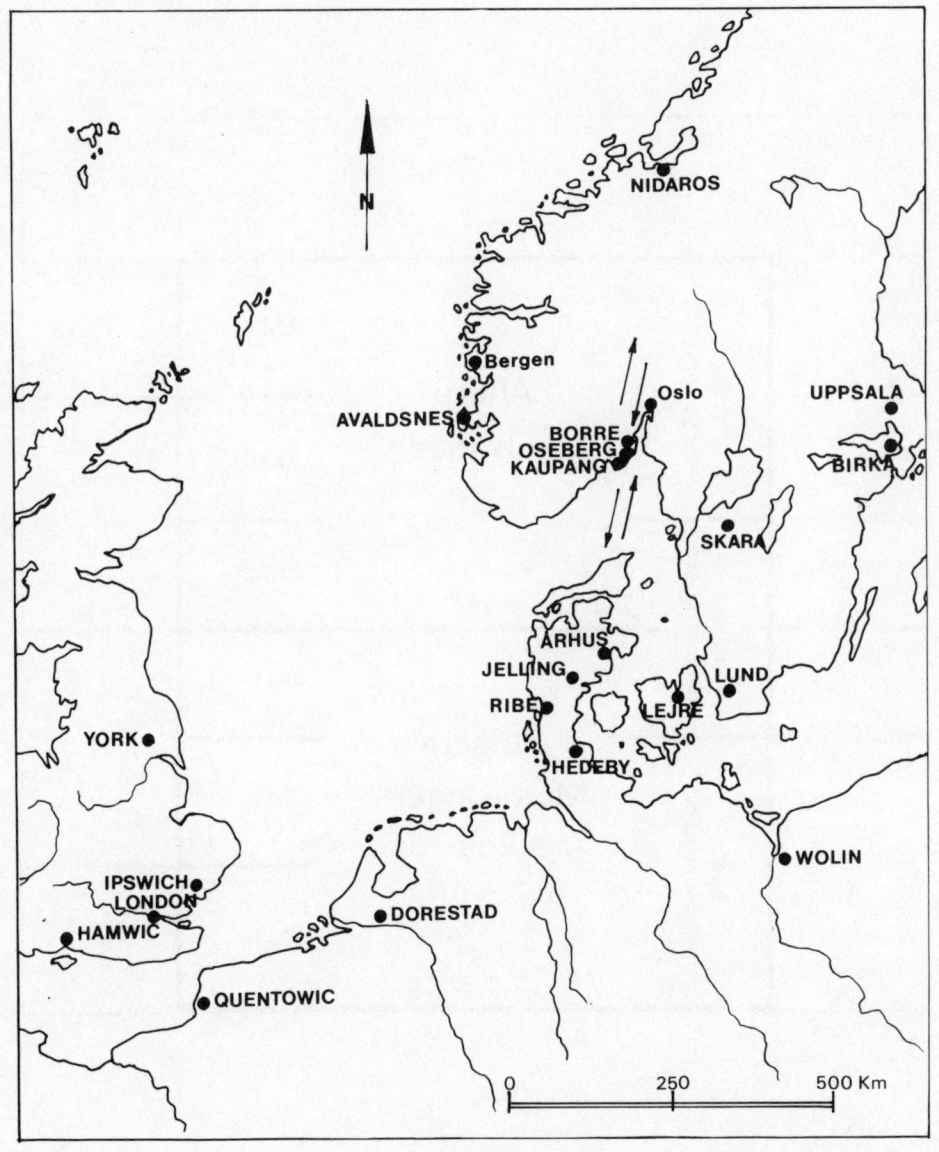

Fig. 1. Major sites and market-places around the North Sea during the 7th to 9th centuries.

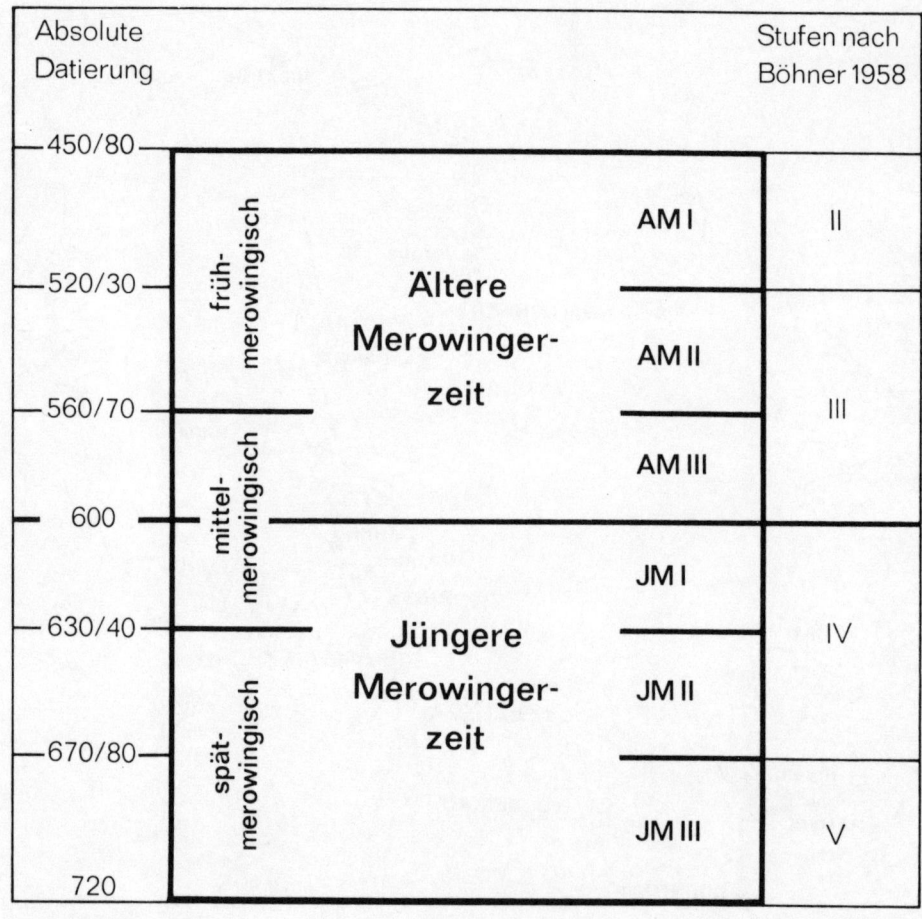

Fig. 2. Ament's chronological scheme of the Merovingian Period on the Continent (Ament 1977, 135, fig.1).

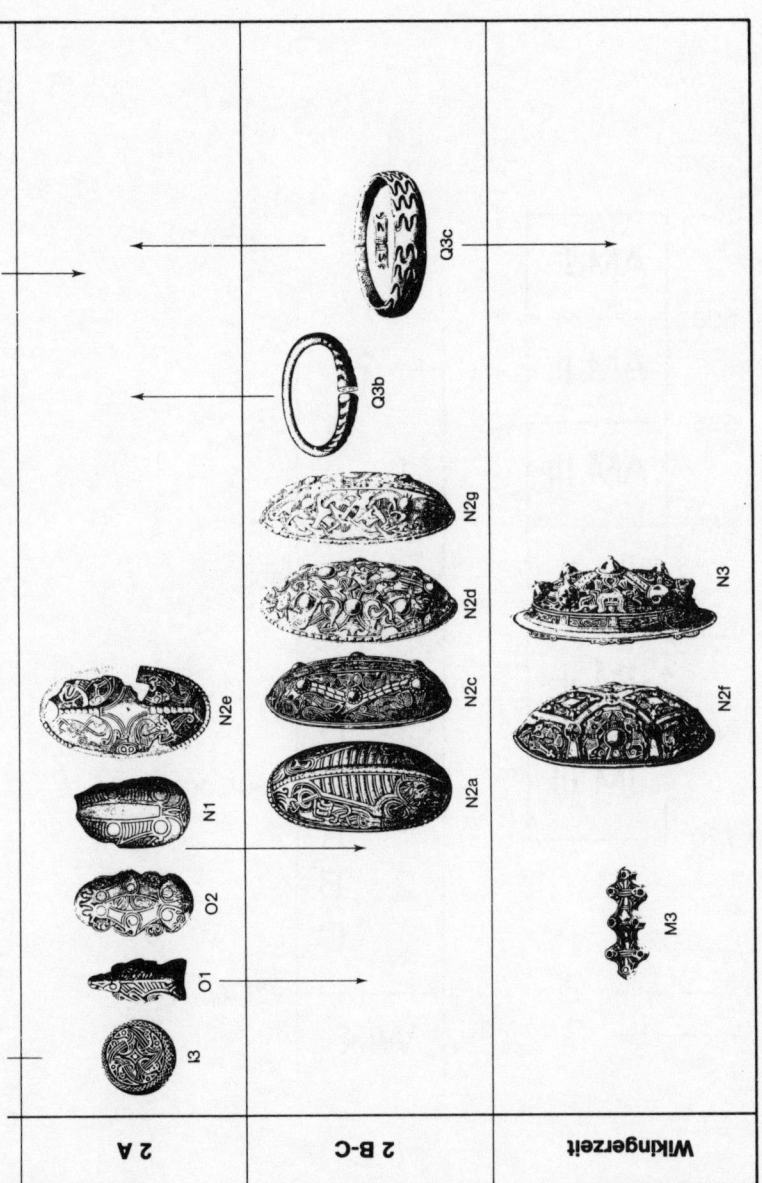

Fig. 3. Brooches and arm-rings from the Vendel Period phase 2A–C and Early Viking Period, from Karen Høilund Nielsen's study of Bornholm (1987, fig. 10). Note that zoomorphic oval brooches occur in phase 2A, Berdal brooches and oval brooches similar to P 27 in phase 2B–C and oval brooches similar to P 37 in the Early Viking Period. Karen Høilund Nielsen has correlated her phases with Ament's scheme (over).

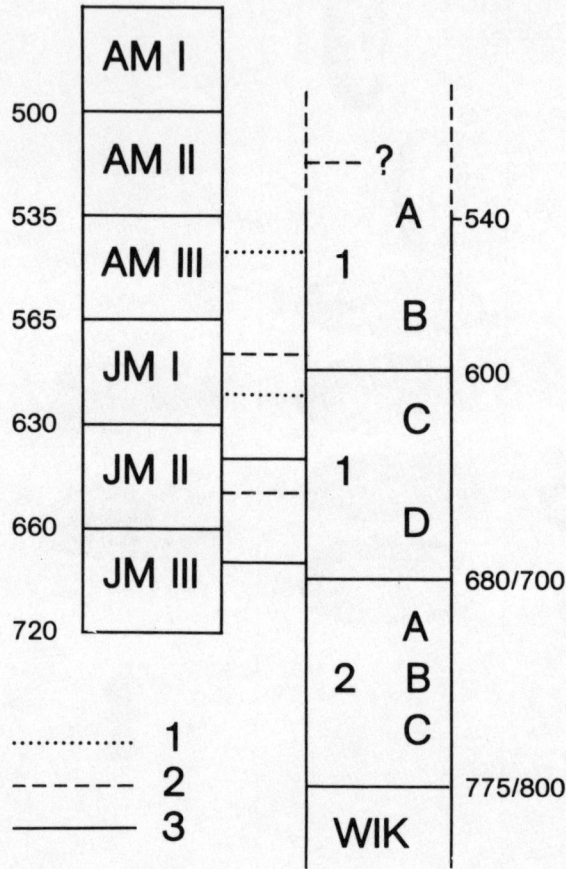

Fig 3a. Høilund Nielsen's chronological scheme correlated with Ament's.

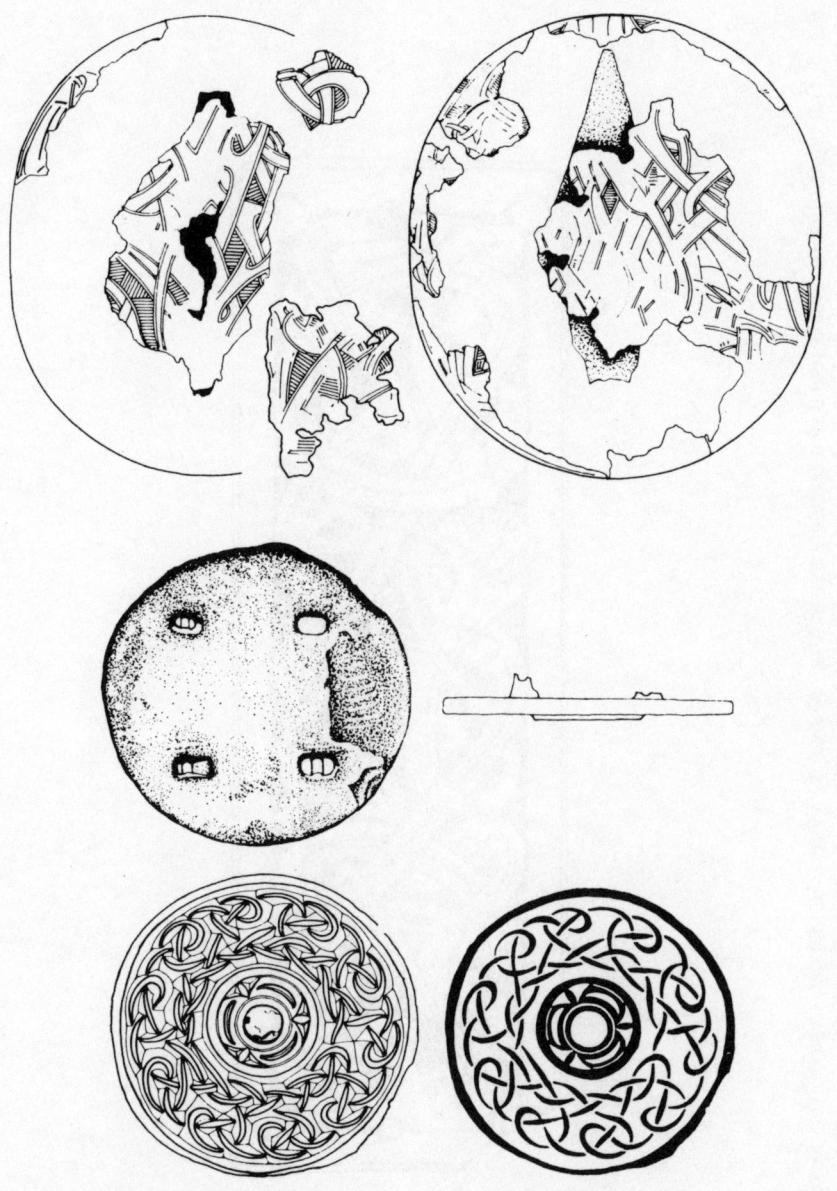

Fig. 4. Objects from a female grave at Fosse, Meland, Hordaland, western Norway: two thin-bodied oval brooches and one gilt bronze Insular mount, reused as a brooch (B. 12012; Bakka 1973).

Fig. 5. Gilt bronze Insular mount found in a female grave at Store Kongsvik, Tysnes, Hordaland, western Norway together with two thin-bodied oval brooches like P 4 (B. 7639; Bakka 1973, fig. 12).

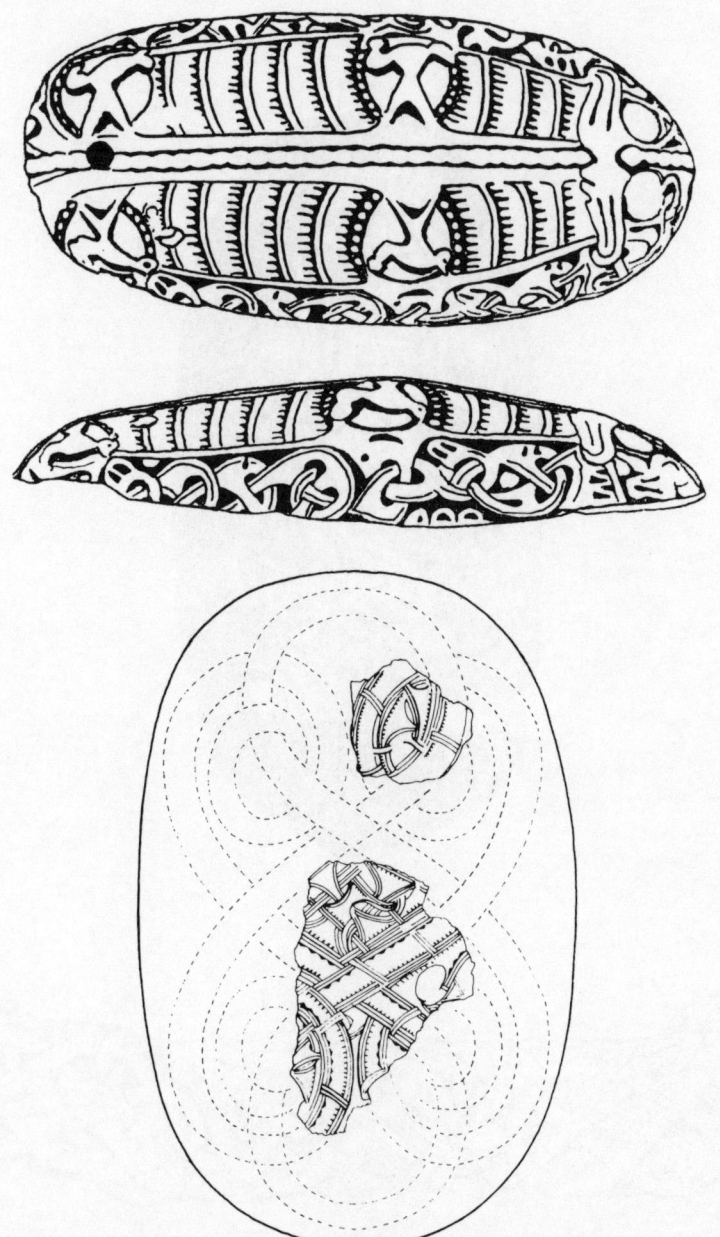

Fig. 6. Zoomorphic oval brooches from Vangsnes, Balestrand (above) and Skjervum, Vik (below), both in Sogn og Fjordane, western Norway. Both were found in female graves with gilt bronze Insular mounts (B. 700; Blindheim 1949, fig. 6 and B. 6700; Bakka 1973, fig. 13).

Fig. 7. Oval brooch and gilt bronze Insular mount from a female grave at Svennevik, Hommedal, Aust-Agder, southern Norway (C. 1970; Bakka 1973, figs 9 and 11).

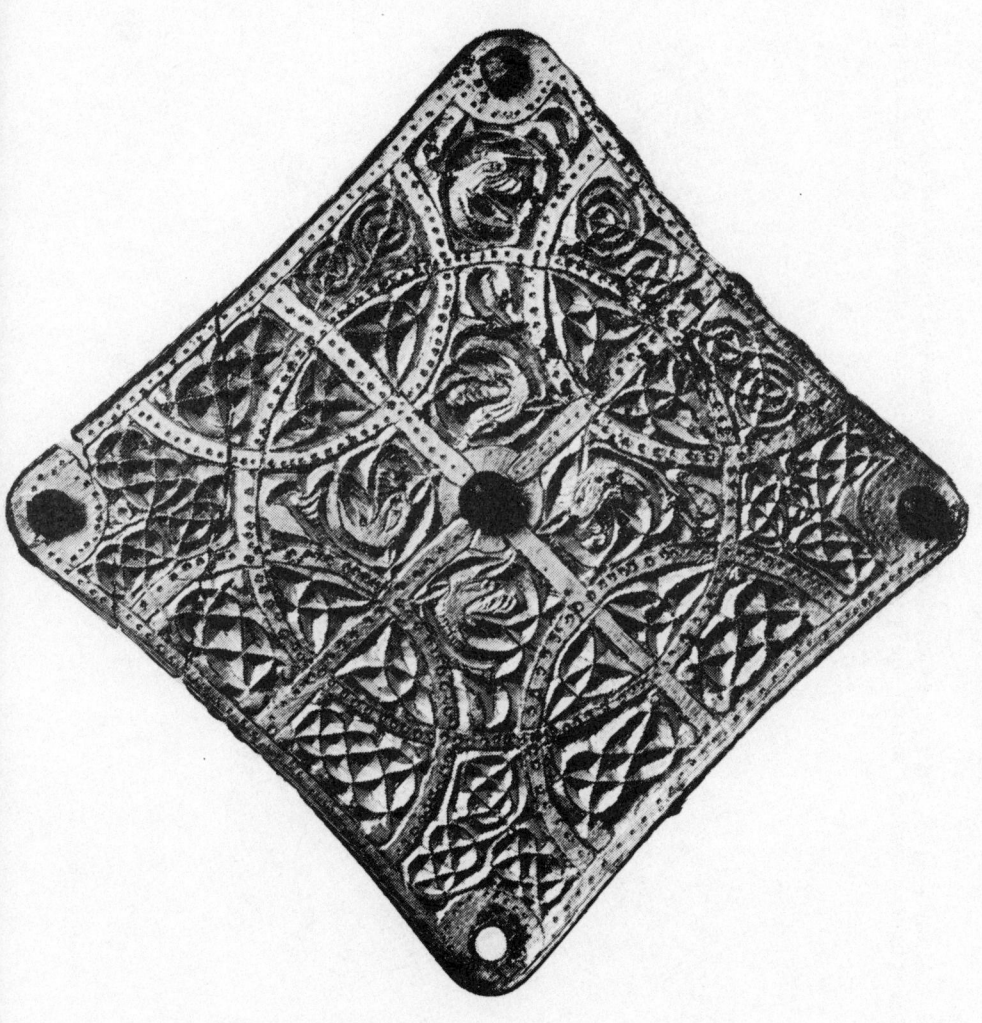

Fig. 8. Gilt bronze Insular mount from Bjørke, Ørsta, Møre og Romsdal, western Norway found in a female grave with two thin-bodied oval brooches, similar to P 4 (B. 8256; Bakka 1963, fig. 8; Bakka 1973, 12).

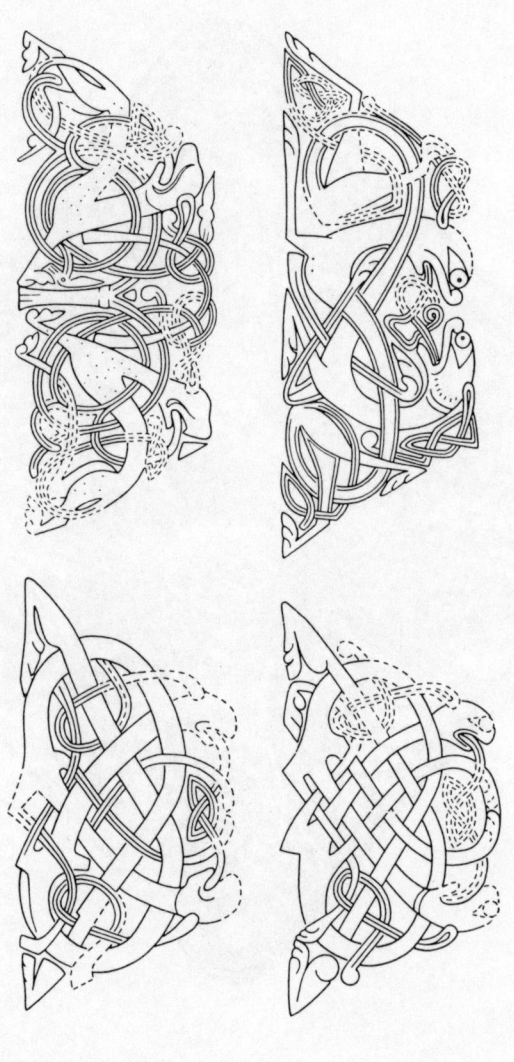

Fig. 9. Animal ornament on a bronze gilt Insular mount from Fure, Askvoll, Sogn og Fjordane, western Norway found in a female grave with a disc-on-bow brooch (B. 4969; Bakka 1963, fig. 54; 1973, 10).

Fig. 10. A Berdal oval brooch from a female grave at Oronsay, the Hebrides (Brøgger 1930, fig. 126).

Fig. 11. A Berdal oval brooch from a female grave at Kilmainham, Dublin (above). Mould impression of an oval brooch of the same type, found in an 8th-century layer at Ribe, Jutland (below; the white part) (Brinch Madsen 1984, figs 105, 107).